PREPARING
FOR LIFE

PREPARING
FOR LIFE

A PARENTS' GUIDE TO THE PSYCHOLOGICAL
AND EMOTIONAL LIFE OF YOUNG CHILDREN

DR ANDREW STANWAY MB MRCP

VIKING

VIKING
Published by the Penguin Group
27 Wrights Lane, London W8 5TZ. England
Viking Penguin Inc., 40 West 23rd Street, New York, New York 10010, USA
Penguin Books Australia Ltd, Ringwood, Victoria, Australia
Penguin Books Canada Ltd, 2801 John Street, Markham, Ontario, Canada L3R IB4
Penguin Books (NZ) Ltd, 182–190 Wairau Road, Auckland 10, New Zealand

Penguin Books Ltd. Registered Offices: Harmondsworth, Middlesex, England

First published 1988

Made and printed in Great Britain by
William Clowes Limited, Beccles and London
Filmset in Monophoto Sabon by
Servis Filmsetting Ltd.
Illustrations originated by
William Clowes Limited

British Library Cataloguing in Publication Data

Stanway, Andrew
Preparing for life: a parents' guide to the psychological
and emotional life of young children.
1. Child rearing   2. Child psychology
I. Title
649′.1′019 HQ772

ISBN 0–670–81044–4

ACKNOWLEDGEMENTS

I should like to thank the Librarian and staff of the Royal Society of Medicine; and Professor Michael Rutter, Professor of Child Psychiatry, University of London, for his helpful comments on the final manuscript.

My special thanks are due to Dr Philip Cauthery who has so generously shared his knowledge and skills with me over the last ten years. His contributions at various stages of the book's life have been invaluable.

PICTURE CREDITS

Pages 12, 45, 54, 73, 74, 82, 105, 111, 115, 153, 181, 190 Vision International; pp. 20, 23, 81, 93, 97, 130, 186 Hutchinson Library; pp. 28, 34, 37, 49, 57, 69, 86, 94, 138, 196 Sally and Richard Greenhill; pp. 29, 33, 42, 61, 63 Camilla Jessel; pp. 43, 56, 107, 123, 127, 141, 158, 179 Bob Bray; p. 65 Barnabys Picture Library; p. 148 Janine Weidel. Book cover: Susan Griggs agency. Picture research: Deborah Pownall.

BY THE SAME AUTHOR:

Alternative Medicine
The Baby and Child Book
The Boots Book of First Aid
The Breast Book
Breast is Best
Choices in Childbirth
The Complete Book of Love and Sex
A Dictionary of Operations
A Guide to Biochemic Tissue Salts
Overcoming Depression
The Pears Encyclopaedia of Child Health
Taking the Rough with the Smooth
Trace Elements – A New Chapter in Nutrition
The Natural Family Doctor
The Complete Book of Sexual Fulfilment
Love and Sex Over 40
Infertility
Prevention is Better

Your children are not your children
They are the sons and daughters of Life's longing for itself.
They come through you but not from you.
And though they are with you yet they belong not to you.
You may give them your love but not your thoughts,
For they have their own thoughts.
You may house their bodies but not their souls,
For their souls dwell in the house of tomorrow, which you cannot visit,
    not even in your dreams.
You may strive to be like them, but seek not to make them like you.
For life goes not backward nor tarries with yesterday.
You are the bows from which your children as living arrows are sent
    forth.

Kahlil Gibran, *The Prophet*

CONTENTS

INTRODUCTION

Until recently, in historical terms, most parents were delighted if their children survived the rigours of birth and the first year of life. Today things are rather different and most of us in the West take our babies' survival for granted. In 1900 around four to five women per 1000 giving birth died; 40 births in 1000 were stillbirths; and 150 of every 1000 children born failed to live until their first birthday. What these figures imply in terms of family distress is almost unimaginable.

Life took an emphatic turn for the better with the arrival of new medical methods and techniques and, probably of more importance, with the improvements in social conditions, especially since the Second World War. By the 1950s the medical profession was sufficiently on top of the child mortality problem to be able to turn its attention to a better deal for mothers. Maternal mortality had already begun to fall, and had fallen by three-quarters in the previous twenty years, but levels were still unacceptably high. As a result of efforts in this area maternal mortality has fallen dramatically and having a baby today is a relatively safe business.

In parallel with the dramatic developments in maternal and neo-natal care, standards of physical health in general have risen throughout the western world. Few parents now need fear that their child will die at any time of any one of a number of diseases that used to be so commonplace. With physical survival assured parents are freed to focus elsewhere, notably on the psychological, mental, social and emotional development of children. Whether this shift in focus is a good thing has been disputed: as with almost everything else in life, it seems to have had both good and ill effects.

In the past children were considered chattels. Parents could do with them what they liked until they reached marriageable age. They were then handed on to their marital partners to become, if they were female, someone else's chattels. Along with a change in the view of women that has occurred over the last thirty years or so has gone a similar change in society's view of children. The two are probably more interlinked than most people realize if only because, until a few decades ago, both were considered to be a man's property and to have little validity outside this context. Against this background there has been a new interest in the welfare of children that would have been incomprehensible to our forebears. Today we look to the mental, emotional and even spiritual future of our children in a way that is almost new for westerners.

All of this has to be put into the context of greater interest in things to do with the mind, the supernatural and the spiritual world. In the last decade especially there has been a real upsurge of interest in all of these areas as

9

increasing numbers of westerners become disenchanted with the rational, mechanistic world in which they live. This interest can be seen in areas as different as alternative medicine and oriental religions, both of which have captured increasing attention in recent years.

A hundred years ago a man would have been lucky to live much over forty but today he'll live until his seventies and, *if* his marriage lasts, he will have been living with his spouse for an average of fifty years. Such changes in life expectancy have profound effects on the whole of our lives and what with technological advances the physical aspects of life have become much more predictable than even very recently. What is *less* certain is what is going to happen to us in terms of experience. Life today is so complex and so long for most of us that the sheer potential for trouble of all sorts has greatly increased.

People today can no longer rely on what their parents or grandparents told them about the world. Indeed, much of what the older generations have to say is considered valueless as the pace of world events increases. A few individual elderly people have personal power and esteem as a result of their age and experience but most ordinary elderly people are not regarded in this way and their viewpoints are often seen as redundant.

This loss of the wisdom of the old coupled with an increasingly mobile society in which extended family units are no longer the norm has meant that many people no longer know where to look for emotional, mental and spiritual succour. Such support as was built into traditional, pre-industrial societies has now been greatly modified or even entirely lost. Although many families *are* still in touch with their older members and, indeed, in times of illness or strife families do tend to pull together, the fact remains that for the most part we live isolated lives. As a result many of us do not know where to turn when it comes to dealing with the inevitable problems of daily life. The medical and paramedical professions have, to a limited extent, tried to fill these gaps but it would be unfair to expect them to fill them well, if only because most of their practitioners have been inadequately trained to deal with such matters.

To many people, even today, the notion of focusing on mental, emotional and spiritual matters seems a waste of time. Such people often say that if everyone led a 'decent' life and kept physically healthy and active all would be well. Unfortunately, in a culture of increasing automation and a shrinking number of jobs the nobility of work as an answer to all our ills begins to look rather less than realistic. People who hold such views tend also to overlook the enormous part played by the mind in all kinds of ailments, be they bodily, emotional or spiritual.

This book looks mainly at the emotional and psychological development of children. I came to write it because as a marital therapist I am moved by the number of patients I see whose problems clearly date back to their childhood. Even this might seem fanciful to some but if they were sitting where I am every day they could not but believe it. Whilst it is all too easy to 'blame' one's childhood for everything, and to some this seems a cop-out of unacceptable proportions, there is little doubt that the very first few years of life do indeed have a profound effect on what is to follow. They are the foundation stones on which we build, and as with any building, if they are poorly laid the building will be in jeopardy. Having said this it would be wrong to assume that good foundations make for a successful or attractive building – they do not. Some people who find themselves in trouble in life have excellent foundations but the superstructure of their building is faulty or dangerous because of what has happened to them in later life. It is arguable that their good foundations stand them in good stead and that they can re-build on them but this is not necessarily always so.

At this point people usually say that I, and others like me, see 'sick people' who have problems and that the rest of society is basically all right and happily going about its daily business. Alas, this is not so. There are more people in mental hospitals than in all other hospitals put together; the biggest single category of drugs prescribed by doctors is the kind that affect the mind; agony aunt columns receive thousands of letters a year *each*; about four out of ten people going to their GP have nothing physically wrong with them; divorce rates in the United Kingdom are higher than anywhere in the western world except for the United States and the Soviet Union; alcohol and illegal drug consumption is running at alarmingly high levels; and so it goes on. These are not indicators of a society that is healthy mentally or emotionally. And what professionals see is simply the tip of the iceberg.

How then does it all start? As we have seen there is little doubt that the story begins in childhood. And recent research suggests that the period when the baby is in the womb can also be critical. What I have tried to do in this book is to look at what we as parents can do to help our children learn how best to cope with the world.

To those with any experience of children it is clear that they are all different in how much they are affected by their early upbringing. Some seem to be very resilient and others terribly vulnerable. Overall though, most parents are loath to accept that what they did had an adverse effect on the personality of their child and many end up blaming others such as school teachers, the child's friends, or even the child itself. Of course, most parents consciously wish their children no harm and the vast majority work very hard to do their best. As we shall see later (see page 103) the old argument about nature versus nurture still rages but it is largely a sterile one as both undoubtedly play a vital part, albeit in different ways.

All of these factors, and many more, slowly build together with the

'There, there, Mummy . . .' Will this little girl grow up 'mothering' her own mother?

child's experiences of life to form what is called its personality. This is created by the blend of emotion, perception, understanding and action which is unique to that child. An individual's full personality is not manifested until late adolescence, or even later, but many parents claim that even in the cradle they can tell what the basic characteristics of their baby are likely to be – and they are often right, especially if they are experienced parents.

But just as most of life's experiences tend to form a positive type of personality, one that can cope with the world fairly well and enables the individual to cooperate with others and contribute something to society, some people's experiences are so adverse, if only cumulatively in small ways, that they end up unable to deal well with the daily rigours of life and some even become mentally ill. To some extent this applies to us all for few, if any, of us are truly 'normal'.

A way round most, if not all, of the emotional and psychological ailments that so plague us as a society is to have a stable family home with two parents who care for one another and who live together in a close bond within which the child feels securely loved. Such parents encourage their child to love itself and to love them and in turn they love him or her unconditionally. They create a realistic world within the family that mirrors the outside world thus truly preparing the child for the harsh realities while he or she is still within the loving, safe environment of the family. They give the child the feeling that he or she is unique and valued, at the very least by its parents. Such parents never reject their child as unlovable and intrinsically bad, no matter how he or she behaves and they try to reduce the negative effects of their own upbringing on their children by gaining insights into their own personalities and behaviour.

Certain types of personality are valued by our society in the way it is currently organized. Some people are needed to be ambitious, for example, or no new businesses would be started so as to create work for the rest of us. Some people will always feel compelled and competent to lead, and others to follow. And in a balanced society there should always be room for the eccentric and for the creative genius. Some need to be 'takers'; some to be celibate; and yet others to spend their lives helping others, to mention but a few of the hundreds of possibilities. (On this last point there is little doubt in my mind that, in psychoanalytical terms at least, many doctors and those working in the caring professions are 'wounded'. Such people then seek to heal themselves by healing others, often for a whole lifetime. Were these individuals perfectly balanced and 'normal' who would there be to help the rest?)

As in all things human the balance is a delicate one. Most of us want to bring up children who are able both to cope with the world and to contribute something to it. And we want them to be happy, in whatever way is meaningful to *them*, even if it is not what we would have chosen ourselves.

In this book I try to give parents insights into what is going on as young children grow up. To cover every detail in a book of this length would be quite impossible so I have decided to focus on five main areas that seem to me to be either exceptionally exciting or important, as judged from clinical experience. These five areas are: pre-natal and peri-natal influences; emotional development in the early years; understanding what goes on inside our children's heads; the psychosexual development of children; and finally those problems in the life of a child that seem to create so much heartache in many families.

This is not a baby book. It will not tell you what to do and how to do it, at least not in the sense that other child-care books do. This is mainly because the more I and others like me in the medical and paramedical professions see of human beings, and especially of those in trouble, the clearer it becomes that there are no universally 'right' ways in such matters. What I hope it will do is open readers' eyes to the effects their own personality can have on the developing personality of their child. With greater insight it is possible to modify your behaviour, and even attitudes where necessary, so that your children experience, by a gentle type of osmosis rather than by 'teaching', a more, rather than less, favourable environment in which to grow up. None of us can transform the way we think or behave overnight and this is a book that you might need to re-read over the years as you change and as your ability to incorporate some of the concepts and ideas broadens.

Although the emphasis throughout the book is on families with two parents I am well aware that this stereotype forms an increasingly small percentage of any western population. However, it is still what the vast majority of children experience and it is a model to which most of us aspire.

As a therapist I, perhaps more than most, am realistic about people's *real* lives. Social pressures on us all as parents, whether we have a partner or not, are enormous and growing. Our children's expectations, too, are considerable and put us under even greater pressure to perform. There are more choices in society today than there have ever been, and while this results in joy for some it produces anguish for many. The changing roles of women and their new views of themselves have dramatically altered things: there are some women who have to work and some men who cannot even if they want to.

A book such as this is almost bound to create some feelings of guilt or dissatisfaction but I make no apologies for this. When my wife and I wrote our international bestseller on breast feeding called *Breast is Best* we were attacked by some women who claimed that we would make many women guilty by saying that it was best for babies to be breast-fed. They thought something less intimidating would be more appropriate. We did not agree then and ten years on and millions of readers later we still do not.

So it is with this book. While I have no desire to worry anyone unnecessarily, and none of us can control our lives so that we can make everything go well, there is little doubt that certain basic lessons come across time and time again when dealing with people whose childhood has harmed them. It is from these lessons that I, and others like me, have learned over the years.

We all try hard to be 'good' parents and most of us are only too aware that this is an ever-changing task for which we have no formal training. Perhaps it is helpful and reassuring to remember what Donald Winnicott, the great psychiatrist and specialist in this field, said. He created the notion of the 'good enough' mother. He maintained that no child needs, or seeks, perfection in order to grow up emotionally well balanced. Perfection is for the gods and to aspire to it in family life is to be perpetually disappointed, guilty and miserable. What I think we *can* all aspire to is to take our roles as parents seriously, to make a major investment in parenting both for our sakes and for those of our children, and to bear in mind that our children did not ask to be born – they are the product of *our* wills, not theirs. This latter point should, in my view, mean that we do everything that is humanly possible to make our children's lives the best possible foundation for their future – if only because we are so vitally central to their personalities.

I hope that you, the reader, will end up after reading this book having rethought some received 'truths' about a few things and as a result might just be able to do better in certain ways for your children than perhaps your parents did for you. Only in this way can we hope to move the world on, albeit ever so little. And this in itself is surely a worthwhile goal when we look around us.

PART I

THAT VITAL START: PREGNANCY AND BIRTH

1

THE FIRST NINE MONTHS

Until fairly recently most people thought that the psychological and emotional life of a child began at birth, though, when pregnant, many individual women have suspected that their babies are being affected by what goes on around them while they are in the womb. Research done over the last ten years or so, however, makes it quite apparent that the fetus has an emotional and psychological life from very early on. Undoubtedly, we are only just scratching the surface of the subject and the whole area is still in need of much more research. Yet, at the risk of appearing fanciful or even unscientific to many, I feel the subject deserves more consideration than it has so far received. Just which way the small amount of evidence will eventually lead us in this ill-understood area is yet to be seen but the whole subject is on the agenda now and cannot be ignored.

In 1982 the founders of the Pre- and Perinatal Psychology Association in the United States found they could not get together enough support to create a group at the annual meeting of the American Association for the Advancement of Science. In 1985 they attracted 400 delegates to their second International Congress in San Diego. Suddenly psychologists, psychiatrists, gynaecologists, general practitioners, nurses, midwives and parents were starting to see that the subject held considerable fascination.

At the heart of all this interest is the notion that human life starts in much more profound a way with conception than was previously recognized. This view asserts that the process of human development starts at conception, is continuous throughout life, and that birth is just one, however important, milestone. Although most health professionals and indeed many others working with children in various ways are unaware of it there is now a growing body of clinical research in this field and some of the findings are turning long-held concepts on their head.

For example, a 'pre-natal university' in California teaches parents in a systematic way how to communicate with the fetus with manuals and cassette tapes which suggest techniques for interaction. In a follow-up of 500 babies born after the programme, researchers claim to have found enhanced physical and mental development, including easy birth, early speech, physical agility and healthy bonding between parents and child.

There is now no doubt that the fetus can see, hear, experience, taste and even, on a primitive level, learn, whilst in the womb. It also seems highly likely that he can feel too. Clearly this latter finding has especially profound implications for the shaping of attitudes and expectations about himself. The mother is a fetus's main source of incoming messages, as we shall see, but this does not mean that, if she gets upset over missing a train, her baby will be irreparably damaged. What it does mean though is that persistent feelings, held over some weeks or months, could affect the baby. This applies to both positive and negative feelings.

Interestingly, although most research has looked at the baby–mother link, increasing evidence suggests that the father plays a vital role too. Several studies have found that women fare better if they have a loving and supportive partner during pregnancy and there is little doubt from research

A happy, supportive relationship with her partner will enhance this woman's chances of having a contented pregnancy, birth and baby.

and clinical experience that a woman who has a happy sex life when pregnant is likely to have an easier birthing experience than her sexually inhibited sister. Many mothers know that a fetus reacts very differently to the sound of its father's voice compared to that of her own and it has been shown conclusively that a fetus can hear clearly from the sixth month. Babies in the womb, it appears, move to the rhythm of their mother's speech and research shows that babies in the womb react differently to various types of music played to them. This has important implications for how we talk to our babies while they are in the womb: calming, quiet talk is obviously preferable to shouting and other loud noises.

Some mothers know that they can calm their baby in the womb by soothing talk or singing. This could be a baby's first lesson in coping with the stressful world, and what a valuable one. As we shall see in Chapter 3 one of the most vital tasks a baby has in its early weeks of life is to learn how to calm down after the disruptions forced on it by the outside world.

During the first few months of life, while a baby is still inside his mother, it seems reasonable to suppose that she can influence his growth and behaviour later on in life. By creating an emotionally warm, safe and enriching environment in the womb a mother gives her baby the best possible start in life. During this time the mother is the baby's window on to the world. Everything she experiences affects him in one way or another. Probably the most important is the relationship between the mother and her partner. Such research as has been done shows that a loving, supportive partner can have a beneficial effect on a woman's enjoyment of her pregnancy and thus on her child's eventual wellbeing.

One study rated the quality of a woman's relationship with her partner as second only to her attitude to being a mother in good child-rearing. One researcher found that a bad marriage or relationship was among the greatest causes of emotional and physical damage in the womb. On the basis of the study of over 1300 children and their families it was concluded that a woman in a bad or turbulent marriage ran a very much greater risk of bearing a psychologically or physically damaged child than did a woman in a secure, nurturing relationship. Even smoking, physical illness or really hard physical labour seemed to exert a less damaging effect, and these are hazardous enough. Babies of poor marriages were found to be five times more jumpy and fearful than the babies of happy relationships and such babies often grew into problem children. At four and five years old it was found that these children were undersized, timid and over-dependent on their mothers.

All such research, and there is a lot of similar work, some of which will be mentioned later, suggests that the psychological and emotional life of a child starts in the antenatal period. It is impossible to deny the very real value of antenatal care and many studies have found that babies are more likely to be born healthy if a mother goes regularly to such clinics. Yet, the average antenatal clinic concerns itself mainly with the physical health of the mother and baby and little, if anything, is ever said about their mental and emotional wellbeing.

This is a major mistake. For many a woman, having a baby, especially if it's a first, is the most psychosexually disruptive event of her life. (When I use the word 'psychosexual' I mean those behaviours, emotions, beliefs and so on which are to do with how the mind and a person's sexuality interact.) Yet she gets little help or support in coping with it and even fewer opportunities to air her problems and fears. In our culture, with its somewhat limited social contacts, many mothers are lonely when pregnant and have few opportunities to learn about the mysteries of pregnancy and birth from older and more experienced women. As a result many worry a great deal, often quite unnecessarily, yet there is, in the absence of the extended family, often no one to whom they can readily turn.

What I should like to see, in the interests of future generations, is the opportunity for all pregnant women, and indeed their partners, to have a session or two with an insight-trained counsellor so that such concerns could be aired and hopefully dealt with. At this time marital and other relationship difficulties could also find an outlet and professional help given that would benefit both the parents and their unborn baby.

Although some readers might find all this somewhat far-fetched it is certainly not a new fad in medical circles. The Chinese established the first pre-natal clinics a thousand years ago and almost all cultures, however 'primitive', have rules about not frightening pregnant women or letting them witness certain events. Thousands of years of human experience have proven that fear and anxiety antenatally can adversely affect the fetus and there is no reason to disbelieve such ancient wisdom today.

To bear a baby that she does not want is, for a woman, one of the most distressing situations in life. Although there are no studies I am aware of which shed light on this subject, it makes sense to assert that a woman who is upset for weeks or months might do harm to her unwanted baby. It is true that many women who start off feeling very unhappy, or worse, about a pregnancy, change their mind and come to accept the baby but it is equally true that some do not. Perhaps for them an abortion would have been in the best interests of the child – not to mention themselves. Given that reluctant mothers will behave differently towards an unwanted baby once it is born it is almost impossible to tell how much of the subsequent harm that is done to the child's upbringing results from antenatal maternal feelings. It seems reasonable to me, and I can only express a personal view, that there is at least a potential for fetal harm in such circumstances.

Perhaps the main problem with any research in this field is the fact that it is almost impossible to get direct evidence about what babies experience in

These women may be well cared for physically – but who is looking after their emotional needs?

the womb, or even for that matter in early life. None of us can remember our moods as a fetus and the vast majority of us have no access whatever even to later experiences such as being breast-fed or potty trained.

But all is not lost because it is now clear, contrary to even quite recent medical 'knowledge', that the fetus and the young baby *do* remember things and that such material is stored away in the unconscious where it exerts an effect on personality development and later behaviour. In many people it is likely that such material remains 'dormant' for a whole lifetime while for others it surfaces in various unconscious ways to affect their lives.

As well as the nervous pathways of the brain affecting the mind of a fetus there is also the possibility that the mother's hormones do so. The hormone oxytocin is present in large amounts during pregnancy and is responsible for the contraction of the womb during labour. Laboratory experiments show that it produces amnesia in animals; even well-trained animals lose their ability to perform tasks under its influence. So it could be that at least part of the reason that we remember so little about our time in the womb and during birth is that the memories are 'washed away' into the unconscious by oxytocin.

ACTH is a stress-related hormone that has somewhat opposite effects to those of oxytocin. This could explain why it is that people appear to have clearer unconscious memories of traumatic and negative birth experiences than of good ones. ACTH floods into the child every time its mother has a fright or even becomes very anxious and it has recently been found that stress hormone levels are extremely high in new-born babies. This too could explain why we retain a clearer unconscious memory of such events than of less traumatic ones.

A lot of work by rebirthers, regression hypnotherapists, psychologists, and indeed in many other forms of psychotherapy, has shown that it is possible to gain access to memories from this time of life, however deeply they lie in the unconscious. This appears to reflect a condition called state-dependent learning, involving an event such as birth which we experience as a state of physical and emotional arousal. It becomes a part of our mind and we retain a memory of the whole event in all its components. However, we can only rarely gain access to the memory directly, as a whole. One way that this *can* be done is to recreate certain of the components of the memory and thus encourage the mind to make up the deficits from the real memory of the events held in storage.

Recent research has found that people's ability to memorize things can be influenced by their current mood. In one study subjects were asked to remember two sets of words, one when they were happy and the other when they were sad. People who were sad during recall remembered about 80 per cent of the words learned when they were sad, compared with only 45 per cent of those learned when they were happy. On a purely practical basis then it can be helpful to try to recreate the mood you were in at the time of an event you are trying to remember.

There are various manoeuvres that can facilitate people's remembering pre-natal and birth experiences. It is difficult to know which of the many methods that have been used to give people access to such memories is best but hypnotic regression and rebirthing are certainly highly effective. With either of these methods it is possible for a substantial minority of people to re-live these earliest months of life and even to go back to their birth and beyond. Many studies have followed up such memories and checked them with the parents of the people involved, usually to find out that something that the individual could not possibly have known was in fact true.

There is such a vast body of such stories that it can no longer be denied that the mind remembers things from very primitive stages in the womb. No one knows how, of course, because as far as current scientific theory is concerned the brain is simply not sufficiently sophisticated structurally to be able to do so. This raises all kinds of interesting, but as yet unanswerable, questions about the possibility of a memory system that rests outside the nervous system. I also mention later something of what the psychologist Jung had to say about the 'collective unconscious'.

It is well known that human beings communicate on many levels, some at least of which are intuitive, the unconscious of one relating to the unconscious of the other. We look at this in some detail on page 114. But here let's concentrate more on the other subtle ways that humans communicate. Whilst no one knows how parents communicate with their unborn baby I believe that 'telepathic' communication is one way. Telepathy, although widely researched by the scientific community for many decades, is still something of an uncharted sea, but it is impossible to deny people's personal experiences in this field.

Many a highly attuned couple, especially if they have been married for some years, find that they can communicate non-verbally with one another, even over considerable distances. Some couples even dream about the same things at the same time. Some people have been declared dead according to all known medical tests and yet return to life to report in considerable detail what went on in the room. They can say what was said and done, describe the expressions on people's faces, what everyone was wearing, and so on.

Telepathic experiences are commonplace and it is increasingly clear that even inanimate objects can retain memories just as we humans do. In a process called psychokinesis a gifted person can hold an object and reveal things about its past history by tuning into some kind of 'memory' it holds.

Clearly memory is a complex and ill-understood subject which will doubtless elude our scientific efforts for many years yet. However, there is now little doubt that, whatever the explanation, many adults can fairly easily be helped to remember events and the emotions associated with them that date back to their days in the womb. Just what effect such unconscious memories from these formative periods of life have on our behaviour as children or adults is difficult to assess but it would be a very brave person who would claim that they have none.

Having seen that many memories of intra-uterine life lie in the unconscious it now makes sense to look at the communications system between mother and fetus that provides the inputs to create these memories.

A major factor is undoubtedly the mother's hormonal state. Quite obviously a mother and her baby do not share a common brain or nervous system yet they do exchange various substances via the placental circulatory system. This means that certain things that happen in a mother's blood will be reflected in that of her baby. This seems to be particularly true for substances such as drugs, chemicals and tobacco products but is also known to be so for maternal hormones.

What usually happens is that the mother, because she is in touch with the outside world, experiences something, be it positive or negative, and then reacts hormonally to it. For example, let's imagine that she runs over a dog when driving. At once her stress hormones are called into play and surge around her bloodstream. They enter her child's bloodstream too, of course, where it makes sense to believe that they have some effect. If these changes are transient they probably do little harm but even this cannot be guaranteed. Mankind has known since time immemorial that extreme stresses to pregnant women can upset or even damage the fetus, perhaps to the extent that it is born abnormal in some way.

But, serious though this is, many such instances are probably not preventable. For example, it is unlikely that the woman could have done anything to stop the dog from running into the road and this is even more true when we look at the effects of women being pregnant in Second World War concentration camps or in other highly stressful situations.

What is of more interest to us is the possibility that lesser, but possibly preventable, stresses might also have harmful effects on the unborn baby. Indeed, this does seem to have some basis in truth. It appears that surges of maternal hormones alter the balance of the baby's biological rhythms in such a way as to predetermine a likelihood that it will be more sensitive to, say, anxiety although research does not yet indicate when in its development the fetus is most susceptible to such overdoses of maternal stress hormones.

A team of researchers studied the records of Dutch women and their sons who had been subjected to famine in 1944. Severe overweight problems were very common in the men born during this time and the differences depended on the stage of growth in the womb that the, as yet unborn, boys were at when the famine struck. Mothers suffering severe hunger in the first four or five months seemed to have the greatest likelihood of producing obese men. The team concluded that nutritional deprivation at this stage of pregnancy seemed to set the body's control mechanisms wrongly, perhaps for ever.

Another study, this time in Finland, looked at people including some who had lost their fathers while they were in the womb. The rates of psychiatric disorder, particularly schizophrenia, were highest in those babies whose fathers died before they were born. Perhaps, something about the distressed state of their mothers had been transmitted to them as unborn babies, although the fact that they had no fathers after being born must also have exerted some effect.

Dr Thomas Verny, author of *The Secret Life of the Unborn Child* claims that excessive stress hormone production in the mother leads to low birth weight, and/or gastric disorders and/or reading difficulties and/or behaviour problems.

Further evidence that hormones can affect personality comes from studies done on mothers and their children who were exposed to female sex hormones. In the early 1970s oestrogen, alone or with progesterone, was used to prevent miscarriages. Women who were about to miscarry were given fairly large doses of these hormones. When studies were done of the temperaments of the children who had resulted from such pregnancies it was found that they had somewhat increased feminine traits. The differences were most marked in the girls but the boys too were more effeminate, less athletic, and were significantly less aggressive towards their fathers than were the non-drug group. All the differences were of temperament rather than behaviour disorders but, having said this, it must be possible that varying levels of even normal pregnancy hormones at various critical times during the nine-month period could just have similar personality or temperament modifying effects.

Perhaps the most obvious way that a baby makes its presence felt when in the womb is by kicking. Many things provoke this response including maternal emotions (such as anger, fear and anxiety), external noise, and certain foods the mother eats. The sensitive mother gets to know what provokes her baby's increased movement and will try to reduce the stresses to a minimum. Of course, kicking is perfectly normal but many women say that when they are upset or excited and elated the fetus seems to kick more.

Physical changes in the mother can affect the baby too. For example, one study found that 79 per cent of pregnant women were planning to change their homes, partly because of the baby. Another found that moving house during pregnancy delayed bonding between mother and baby after birth, arguably because of the stress involved in the move. Perhaps a way around this is to ensure that you get enough rest and that the move is made as stress-free as possible. Some experts also advise 'explaining' to the baby what's going on. You can plan for the stress of moving house in general, so try to make things easier for yourself.

There is little doubt that mothers communicate with their unborn babies at an extrasensory level. Many pregnant women feel that they have a relationship with their baby while it is still in the womb and many more dream and in doing so confront conflicts that they are unaware of over the pregnancy or the birth of the child. A surprisingly large number of pregnant women dream about giving birth to monsters, dead babies, or even sometimes to animals. What is interesting is that research has found that women who have such anxiety-provoking dreams are more likely to have shorter, easier labours than those who don't. It appears that in their dreams they are confronting and dealing with their unconscious fears and anxieties and are thus better able to cope when it comes to the real thing. In a sense they are unconsciously rehearsing their worst fears and so defusing them in their minds. What the effect of these alarming dreams is on the child no one can tell but they are without a doubt yet another form of communication between the mother and her unborn child.

When it comes to looking at things from the mother's point of view, her maternal emotions seem to be paramount. Study after study has found that

Will the stress of moving house have an adverse effect on this mother's relationship with her baby?

happy, contented mothers have bright, outgoing babies and that on average the reverse tends to be true. Almost every woman will be ambivalent about her baby, however unconsciously, and to however small an extent. That we can hate the ones we love is plain to most of us. In fact hate could be said to be an integral part of love. Few women are totally without negative feelings, even if most such feelings are unconscious, about a new baby and there is little doubt that the love they feel is to some extent modified in its effects on the unborn child by their negative feelings.

Therapists who work with women who miscarry sometimes find that there are unconscious reasons for the loss of the baby. Indeed there is good research showing that persistently miscarrying women who have psycho-therapy can sometimes be helped to hold on to their babies, so it does appear that a woman's unconscious attitude towards her baby can be critical in the matter of 'holding on to it' or 'rejecting' it. One major study of more than 400 miscarriages found that a fear of responsibility and a fear of having an abnormal baby greatly increased a woman's chances of having a miscarriage. In another study women who had miscarriages were found to have unconscious fears of being abandoned by their husbands, friends, family, or even by their doctors.

Without a doubt physiological changes are produced by drugs, chemicals and alcohol. Smoking and all these other noxious substances have a profound effect on the fetus and might well provoke unconscious memories of one kind or another in the baby. Alcohol is the most obvious of these because at its worst it can kill the unborn child. Clearly both of these toxins have physical effects on a baby and it seems reasonable to suppose that they have emotional and psychological effects too. There is now little doubt that the best policy over alcohol in pregnancy is DON'T.

Cigarette smoking presents much the same problems. The odd cigarette probably does little harm but women who smoke forty a day or more seriously run the risk of having a small baby in poor physical condition.

Smoking may relieve the stresses and strains in her *life – but what is it doing to her baby?*

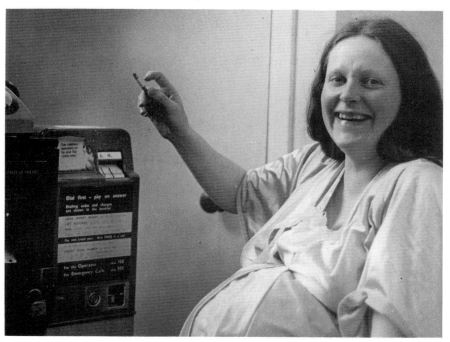

More to the point in a book such as this, such children are affected mentally in no small degree. At the age of seven they will be more likely to have problems learning to read and will have a higher rate of psychological disorders than children of non-smoking mothers. A father's smoking can affect his unborn baby too, of course, as the woman breathes in his smoke and delivers it second-hand to their baby. So once again, it appears that what we do pre-natally affects our children not only physically but also mentally and emotionally. Any chemical substance that adversely affects the growing brain could reduce the child's abilities to express positive emotions and to relate positively to its parents.

For this and many other reasons it makes sense to go out of your way to keep exposure to chemicals and noxious substances of all sorts down to a minimum during pregnancy. This includes things like not painting the sitting room because the fumes might just harm the unborn child and his future development. If readers think that this level of care is rather obsessional they should reflect that pregnancy is a relatively short time in a woman's life yet if she behaves thoughtlessly or recklessly she could end up regretting her decision at leisure.

Whilst this does not mean living in a sealed room for the whole of pregnancy it does make sense to avoid X-rays, industrial chemicals, domestic chemicals (including weedkillers, dry cleaning fluids etc.) and, of course, all but the most essential of life-saving drugs and medications. Think twice before you put anything on your body or take anything but healthy food into it. Even repeatedly dyeing your hair during pregnancy might just be harmful so it pays to be vigilant.

Just as a baby grows physically from one cell to a highly complex and well-differentiated child and then an adult, so the same things happen in his emotional and psychological development. Every baby starts to develop its own concept of 'I' – ego, as it is called – during his stay in his mother's womb. Some experts now believe that a fetus has the nervous apparatus to start on this process as early as three months.

When a mother becomes anxious her feelings are transmitted to her fetus in various ways. Her hormones make him agitated and he kicks and moves about, as we saw earlier. He might well also be capable of thinking about how to reduce this unusual and none too pleasant sensation.

It also seems sensible to suggest that babies of persistently depressed mothers are more likely to become miserable themselves. Clinically this appears to be the case. Unhappy, depressed or ambivalent mothers do indeed seem to produce more neurotic children, perhaps because their children's poor sense of self is born out of their own negative emotions.

If all this sounds fanciful, bear in mind an experiment that was done in the United States. A researcher took three flasks of a bacterial culture whose rate of growth was known with considerable accuracy. That is, the numbers of bacteria that could be expected to be present at any time in any given condition could be predicted from long experience.

She then gave one flask to a 'normal', healthy person to hold; another to a healer; and the third to someone who was depressed. After a fixed time the bacterial contents of the flasks were counted: the normal person's flask was found to contain exactly what would have been expected had it been left on the laboratory bench; the healer's had considerably more bacteria than would have been expected; but most interestingly of all the one held by the depressed person contained substantially fewer. Her depression had stopped the bacteria growing and reproducing at their normal rate.

We have all experienced the negative effect of being with someone who is 'down' and there are those with psychic skills who can detect depression even when it is unrecognized by the person himself. All of this makes it highly likely that a baby in the womb will be affected by its mother's moods and especially by depression. It is my belief that some miserable adults started life as miserable fetuses because of their mothers' ambivalence or even frank hostility to them. There is regression evidence that suggests that this is not as unlikely as it at first might appear.

In *The Secret Life of the Unborn Child* Thomas Verny details the findings of a study he did into what people thought influenced them and what actually did. His group had highly charged pre-natal and birth histories. The results showed that an individual stood a much better chance of growing into an emotionally stable adult if his mother had looked forward to his birth. Verny also found that the more positive a mother felt about childbearing the more likely her son or daughter would be to grow into an adult that had a healthy sexual attitude. The best possible outcome, he found, was when a woman who looked forward to having her baby, enjoyed her pregnancy, and ended up with a child of the sex that she wanted. This combination seemed to produce adults who were less prone to depression and anger and who were better adjusted sexually.

From all of this it will be plain that a baby doesn't just emerge after nine months in his mother's womb as the person that we know him to be right from birth. He was this personality before and probably for some months. Many women say that they can tell how placid or active their baby will be simply by his responses in the womb to all kinds of stimuli. This is an especially common story in those women who have had several babies. Indeed, experience bears them out because highly active babies and children tend to have been very active fetuses.

Just how much of his personality is the result of his intra-uterine environment and how much can be attributed to his genetic blueprint no one knows but there is little doubt that the early environment plays a much larger part than was previously suspected.

2

THE IMPORTANCE
OF BIRTH

Although giving birth is a happy and momentous event for many women the whole subject of birth and its importance in the scheme of things is strewn with problems, heartfelt emotions and guilt. Until fairly recently mothers were happy to end up with a live baby as a result of their birthing experience but today things have changed in that they are looking for a better outcome overall and one not simply judged in terms of the immediate health of the baby.

In the last few years there has been increased interest in the way in which birthing is conducted in the West and there have been important moves to make birthing less technological and more instinctive, especially in France. There, Frederich Leboyer and more recently Michel Odent have laid great emphasis on gentle birthing as a way of making a baby's entry into the world less traumatic and more pleasurable for all concerned.

Just how valuable such measures are from the child's point of view is hard to know. We shall look at some of the evidence in a moment. Whatever the value to the child though, there is little doubt that the majority of mothers who have experienced gentler, more instinctual birthing methods prefer them and as a result feel better disposed towards their babies. This in itself probably bodes well for future mothering (and indeed fathering) so there could be an argument for such methods on these grounds alone.

There is little doubt that being born is just about the most stressful event both physically and emotionally that a fetus has gone through. That the whole process might also be pleasurable can only be surmised but this is almost certainly likely to be true given that he is bathed in sensuous fluids and massaged as he passes through his mother's birth canal. However, what is not disputed is that it must also be very painful as the gentle massaging motions give way to a substantial amount of pressure and presumably pain.

That the pain is considerable can be deduced from the fact that newborn babies have very high levels of naturally occurring painkillers called endorphins. Indeed, some of the highest levels of endorphins measured in humans have been found in the new-born. As the birth progresses modern medicine may step in and apply further painful stimuli in the form of obstetric forceps, an electrode in the scalp to measure the fetal pulse rate, considerable stresses and strains on various parts of the body as he is pulled out, a cold, noisy environment, and so on.

Even though this is how it was, few if any of us can consciously remember the events, however hard we try. But such memories exist, as we have seen, and can be retrieved in several ways. Many studies have looked at what people remember about their births under various forms of regression therapy such as hypnosis and have checked back with their parents to see how the facts correlated. Almost always they are accurate, sometimes down to the most intimate of details. One study asked people re-experiencing their births what the position of their head was at the birth. This is clearly something that even the mother couldn't have known and therefore could not have told her child. The researcher then went back to the obstetrician's notes and found that the subjects had described exactly the position of their head and shoulders in the last stages of labour and how the head was delivered.

Clearly, if a child can remember such small and insignificant details

Even the most normal birth can be stressful.

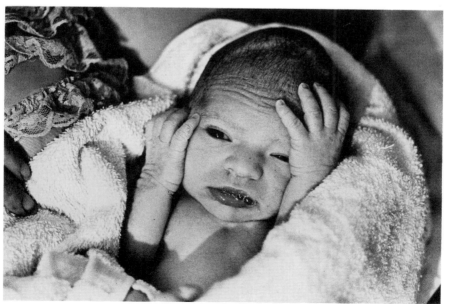

about its birth it is highly likely that it will remember the more traumatic events. It also seems possible that it will be able to remember its mother's emotional state.

One study found that the simplest of births (unassisted and uncomplicated vaginal births) gave rise to outward-going people who were optimistic and trusting. This has been borne out in animal studies too, especially when comparing vaginally-delivered with Caesarean-delivered monkeys. Next up the scale, according to the study, came breech births (babies born bottom first) which, some studies claim, suggest that the child will be more likely to have learning problems later in childhood. This latter point has not been confirmed in later studies. At this level too came the minor abnormalities of labour which correct themselves.

Higher up the scale of birth traumas though come such things as the cord being trapped around the neck. This, it is claimed, gives rise to a greater number of throat problems, speech impediments and swallowing difficulties later in life than would be expected.

Premature babies can be very disadvantaged both physically and emotionally although, to be fair, the vast majority are not. A few days' prematurity is probably of little importance but as the degree of prematurity increases the effects become more marked. According to those who advance these views, some such babies seem to be rushed all their lives. It is claimed that the reason for this is that they feel they will never catch up as a result of their prematurity.

This couple are doing all they can to improve the odds for their premature baby.

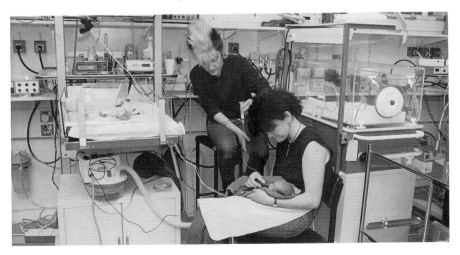

But at the top of the scale of birth hazards come events such as very high blood pressure in the mother (eclampsia); serious cord problems; placenta previa (an abnormally placed placenta that can actually get in the way of the baby as it comes to be born); and severe distress in the fetus. These so endanger the life of the baby, however temporarily, that they must have mental and emotional as well as the provable physical effects on both mother and child. Certainly, mothers who have had such birthing problems seem to cope less well with their new-born; do not appear to bond as well with them; and are less likely to breast-feed successfully. So obviously such momentous events in the delivery room can have profound long-term consequences.

The effects on the babies are more difficult to prove because so many other events affect a baby's life between birth and any measured parameter in later life but there are those who are experienced in regression work who claim to be able to detect in adults the personality types and problems arising from say, a caesarean birth.

In 1985 the *Lancet* published a paper that showed a correlation between adolescent suicide and birth events. The birth records of suicide victims, all teenagers, were scrutinized for forty-six risk factors and compared with those of a control group of teenagers. The results showed that there were statistically significant differences between the suicide victims and each of the controls and no differences between the controls themselves. Three specific risk factors were found to be powerful indicators of teenage suicide: breathing problems lasting for more than an hour at birth; no antenatal care before twenty weeks of pregnancy; and chronic disease in the mother during pregnancy.

Of course, as with all the effects I discuss in this section, by no means all babies who suffer such events end up committing suicide. What this study does suggest is that when other pressures at home, school or whatever, make a teenager's life, however temporarily, unbearable, those who have this kind of birth and pregnancy history are more likely to kill themselves than are others. The question that cannot be answered but which is likely to be a subject of endless fascination is, why? Could it be that at this highly impressionable stage in life around the time of birth such children 'learn' somehow that life can so easily slip away from them? Could it then be that later in life rather than cling on, as most do, they let go more easily?

Whatever the answers to such questions there seems little doubt that we should do everything we reasonably can to prevent such birth traumas. It could even be argued, for example, that saving babies who have bad breathing problems around the time of birth leads to a larger number of potential suicide victims in the teen years. This is certainly what the authors of the above study have suggested and it deserves consideration.

There is also no doubt that many of the interventions of western

technological birthing methods do at least some harm and no one denies
that once we start on the road of medicalizing any given birth we end up
using more and more technology in a sort of cascade that becomes ever
more likely to produce hazards. No one would want to see birthing
returning to the dangerous business it was in Victorian times but there is
increasing concern, among even some conservative obstetricians, that
medical intervention in birth has gone too far and now needs to be looked
at in a new light. This does not mean throwing out all the advances that
have been made but rather seeing how they could be used only when
absolutely necessary so as to protect babies and mothers from their
provable side effects.

We have looked so far at the baby and the effect of birth on him or her
but it is becoming increasingly clear that the mother's state of mind at the
time also plays a vital part in the eventual outcome. Several studies have,
for example, found that mothers who are sexually aware and at ease with
their bodies are more likely to have uneventful births than are sexually
anxious women. Relaxed, confident women who are looking forward to
the birth of their child also tend to have trouble-free birthing experiences.
We have already seen the effect of ambivalence on birth and it is possible
that some such women struggle unconsciously to hold on to their babies
partly because they have considerable anxiety about being separated from
them. Studies seem to bear out this hypothesis. One heartening fact to come
out of all this is that normal anticipation and worry about labour and birth
seem to have no adverse effects at all on the duration of labour or on
uterine contractions.

What can be shown for sure, however, is that troubled women are more
likely to have delivery complications, and so might stand a greater chance
of having a child that is, in its turn, damaged emotionally or physically.
One study looked at two matched groups of women, one that had serious
problems during pregnancy and another that hadn't. Independent obstetricians who knew nothing of the personal histories of the women reported
the birthing events of all of them. Those who had at least one serious
birthing complication all belonged to the 'troubled' group; none of the
'normals' had any birthing complications.

This seems to point to the crucial, yet almost totally ignored, need for
women to have better emotional and psychological care during pregnancy
than they currently receive. What are needed are trained counsellors who
can detect the woman in trouble and help her with insight-giving
counselling of some kind. This would be real antenatal care and true
preventive medicine such as we currently don't see.

Against a background of increasing technology in the birthing room it
now seems sensible to look at what we are doing both before, during and
after birth to see what effects any or all of it might have on the emotional

Mother and baby are already enjoying one another and he's only been born for a minute.

and psychological state of both the baby and the mother. Much is known already about the difficulties some women have in bonding to their babies and in turn the effects that this can have on such babies. Anything that can be done to help a women enjoy her pregnancy and birthing experience more must have positive effects on her attitudes to the baby which, in turn, could have long-term positive effects on his personality and emotional growth.

It is, as with so many things in medicine and health, all too easy to look at a situation and see the results of the worst kind of behaviour. However, what are impossible to assess are the shades of grey between the black and white that seem to be obviously harmful and helpful respectively. This is reflected in the various studies that have tried to assess the work of Leboyer and like-minded 'natural birth' experts. As one would expect, the results are mixed but my reading of them is that overall, and judging by what the studies have set out to test (which could, of course, be inappropriate), there are no grounds for pursuing the proposition that all babies should be born in a 'natural' way or they will be disadvantaged. Certainly I should like to see all those women who want a 'natural' birth being able to have one – indeed my wife and I did so ourselves – but having said this it would, in my view, be quite wrong to suggest that those who do not do so harm their babies in any way. On the contrary, even though I am no fan of interventionist obstetrics and think there ought to be far less interference with birthing, there is no doubt that most babies born using such methods fare perfectly well, especially if they have loving parents who really want them. Such small 'harm' as might be caused either emotionally or psychologically can, almost certainly, be remedied by caring parents. When it comes to very difficult births the picture is without a doubt less rosy but even here a loving, caring family, and especially a wholehearted mother, can rebalance such disadvantages as there may be so as to minimize the effects that such birth traumas have.

Given that the practice of obstetrics is unlikely to change in the near future and that there will always be a certain number of unforeseeable and unpreventable birthing problems, the major emphasis in the emotional and psychological care of young children will almost always fall on the early years of life. How we as parents deal with our children's earliest development is what the remainder of this book is all about.

PART II

LAYING THE EMOTIONAL
FOUNDATIONS

3

CALM YET AWARE

Not many years ago most people, even (or especially) the 'experts' thought that young babies were simply a collection of primitive reflexes that kept them alive – rather like simple forms of life. They certainly weren't thought of as little people in their own right and, as such, had few rights. Even today many adults still treat babies as if they were things and really cannot understand how it is that such a small, helpless 'object' could be truly human with a range of emotions, complex sensations and so on.

But babies are people right from the start and it is helpful, if not vital, successfully to negotiate each stage of psychological development before going on to the next. It is important to remember that we as adults should be interested not only in what our children will turn out to be like when they are *adults* but what they are like *now*.

The emotional needs of children include love, pleasure, the need for intimacy, assertiveness and discovery, anger, self-discipline, loss, guilt, fear, dependency and many others. The way children learn about their emotions and the way parents handle them have a lasting effect throughout life. We as parents have a big influence over our children's lives – an influence that can appear awesome to many. But if we can have adverse effects by behaving inappropriately, we can certainly have positive effects by taking into account our children's emotional needs and by reducing the harmful effects on them of our own personalities. Recognizing and correcting problems early unquestionably produces happy, self-reliant and loving children who, in turn, become well-balanced adults.

We saw in Part I that babies have a vigorous life, both physically and emotionally, in the womb, and at birth are capable of an astonishing array of activities and can even learn simple tasks. In this chapter we look at how the new-born baby starts to experience the world by interacting with it emotionally and learning to use his senses.

In the very earliest weeks of life a baby seems to be doing two main things with his time. First, he is interested in the world around him and second he seems to be self-controlled – he isn't overwhelmed by all the inputs from his environment but somehow seems to be able to come to terms with them, however strange they may appear.

Babies are people right from the start – many parents can tell their child's personality from the very earliest days.

But however calm and collected a baby seems to be much of the time it doesn't take much to disrupt his world. Because he is so totally helpless and relies for his food, and indeed everything else of importance, on his mother, any failure on her part to fulfil these needs almost certainly results in distress of some kind. Of course, we have no way of knowing what babies are thinking but the way they *behave* tells us a lot. A baby who is hungry will cry to gain the attention of his mother. If she recognizes that the call is for food she will feed him. But she may not be good at recognizing his needs and may react inappropriately or leave him to cry in increasing distress because she has been told that babies cry for so many reasons that it is virtually impossible to sort out why. Evidence suggests that this is not so. Indeed, many mothers can detect very different types of cry in their children and this is especially true of experienced mothers. So it is that such a mother can tell if her baby is wet, hungry, angry, tired, or whatever, just by his type of cry. For more about this, see page 216.

How we respond to this picture says a great deal about what kind of parents we are.

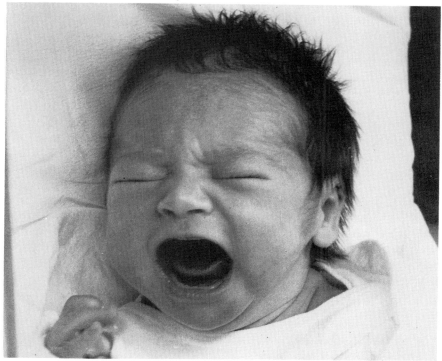

How we respond to our baby's crying depends to some extent on how we ourselves were treated in childhood. If we have learned, however unconsciously, as children ourselves that our crying was ignored then we will be more likely to react in the same way to our own children. When I hear of mothers who leave their baby crying in a bedroom while they remain downstairs ignoring it I sometimes wonder whether this is the way they would behave to an adult who was crying. When the matter is raised with such mothers they say that they wouldn't behave in this way to an adult but seem to think it acceptable to do so to a baby. Many a woman has never thought this through before and it comes as a considerable shock to her to realize that she really has been mistreating her baby, perhaps from the very first day she brought him home from the hospital.

A crying baby always has a reason. Crying is a way that he communicates his needs and all crying should be taken seriously. It will probably seem unlikely to the reader but it is quite possible to bring up a young child in such a way that he almost never cries and certainly doesn't cry inconsolably. Mothers who have their young babies with them all the time wherever they are and whatever they are doing can often tell what their babies' needs are in advance of actual crying. A baby who is responded to willingly and generously doesn't need to create a fuss every time he needs something and as a result he spends a lot less time being unhappy, frustrated and crying.

It is easy to see then that even the very youngest of babies can start to learn that the world is a good place in which needs are answered fairly quickly or that it is a bad place which involves a lot of yelling and screaming to get what you want, or perhaps even to end up not getting it at all. You don't need a PhD in psychology to recognize these two types of behaviour in adults, some of whom know no other way of behaving than to yell or scream whenever they want something that they can't immediately get. We condemn such behaviour in adults yet we all too often unconsciously encourage it in babies – at a time of life when they have everything to learn.

For a baby it is a vital part of learning about his emotions to find that he has the capacity to return to being calm and collected after a big emotional upheaval. Some babies are over-excitable; some babies find it difficult to be calm; and some are difficult to excite. An over-excitable baby may be overstimulated and efforts to improve matters will usually make things worse. At the other end of the scale is the baby who has little interest in the world around him. He may be physically droopy as well as emotionally so.

A way of understanding all this better and coping with it to your baby's advantage is to become very aware of your child's senses and how he or she uses them. Look at how he reacts to his world and try to see which senses he uses most and which he uses hardly at all. The way ahead then involves encouraging those that he doesn't much use and playing down those that he

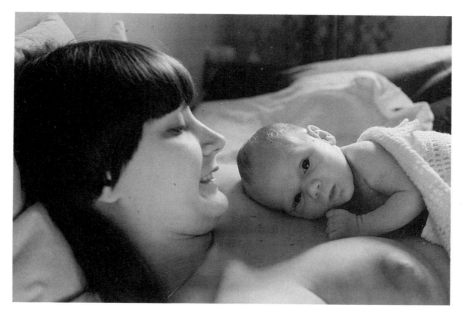

This baby has just had a fit of rage but is now calm and 'connected' to his mother again.

over-uses. If a baby is very poorly aroused, for example, try to engage him in activity that stimulates his under-used senses while at the same time keeping him 'controlled' and engaged in what he is doing using his other senses. An excitable baby can be calmed, for example, by being rocked or walked around in a sling or a baby carrier. He will quickly associate the pleasant rocking motion which calms him with the comforting talk and you will have added to the collection of sensations that can calm him down and keep him calm.

If a baby is to learn how to cope with itself and to take an active interest in the world you will have to be prepared to do whatever it takes to keep him calm yet open to new experiences. This will mean a lot of close observation and involvement on your part. Helping your baby be calm and return to calm after crying is an important lesson that teaches him that the world is not always horrible and that even very bad feelings disappear to be replaced by good ones.

You may hear it said that spending so much time with your baby will mean you are spoiling him and that children should learn from day one that the world is a harsh place which they had better get used to dealing with. Nothing could be further from the truth. Clinical experience suggests exactly the opposite: babies who are helped to be calm and in control are more likely to be independent and resilient later in life because they have inner resources to enable them to cope with the world and, as a result, can return to being calm once a disruption is over. Babies are not born with this skill; they need to learn it.

At this point many parents become somewhat anxious and ask how much they will have to invest in their baby to achieve this. There is, of course, no absolute answer but the truth is that it is almost impossible to invest too much in a young baby and that they vary greatly as to how much attention and sensory input they need if they are to stay calm yet alert. Unfortunately, we live in a culture that has become used to putting babies aside as much as possible and to ensuring, or rather trying to ensure, that they interfere with our adult lives as little as possible. Some young parents try to do the least that they can get away with compatible with continuing their own lifestyle with the minimum of interruption by the baby. A baby who persistently intrudes too much can be in danger of being battered.

There is no doubt that the approach to helping your baby to learn about staying calm that I have outlined above is hard work, but the bigger the investment you can reasonably make, the better the rewards will be both in the short and the long term. Even if your baby seems calm and alert most of the time you can still improve on this by reinforcing calming behaviour and adopting a parenting style that increases his or her interest in the world around. The answer here is to try giving lots of different types of sensations to your baby and by learning how best to entertain him to encourage him to use all his senses. There is evidence from both human and animal studies that what really matters are *active* experiences like showing your baby things and doing things with him. Simply turning up the television or surrounding the child with flashing lights does nothing to aid its development.

In practical terms helping him to use all his senses will mean that you will be able to prevent over-activity and disruptive behaviour by spotting it early and dealing with it and pre-empt under-activity by learning how to stimulate your baby to use his senses and to take a delight in the world around him. This latter can be exceptionally time-consuming especially for the parent who believes that a good baby is a quiet baby. Many such parents say that they are grateful to have a calm, quiet and understimulated baby because it makes fewer demands on them. This is understandable as far as it goes but doesn't take account of why the baby isn't making the most of the stimuli about him and what he could learn from his environment if he were more actively encouraged to do so. At one extreme end of the scale the baby could be depressed yet the mother would think he was simply being good!

Just how effective you are at this will depend very much on your own personality style, your marriage, your partner's personality, your own childhood, and the current environment you find yourself in. Life can be pretty stressful even without a baby and of course all these stresses and strains continue and influence not only you as parents but also your baby. Conflicts with older children, the threat of redundancy, money or housing problems, persistent marital difficulties and so on can all produce problems that will make it more difficult to relate well to your baby. He too will pick up the body language and the negative feelings around the home and will quite likely be more fractious as a result. This can all too easily lead to a situation in which the baby and his parents wind one another up.

Something that most parents tend to forget is that we adults are developing as human beings, and as parents, all the time. People often ask why it is that they seem to have babies of such different temperaments even though they are the same parents and have given the same genes to their children. The answer, of course, is that they *aren't* the same parents and that they *don't* give an exactly similar collection of genes to each child. As we age we change, often quite dramatically, in the way we behave and think. Not only do we change as individuals but the nature of our partnership changes too. So it is that a first-time parent can be very different indeed from a third-time one, even if they are the same individuals. This comes about because over the, say, six years between the three babies the world has changed, the mother or father has changed, their relationship has changed, the family situation is different, and so on. At the very simplest level people realize that they are more anxious and aware of themselves first time around and that they gain in confidence as they become more experienced in family life, but this is only a superficial approach. The nature of the relationship between a couple does change, sometimes dramatically for the worse, once they have children and as the power balance within the relationship shifts new personality traits begin to appear. As more children come on to the scene more personalities have to be accommodated under one roof and again the picture changes. As the children grow older and begin to assert their own personalities this once more alters things and a parent who coped very well with babies may now have trouble – or vice versa.

Women who, for example, love their babies because they give them, the mothers, the unconditional love they need and perhaps haven't ever really experienced before in life, often find that once these same babies become children who have their own minds – and by definition the power to reject their mother – they go off them or find them difficult to cope with. Some such women unconsciously prolong the baby business by having several so that they can always be sure to have at least one human being at any one time who loves them in this total, unconditional way. This has been called 'smother love'. When such women come into therapy they turn out to have had emotionally distant mothers or fathers who never really gave them the love they needed. Such women – and the same can be seen in men – are love-hungry and seek to satisfy their appetite with their children. If such a woman grows in her marital relationship over this early babyhood period she may well be able to find the unconditional love she craves in her adult relationship and so won't need to look to her children for it. This is much more healthy because it does children no good to be thought of as love objects, only to be rejected in various subtle ways as they get older and start to become less attractive in this context. This is just one of many ways in which our unconscious minds influence the way we behave towards our children – even to the extent of whether or not we decide to have them in the first place.

Whatever the reasons for a woman's displeasure or dissatisfaction with her baby they tend to reduce her delight in him and her willingness to devote time and love to caring for him in the earliest days. Much of this goes on at the unconscious level and the father may be totally unaware of what is happening. All he sees is that his wife doesn't appear to be attracted to or particularly loving towards the baby.

If any of these things seem to strike a chord in you perhaps it would make sense to seek professional help to talk things over. It is a sad but real fact that most people, and not just young parents, focus much too closely on the immediate problem when trying to find answers to their worries with their children. The real answers almost always lie much deeper and have their origins in the childhood of the parents themselves or perhaps in the ante-natal events surrounding the child.

Some fathers – and indeed mothers – are intensely jealous of the new arrival, however unconsciously, and this can wreak havoc in the relationship not only between the jealous parent and the child but between the adults too. Again someone who had little love shown to them as a child can be very sensitive to the loving and close relationship the other parent has with the baby. He or she may then, again unconsciously, apply pressure to the loving parent to show less affection to the baby in some way (for example, by stopping breast-feeding early) in the hopes that the woman, in this case, will focus the 'spare' love she will then have on her husband. Many men experience jealousy like this on the arrival of a new baby and this can so colour the situation that they virtually disable the mother and make it nearly impossible for her to mother her baby naturally and wholeheartedly.

Add to this the concept of the 'ideal' mother and in our culture we have a mix that can all too easily make it very difficult indeed for the baby to receive the kind of care, time and love that will enable him to be calm and attentive. Many women (and their partners) have an idea in their heads of an ideal mother but the main thing to remember about the ideal mother at

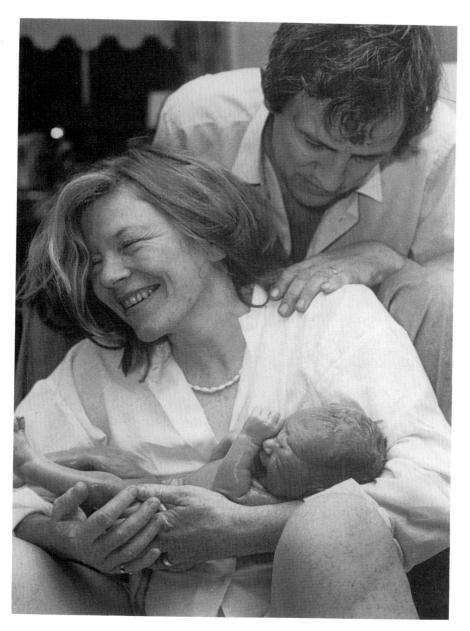

Moments after birth. Mum is delighted. Dad's face shows some mixed feelings – will his life ever be the same again?

this, or indeed any other stage, is that there is no such thing and that provided that you can throw guilt out of the window you will almost certainly do well for your child – as most parents do. This can be very difficult to do though because of the way we bring girls up in our culture. (See also page 228.)

We can all look back in middle age and blame ourselves for something to do with our children. In fact it is terribly easy to blame ourselves for *everything* that goes wrong with them. But this is too harsh a judgement. In practice the vast majority of half-way decent parents do the best they can for their children in the circumstances. Having said this it is vital to be self-critical to some extent if only to ensure that we are aware of those things that *do* harm our children so that we can do something about them.

But it is during the earliest days that most of us are dogged by fears. Fears of actually damaging the baby, of being inadequate as parents, of not having enough to give emotionally, of being a bad mother, of being tied down, of being controlled by a little tyrant, of his disruptive effect on the marriage, of the baby's emerging sexuality, and so on. Any new experience in life is accompanied by at least some anxiety and this is perfectly natural. However, it really helps to talk these fears through with someone who has insights into them if you are to do the best for your baby.

During this early phase and indeed later in life there is no reason to believe that every moment will be a joy with children. The danger is that when it is not – and it often isn't for reasons that are beyond your control – you will blame yourself and eventually even give up bothering because it all seems so hopeless. Even the most overwhelmed of parents can, with a little insight, see what is going on and then do something about it. No situation is truly hopeless. The trouble is that babies, even when they are at this very early stage of their development, push all kinds of buttons in the unconscious minds of their parents – buttons which in turn produce behaviour that can be detrimental to either the baby, the individual adults, or the parents' relationship. Some, women especially, become so over-whelmed with feelings of inadequacy and self-hate that they become depressed. This leaves them with few or no resources to be able to invest in their babies and understandably the babies suffer. Apart from the briefest of baby blues, all depression in young mothers is worth taking very seriously because a baby needs stimulation and loving inputs at this stage or it won't successfully negotiate it and be ready to go on to the next. On page 265 you will find details of helpful agencies to which to turn if your depression seems to be hanging on.

All of these problems can be greatly reduced if the parents have other adults who can help care for the baby in the earliest weeks and months. In this way a grandparent, or even a close friend or relative, can to some extent compensate for the inabilities of the parents, especially if one is depressed or absent. Of course some parents find themselves with little or no such support from even their extended families, but all need not be lost if you look for other sources of support in the community such as a mother and toddler group.

The trouble with all of this is that having a baby and trying to do the best for it brings out many of our old unconscious feelings and quite consciously makes us realize our personality faults and failings. Many of the qualms people have about being 'perfect' parents are simply reflections of their feelings about their own sense of inadequacy. Western cultural stereotypes about parenting aren't much help either. The arrival of a baby simply highlights these old insights and brings them into focus.

A new baby also means change and many people are not good at it. Realizing that you are pretty impatient, intolerant, easily made to feel guilty or whatever, perhaps for the first time in such a real way, can come hard and making changes to cope with such revelations can be very tough. The reality of having a baby for many people then is that it shows up (or they fear it will) their own personality failings. If we have problems in our marital relationship we can always, however unconsciously, blame our partner for being so difficult. It is almost impossible, though, to blame an 'innocent' little baby so we can only reflect our negative emotions and shortcomings back on to ourselves, which is where they really belong anyway. For some parents this can be a bleak experience.

But having said this, for the aware individual who has at least a few insights these lessons can be some of the most valuable they will ever learn and is undoubtedly why many, especially women, say that having children is so rewarding. Through the self-knowledge they gain they find themselves and through their love for their baby they modify their behaviour and expectations in a way that probably wouldn't have been possible in the context of any other human relationship.

We have seen then that the first phase in the emotional development of a child is his ability to stay calm and to get the best from his environment. But what are the implications for later life if this phase isn't successful?

The world is full of things that disturb our calm. Let's focus on emotional factors here though because a book such as this is no place to consider all the other, more obvious ones – most of which have emotional effects anyway.

We are all exposed to situations that make us angry, fearful, anxious or whatever, and how we deal with these emotions is important not only to ourselves but to those around us. We all know the individual who, when made angry, for example, seems to go to pieces for the rest of the day, or even longer. They appear to get stuck in an 'anger mode' and can't get out of it. Something somewhere, deep down locks them in, often quite against their will and much to the distress of all around them. The same applies, of course, to other negative emotions. Such people have never learned to calm themselves – and this probably dates right back to babyhood. They have mislearned that a negative emotion such as anger should not be expressed (for more on this see page 206) or that if it is people will be angry in return, will punish them, or withdraw their love. Whatever the reason they internalize their anger and brood on it. This not only makes it impossible for others to help them out of it but actually makes them less lovable, thus fulfilling their own prophecy that it is unlovable to express anger. Of course it isn't; it is perfectly reasonable to have negative emotions and to express them appropriately *but* most important of all is to have learned very early in life that this is OK and that you will still be loved afterwards. A part of this is being able to return to a state of calm in a relatively short time so that life is not totally disrupted by the original cause of the anger.

It is almost certain that all of this starts to be learned very early in life. A baby who is taught early on to have confidence that bad feelings don't last for ever is likely to grow into an adult who treats the world as if it will behave in the same way. Brooding, sulking and moodiness in many adults would be greatly reduced by such lessons in the first few months of life and society would be a calmer, more peaceful place. As we shall see, many of the battles and 'scenes' of adulthood originate from conflicts in the first months of life at a time when babies are learning most about the world and how it will treat them.

The implications of all this for babies who are left to themselves and not stimulated are many. It appears that babies who are stimulated, and whose senses are all being used much of the time, grow up to achieve more and to enjoy life more. The consequences for babies who have severely depressed mothers, for example, are well known and children who are brought up in children's homes have perceptible disadvantages compared with those who have two parents to care for them on a daily basis. However, stimulating a baby so that it gets into the habit of relating to the world does not only have effects on the baby itself but also on the mother who, because she sees results for her effort and time wants to invest more in her baby. This mutually rewarding behaviour is the essence of any successful human relationship and makes it all the more likely that the next vital stage of a child's emotional development will occur.

4

THAT FIRST LOVE AFFAIR

In the first two or three months most babies are mainly involved with their physical sensations. This is not to say that they have no feelings because it is obvious to any parent that they do. However, their main preoccupation is with what their bodies tell them about the world outside and within them.

Around this time though a baby starts to recognize its parents and a true interpersonal relationship is struck. Many a mother, picking up the cues, starts to court her baby, as in any other loving relationship. They 'talk' to one another, smile a lot, use body language, kiss and cuddle and slowly learn to trust and love. This is probably the most vital stage in the emotional development of a human being and how it is negotiated will influence much of the individual's future.

If at this stage your baby isn't showing any signs of falling in love, try spending more time with him, taking more interest in him and courting him more. As his abilities to love you grow he will relate to more people around him, especially those who care for him for any length of time. At this stage mothers may become jealous if the baby shows a preference for another adult rather than her but she will probably be the main care-giver and so the baby's main love, so long as she is around. If the mother is out at work or away from her baby for whatever reason, this relationship will, of course, be hampered and the baby might well fall in love with someone else. This can be very hurtful to many mothers but is a price they pay for leaving their baby. Everything in life has a price – nothing we choose to do is without some sort of cost. I consider the subject of mother-substitutes in more detail on page 238.

Just as with everything else loving has to be learned and your baby will need to have his emotional and physical responses reinforced if he is to realize that this new skill is worthwhile and enjoyable. Lessons learned earlier about returning your baby to a calm, relaxed state can now be emphasized when courting. If his attention is distracted, gently soothe him and bring him back to a stable, balanced position with a calming smile, soothing voice, gentle strokes, or whatever. Encourage him to give and receive love using all his senses. We all tend to grow up using fewer of our

Wooing and courting a baby is a vital way of helping him to feel loved.

senses than we could and many people go through life virtually crippled in the under-use of one or more of their senses. Some, for example, cannot bear to be touched; others cannot say what they feel; some never really listen to what is said; and yet others don't see what is there clearly to be seen. Such poor learning of sensual inputs is at the heart of millions of poor relationships and is especially damaging when one partner in a relationship communicates largely on one level (using one sense) and the other on another. At the simplest of levels some are more verbal and others more intuitive and feelings-centred. To the 'feelings' person all the talking in the world won't help and a very verbal adult can become intensely frustrated with a partner who can only 'feel' and not verbalize their feelings so that they can be dealt with. More to the point, many couples never really communicate well because they each have a sensory blind spot which the other keeps aiming for. As a result little ever gets communicated. All the cues, which are perhaps obvious to others, are missed and the relationship sinks into trouble. This sort of thing goes on in all human relationships, not just those between partners in a marriage. In fact, of all the reasons people give for divorcing their partner 'poor communication' almost always comes top of the list. Communication failures start in the earliest days of the formation of a baby's first love bond.

Most women believe that they will fall in love with their baby as soon as they see him but it usually takes some time. At first a mother's love may appear to be ignored by her baby but within a few months most mothers perceive that the baby becomes warm and responsive, communicates using all his senses and is able to get back to loving them easily even if their courtship is interrupted briefly. A baby who reacts like this, and most do, is a joy to be with and this is just as well because human babies are so demanding for so long that were they not lovable we'd probably be loath to keep on caring for them.

Of course babies, like adults, vary in their lovability and their ability to show love. This might be just the way they are or could be a reflection of the way you are feeling. Perhaps domestic, work or marital upsets have unsettled you. If you feel as though this is your problem it would be sensible to spend more time interacting with your baby and trying consciously to build up the love bond. Seek help with any other problems you may have, too, of course. To improve your relationship with your baby you may need to set aside more time for him which could seem like hard work and even burdensome, especially if you are unhappy about some other area of your life but it will repay you later on.

One of the greatest problems with some babies, if only at certain times, is that they appear rejecting, angry or frustrated. Few mothers find this easy to take. 'After all I've done for you – all you can do is reject me' is the kind of painful thought that goes through most mothers' minds at one time or

This little fellow isn't feeling very lovable at the moment. Hopefully his mother will show him that she still loves him *and then they will be 'in love' again.*

another and such rejection can be one of the reasons why babies are physically abused. A woman who is unhappy or unsettled for other reasons, whose housing or health is poor, or whose husband is absent or a problem, won't need much in the way of even apparent rejection by her baby to feel thoroughly unloved and that the whole world is against her. If such an 'innocent' can let her down it's the final straw – or so she thinks.

How we react to rejection is conditioned in our early childhood and we as adults tend to react in a knee-jerk way, often experiencing great hurt. Anything or anybody that can inflict such pain is then hated, albeit temporarily, and wanting to hurt the person who has rejected us is the feeling that follows. Unfortunately this is exactly the reverse of what a baby needs. He needs to learn that even when he is expressing negative emotions he will be loved and that negative emotions are an acceptable part of being human.

The love affair we are discussing usually develops most powerfully with a baby's mother – mainly because it is she who is the baby's main caregiver. Fathers too can form a love bond with their child in exactly the same

Not quite sure what he feels – yet this Dad will soon become a central part of his baby's life.

way and having both parents makes the child's experience of love all the richer because he will gain from different expressions of love. One partner may, for example, be very vocal and another very physical, and so on. If either parent is depressed this can hinder the process of falling in love but the other can make up for the loss.

Most of us marry people who are somewhat like us in personality and past history, but often there are substantial differences too. So it is that most successfully married couples have a core of similarity that they can share and live with easily yet they also have sufficient differences to remain individual and interesting to one another.

Unfortunately, babies are not wholly lovable and attractive, just like other human beings, and they have an unfortunate tendency to exhibit the least attractive traits of their parents, or even of a more distant relative. Many a parent sees an annoying characteristic of themselves or their partner in their baby even when he is quite young and this can get in the way of falling in love.

Another hazard to be aware of is thinking of a baby as a doll. Quite a few, women especially, have the romantic storybook notion of babies which, when unfulfilled or frustrated, makes them feel rejected, guilty or a failure in some way. Such a mother believes, however unconsciously, that babies are all fun and as soon as hers starts to grow up and shows it has a mind of its own she can't cope. Some women who feel like this were undoubtedly brought up in a way that made them feel like a plaything until they were quite old, at which point they were expected to become 'real people'.

Obviously such a woman is quite liable to let her baby down as soon as it stops conforming to her stereotype of an 'ideal' baby and she is in real danger of losing touch or falling out of love with it. Such a baby now becomes irritable instead of smiley; inward-looking instead of extrovert; lonely instead of interacting, and so on.

A bigger problem that most parents experience at this stage of their baby's emotional development is to do with intimacy. Some parents, for example, especially if it is their first baby, fear that the baby's needs for intimacy will somehow overtake them or even their relationship. Some, women in particular, fear being 'taken over' by the baby if they give in to their feelings for intimacy wholeheartedly. Many adults are, of course, very bad at being intimate – they have had poor training or negative life experiences that have taught them that intimacy is risky – perhaps unacceptably so. They fight shy of it in almost all situations and it's not difficult to see why they have little, if any, to share with their baby. Fathers could be in greater danger because they are not compelled to interact with their babies and young children. This means that some at least withdraw and become distant. In some instances the mother, because of her love-hunger, wants the child all to herself and more or less excludes the father from contact with it. This is ultimately likely to affect a baby of either sex.

Clearly few people will be able to seek professional help to sort out why it is that intimacy is so difficult for them but they can, and must, make every effort to get a handle on their uncomfortable feelings and modify them. If you get your partner to help, together you will be able to pinpoint ways in which you seem to get it wrong. For example, when you really should be close and intimate do you avoid your child, reject him, or perhaps stimulate him too much? Your family or even close friends who really care for you might be helpful at pointing out where you get the emphasis wrong.

Closely linked to this is the fear of rejection already mentioned. 'If I invest all this love and intimacy in the baby and then he seems to reject me I've lost everything' is the argument. In fact the opposite is the case because the more you invest the less chance there is of the baby rejecting you. He may do so temporarily, but this happens in all love relationships and you should not perceive it as more important than it actually is and as a total withdrawal of love. Many people with marital problems have mislearned this from a very early age. They look at a small lapse in their love bond, decide it is a withdrawal of love and before they know where they are they have thrown the whole relationship into the ring, whereupon anything can happen. Most parents who fear their baby might 'reject' them also have similar fears in their other relationships. The way we behave as parents is simply the way we actually are – we don't have a separate personality we wheel out called Parent. Some people are so fearful of rejection that they never dare make a commitment to anybody in case they are rejected. Once again this is at work in troubled couples who, for fear of rejection, offer little or nothing to their partner and then wonder why they get nothing back. In interpersonal relationships you get out mainly in proportion to what you put in, though sometimes one can be lucky and get the occasional emotional bonus for no effort.

So it is clear from all of this that falling in love with your baby may not be that simple – it often needs working at, just as in an adult loving relationship. It usually occurs automatically if all goes well but there will be times when it's great and times when it isn't. Your baby will have its off days and so will you and your love bond with your partner will interfere with things from time to time. But overall if your baby feels loved and comfortable with you and your emotions, and you can be freely intimate with him, he will have the best possible start in life.

5

COMMUNICATION

From about the third or fourth month of life until the end of the first year a baby really begins to learn to communicate with those around him. A part of this is learning to give and receive love as we have seen but this is just the start. Very soon he adds in physical, mental and emotional developmental skills that increase his ability to interact with the world around him. He now realizes that what he does affects you and what you do – in short he responds and creates responses.

A central feature of all communication is that it has an effect on those who receive it. At this stage a baby is learning very fast what these effects are. The central rule at this time is to return your baby's positive efforts at communication with equally wholehearted positive responses. In other words, you act as a sort of mirror for him. In this way he learns that a smile brings forth a smile and, eventually, a word another word. Long before we communicate verbally we do so non-verbally and it is thought that this is why we can remember so little of our non-verbal memories – we simply didn't file them away in areas of the brain that can be accessed using adult concepts of language. (They can, of course, be tapped non-verbally – the way they went in – using techniques such as regression hypnosis, various types of body-centred therapy, and rebirthing.)

This stage then is the vital time when a baby learns that the world responds and creates responses in him. Slowly he learns – it is not inborn – that actions cause reactions. In other words the world is run on a cause-and-effect basis. If he throws a ball out of his pram it disappears from view and at this stage ceases to exist. His model of the world tells him that if you want something to cease to exist, throw it out of your pram.

But although physical things such as balls can be readily predicted to react in a certain way – all balls thrown from prams fall to the ground – the same cannot be said for emotions. He may smile at his granny but she may *not* smile back at him. She may even do the opposite. Confusion reigns. Suddenly the world isn't cause-and-effect any more. Slowly, if an action doesn't provoke the expected response he'll stop doing it altogether on the simple, learned basis that it doesn't work so why bother. Alternatively, he might mislearn that certain behaviour provokes a response which most of us would call inappropriate. For example, a child brought up by a very obsessional mother will learn that creating even the slightest mess brings forth displeasure from her. He then learns to associate the production of messes with bad feelings. Such a baby or young child subsequently goes to extreme lengths to regain its mother's love by not being messy and so grows up to be another obsessional individual whose life is plagued with concerns over cleanliness and other notions of perfection.

Probably the best way to help babies of this age to communicate is to encourage them to be calm, if they are excited, or more active if they are very quiet or subdued and then to be really inventive about how you

Even a simple task like making the tea can be a time for communication.

stimulate them. Cooing games, little songs, give-and-take games, and so on, all work well and can keep a baby interested for minutes at a time. If he shows a lack of interest, as he will almost certainly do at this age, let him rest and do something else and then start again when you judge he is ready. Don't overwhelm him – his attention span will be very short. What is far better is to have a wide range of sensory and emotional inputs so that he is learning and communicating in many different ways. Obviously we are all different, especially in our emotional characteristics, but it is important to ensure that all the major emotions are freely expressed, including the negative ones.

Some parents try to protect their young children from experiencing negative emotions but this is not wise because it is now that they can learn to cope with them within the close, safe relationship of parental love. Life is punctuated with negative emotions such as anger and frustration and we need to learn how to cope with them and then to return to a calm state unless we are to be tyrannized by life's setbacks. It is arguably more important for a child to learn how to cope with negative emotions than with positive ones because, by and large, positive emotions such as curiosity, assertiveness, pleasure, excitement, joy, dependency and love are valued and encouraged in all kinds of ways. Even at this early stage a child can start to learn that it is not wicked or unloved because it feels angry, stubborn, demanding, jealous or possessive, for example. All these emotions are appropriate at certain times and should be accepted for what they are. Unfortunately, as we saw earlier, many adults find they feel so bad when they have negative emotions that they make all kinds of erroneous assumptions about being unlovable, unworthy, sinful or whatever. They then project these feelings on to their child.

When learning to communicate at any age there's a fair amount of frustration to be coped with. Parents cannot be expected to respond to everything their baby does and a baby must learn to accept this. Delays, too, are inevitable and, unlike in the first few months of life, towards the end of its first year a baby will be able to accept delays within reason. Frustration is a part of all of our lives and it is now that it can be dealt with in a loving atmosphere. The child must know that its needs *will* eventually be satisfied but that the whole world can't revolve around it alone. Once more one sees the results of such mislearning later in life in those who cannot tolerate frustration because their parents have brought them up to think that every whim should be gratified at once. Such parents are often very insecure in themselves and cannot bear to think that their child might not love them. They then drop everything at the slightest demand from the child – who, as a result, thinks the world owes them a living – and double quick too. When the realities of life hit them they become frustrated and even angry because it is all so out of line with their experience of immediate

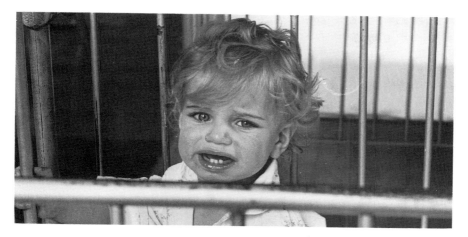

Babies and very young children can't explain their needs.

gratification. Such parents have done their child a disservice by bringing it up in this way.

When learning to communicate with your baby so as to get the best out of him and to teach him to be an effective communicator you will need to pay attention to several things. Being able to read his emotional signals is a vital start. It is also valuable to watch very carefully to see how your baby communicates and then, as we saw earlier in Chapter 3, to encourage the senses that he doesn't much use. But all of this needs to be done against a backdrop of supporting and building up his earlier achievements.

Much of this effort on your part will throw up all kinds of problems about how you as parents communicate, not only with one another but also with other people. This can be pretty disruptive as you realize that your problems in communicating with your baby are simply a reflection of your own general problems in communication. If you are, for example, easily made to feel guilty; if you readily feel inadequate or that you are a failure at most things you touch, it's hardly surprising that even the tiniest sign of any of these in your baby will trigger your old responses and make you feel bad. This will then make you retreat into your shell and you will communicate badly with your baby.

Once again, your partner, close friends and relatives, or in the last resort a professional, can help you gain insight into your behaviour. You can then come to terms with your guilt, realize that you are no more inadequate than the next person, make an effort to tolerate anxiety better, and so on. If you don't, your child will almost certainly grow up learning inappropriate communication skills.

As in any communication system it's very easy to misperceive what your baby means. Babies can't explain what they need and it's very easy to misread what they really mean. A baby who wants to stop breast-feeding may start to fight or actually stop and pull its head away from the nipple. He is saying 'I've had enough' but his mother may see the behaviour as cussedness because he hasn't fed on that breast for as long as he normally does. She persists and a fight ensues. Both mother and baby become fractious, the mother doesn't let down the milk in the other breast and feels she is a failure. A few more feeds like this and the baby is on the bottle. Had such a mother read the baby's cues and signals and been more willing to be led by her baby rather than by her own needs all would have been well.

All babies are different. This is a frustration to parents who have had one child who behaved in a particular way because they then think that they understand children in general. It isn't until such parents have had several children or have perhaps worked with babies and children that they realize that they are all so different that they need to be communicated with in a unique way, just as do adults.

Just as with adults too we tend to project our own desires on to our babies (for more about this process of projection see page 110). The mother referred to above was keen to go out to her evening class and couldn't wait to get going. The baby's playing around frustrated *her* need to get the feeding over with and so produced a problem for them both because the baby wasn't aware that he had to drink up quickly that particular evening. She dashed out to her class feeling terrible, guilty, a failure and a poor mother and her baby cried for an hour with the babysitter. The baby may well have sensed her impatience and the mother for her part was, indeed, in no mood for any messing about but the result was poor communication because both parties had different expectations of the event. We misperceive messages like this all the time as adults – and we can communicate with language – so how much easier it is to get things wrong when one party cannot talk.

Having said this an intuitive and sensitive mother communicates with her baby all the time and knows much of the time exactly what his needs are by carefully reading the tiniest changes in his body language and his moods and expressions. This then is the basic skill of communication, as in anyone of any age. Learn to read your baby's signals and teach yourself to respond to him in a way that satisfies him most. After love, this is probably the most important lesson that you teach your baby.

PLAY

Perhaps one of the most interesting and arguably most valuable things a parent can do with their child is to play with them. Play is helpful to a child's development at almost any age but perhaps especially so in the first five years.

Whenever a parent, or indeed any adult, plays with a child the adult lets down his or her guard of 'adult respectability' and comes to meet the child at his or her own level. In short, the adult lets his or her own inner child out to play. For many this is a wonderful experience in itself especially, and perhaps surprisingly, for men who, in our culture, have few culturally sanctioned situations in which this can be done. The child sees the parent now as much more like them and thus more accessible and approachable. Real communication can occur in such play situations partly, of course, because the adult is functioning on the child's level and on his or her terms. Usually the world runs to the advantage of adults and is run according to their rules. But when playing with a child the adult has to rethink the rules and work within the world of the child's mind and imagination. This is why play therapy is so valuable – sometimes it is the only way of communicating with an emotionally hurt or damaged child.

In the earliest days even a simple game such as peek-a-boo, or tossing a rattle up and down becomes the focus of attention for a young baby and a sign that he is worth paying attention to. Some parents still feel that play

This little girl isn't just amusing her brother, she's enriching his life.

must have some sort of structure to it or that it should involve costly equipment. Nothing could be further from the truth. The real business of play is the interpersonal communication that occurs. It hardly matters whether this is over a supermarket box that is acting as a sledge or over an expensive train set. Arguably the less structured and contrived the toy the more the child's imagination can be called into the game and the more he or she will enjoy the game and benefit from it. Formalized toys and games tend to encourage adults to take over, if only because there is a 'proper' way to play the game. Anyone's game is as good as another's when it comes to a cardboard box and the sensible parent will be happy to defer to the child's interpretation of exactly what the game is.

Early on in life play is the main way that children learn about most things. Making such learning enjoyable is the basis for school learning. Through learning to play with someone else he will eventually learn to play alone and then to become self-reliant and confident as a result.

There are whole books about children's play and this is no place to go into the subject in any great depth. Suffice it to say that play, because it is about communication, tells a child a lot about the adults who care for it.

A father who is never there, or who is reluctant to play with his young child, the mother who is always 'too busy', or the parent who always dominates the games or has to win, say more than they realize about their child's worth to them. And the child usually picks up the message loud and clear. Children learn a lot about the personalities of their parents when they play with them and there is little doubt in my mind that this is why some parents at least are none too keen to play with their children.

Another feature of children playing with their parents is that two generations with very similar genes come together in competitive situations. When playing, a child's true personality will often show through, especially as he gets older and starts to assert himself. Many's the parent who finds this hard to deal with especially if the child starts to exhibit features of their *partner's* personality that they dislike or find hard to cope with.

For many parents today life is a very serious matter – they hardly ever play themselves – so it is not too surprising that they sometimes have trouble relaxing enough to play with their children especially when this involves playing the games on the child's terms. This can be made all the more difficult for the parent if the child is very bright or very dull as either can call for levels of patience that the parents may not normally have.

As children grow physically they can come to out-perform their parents physically, let alone intellectually and this can be hard for some parents to take. It's bad enough if your eleven-year-old knows more maths than you ever did but when he can beat you at football too things can look grim! Many's the man, especially, who sees this as a reminder of his advancing age and for those that cannot cope well with the implications this too can be a handful emotionally.

As in so many areas of a child's emotional and psychological development it behoves us as parents to ensure that when we play with our children we put *their* needs as the priority. If we are determined to win at all costs or to show how clever we are then we can hardly blame a child if he comes to think of himself as something of a failure. If we are aggressive then we should expect our children to follow our lead. If we are always unavailable to play or do so half-heartedly how can we be surprised when our children take no pleasure in play and seem to lead dull, joyless lives?

I believe that we as parents can learn a lot from our children when it comes to playing. Most of us keep our inner child well and truly controlled, or even locked up much of the time. One of the joys of parenting is that under the guise of doing something with or for our children we can let our own hair down and share in the pleasures of childhood again.

6

BECOMING A PERSON

From about nine months until the middle of the second year your baby changes from being a baby to being a toddler. He starts to develop more rapidly as a person in his own right and his biggest problem is coping with all his new-found skills and the emotions he experiences. He begins to make his own contribution – not just to mimic what you do – and this involves a lot of experimentation. As with any experiment, or indeed learning anything new, the potential for failure is high and most lessons, at this age, as at any other, are hard learned. Now is a time for integrating physical and sensory skills with emotional ones as the child becomes more sociable.

The child begins to express his emotions more openly, freely and wholeheartedly; he starts to learn to control them and to realize that his emotions can affect other people. Sometimes limits have to be set to emotional expression: negative emotions such as anger or frustration can become too powerful for the child to control. The overpowering effect of negative emotions can be truly terrifying for children of any age, but now is a vitally important time for boundaries to be lovingly set. You will need to step in and defuse, with love and calming activities, any negative emotion that is getting out of hand. Some children are never taught to do this and go on to frighten themselves all their lives – right into adulthood – experiencing almost any negative emotion as overwhelming. Feeling totally at sea and unable to see any way out of the awfulness, they are frightened of the destructiveness of their own physical and emotional sensations. And yet much of this kind of adult behaviour could be prevented if babies as young as a year or two were helped to return quickly to a calm state after experiencing negative emotions. Babies need to be reassured that they will still be loved and wanted by their parents after displaying negative and 'unlovable' behaviour. Stern handling can make the child feel evil rather than temporarily out of control of what is, after all, a new experience for him.

During these nine months a child begins to imitate parental or other adult emotions and behaviour and it is now, perhaps for the first time, that you will begin to see that your emotional state profoundly influences that of your baby. It cannot be stressed too often or too strongly that children, even very young ones, learn much about emotional responses from us, their parents, and we are usually quite unconscious of how we display our emotions at any time because it is such a natural response – it is part of how we are. But young children are like blotting paper, they soak up everything that is going on around them and even unconscious messages are perceived by them and incorporated into their model of the world. If parents are happy and positive this will usually work out well but more worrying is when parents are not happy either in life generally, with one another, or with themselves. This too communicates itself, quite unconsciously, to the baby and his mood and behaviour change as a result. In this respect it could be argued that an intelligent and perceptive child might both benefit *and* suffer more from his domestic emotional environment – and indeed this is the experience of parents with bright children.

But probably the most vital developmental factor at this age is the capacity the child has to feel attached to his or her main care-giver. From this loved and secure position the toddler can start to explore the outside world – a vital part of growing up both physically and emotionally.

When a child copies what we do it's easy to see how he learns. But he learns about our emotions in exactly the same way.

Children of this age are still very mother-centred but slowly start to explore at greater distances from her. Gradually the distance increases and the time apart grows but the central and important thing is that the child knows that even if he can't see his mother she will still be there when he returns.

At the middle of his second year, and some experts think it begins earlier, a child starts to realize that he is physically separate from his mother – not just an extension of her. This also goes for emotions. At a year a baby feels one emotion at a time and probably fears that a display of negative emotion might cause rejection or even a total loss of his mother. As the second year progresses most children realize that they can be angry with their mother and yet loved by her the next moment.

Now the baby begins to realize that people, including themselves, are made up of complicated combinations of emotions. His mother, whom he generally perceives as 'good', can also be 'bad'. This is the basis of all of our adult battles to come to terms with the apparent contradictions in human emotions. That love and hate are so closely linked is well known by everyone who has truly loved. Love is in fact a highly ambivalent emotion, because if we are to feel it for someone we also know that they have the power over us to withdraw it and so hurt us. This ambivalence about people starts very early in life, probably in the cradle, and lives on into adult life, at least to some degree, in all of us. In some people, and they number very highly among those who come for marital therapy, these battles rage daily in their lives because they were never settled in their early childhood. They have never obtained an integrated view of themselves as people who can be loved and hated in the same breath. At any stage of love withdrawal they panic and retreat or want to end the relationship completely on the basis that 'if I can't be loved wholeheartedly and unconditionally, I don't want any of it'. Such people hurt themselves and their partners terribly but the trouble is rarely within the relationship itself. It dates back to the earliest days when they failed to learn, in a loving and secure atmosphere, that love, hate and the whole gamut of emotions that goes along with them come as a package in a balanced human being and that they are all acceptable and able to be coped with if the background relationship is one of unconditional love and care. It has been observed that when we fail to acknowledge one emotion, as a result of having built up unconscious defences, we also smother the ability to recognize others. An individual can, for example, grow up unconscious of anger or other negative emotions, often for a lifetime. Unfortunately, this spills over into all other emotional areas and he or she is often unable adequately to recognize or express positive emotions either. It is as though the psychic effort needed to suppress the anger and keep it in the unconscious is so powerful that it contaminates, or even cripples, all other emotions too.

SETTING LIMITS

As your child becomes more independent he or she will need to have limits set. This is vital if they are to learn to come to terms with the world and be successful in it. We all have to set limits on our behaviour and then act within them, and childhood is the time to learn this. As with learning to cope with negative emotions, a young child has to make some sort of sense of a confusing world that seems to offer endless choice. He may choose to do things which we, as adults, know will end in disaster or at the very least in trouble. Our job now is to set sensible limits so that the child can see that the world *can* be controlled. If he doesn't learn these limits he could so come to grief that he would stop exploring at all for a while, if not permanently.

Children need to feel that their parents are affectionate to them. Clinical experience suggests that girls find it more important than boys which means that they are exceptionally vulnerable to the threat of losing their parents' affection. Parents may make use of this as blackmail when setting limits: 'If you do/don't do this I won't love you.' If a child of this age has problems with limit-setting it's a sign that he or she needs more love and affection. They may, of course, also need more experience in limit-setting. If a child is to grow up to respect first your authority and then that of others the basic foundation is a secure love base. If this is present the child knows that what is being expected and demanded comes out of love and not out of a need to control him or her for the sake of it. Quite a few parents feel a sense of power, perhaps for the first time in their lives, at this stage of parenthood and they wield it without much care. Some are even frankly tyrannical, so hurt are they themselves.

Control often crowds out love in human relationships and a young child often knows whether the motives behind its parents' authoritarian demands are of love or a desire to control. A child that is secure in its parents' love and has a good intimate life with them will take kindly to limit-setting and will tend not to rebel. If you find your child rebelling, go back a few stages, love him more, be more affectionate, court him and help him to learn how to communicate. *Do not* avoid situations in which conflict occurs or you will be treating him quite wrongly. Conflict will always occur in life and has to be dealt with, not ignored.

But as soon as you start to set limits your own emotions will come into play and this makes the whole thing difficult. 'Am I being too fussy?', 'Why should this be considered inappropriate behaviour anyway?', and so on are the sorts of questions you will begin to ask yourself. Perhaps for the first time you will begin to question widely held 'truths' about what various limits are, or appear to be. Some parents find this quite shocking because it means they have to examine themselves and what *their* limits in life are. If, as a result of your personality and upbringing, you have been used to very strict limit-setting there can be real conflict as other people's children are allowed to behave in ways which create anxiety and other negative emotions in you. This anxiety is sensed by your child who then becomes confused as to how to act. Other children clearly seem happy enough yet *their* mothers aren't ill at ease. Of course, as anyone who has had children will tell, having little children is a time of considerable personal change for the parents and for the mother especially. Almost every day she will have to question and possibly modify her old, long-held views about most things as her toddler challenges her ideas. This probably never happens so obviously in a parent's life again except perhaps in early adolescence when we, as parents, try to come to terms with our children's emerging sexuality.

So you can expect limit-setting to cost you something emotionally. On the one hand you will want to love and please your child but on the other you will have to protect him from danger and inappropriate behaviour in a social setting. This is the first time that you will have had to exert real control over this new little person and he may not much like it. Many a mother, fearing that her child will stop loving her if she sets limits, backs off and lets the child do virtually what it likes, apart from things which are frankly dangerous. At first sight this seems an attractive approach but in practice it isn't because we all need limits within which to function if we are not to be overwhelmed by choice, indecision, fear and insecurity. By limiting our toddler's behaviour we control his environment so that he can more easily make sense of it and in this we help teach him to behave in a socially acceptable way.

EXPRESSING EMOTIONS

As all this exploration occurs it is vital to keep an eye open for how your child's emotional development is progressing. Most of us, toddlers included, can cope fairly well with pleasant emotions, though even these can lead to over-stimulation and excitement which are wearing both for the child and the parents. However, it is much more difficult to cope with emotions that make us feel unpleasant. Some toddlers cope well when the world treats them well but go to pieces as soon as the balance tips even ever so slightly out of their favour. Anger and frustration overwhelm them and they become unreasonable. To an adult the situation appears impossible because the child will not be calmed. Once again these negative emotions call on the parents' underlying emotional skills and in many cases they are found wanting. To cope with your child's frustration, anger, jealousy, or whatever, you have to have coped with your own emotions in these areas or you can be of little or no support to him. If every time he feels angry or frustrated you too revert to being a toddler you are no good for him and you will end up having temper tantrums together. As parents and adults we have a responsibility to be above this sort of behaviour yet all too often our children seem to pull exactly the right strings to make us react, in a knee-jerk reflex way, to their emotions.

We as parents should have the emotional maturity to be able to support our children when their emotions overwhelm them. This proves to the child that they are acceptable and loved, temper tantrums and all. It also gives us as parents the chance to teach our child that pure negative emotions, like rage, achieve little in themselves. The lesson we have to get across is that when they feel negative they should communicate it at once. We can then, calmly and in a controlled way, find an answer to the problem. The implications of this kind of learning *not* taking place are numerous in adult life. Many an adult reacts like a toddler simply expressing and feeling emotions yet never understanding or communicating them. Those around cannot begin to deal with the problems causing the upset and the situation often goes from bad to worse. This happens with toddlers during the 'terrible twos' stage of their lives (which I look at in the next chapter) and in some becomes a permanent way of life.

Powerful negative emotions, such as anger and frustration, can be harder to cope with than 'positive' ones. Try to avoid leaving your baby to suffer alone.

It's healthy for children to let off emotional steam in play.

The way to handle this is to calm the child in any way you can and to get him to tell or show you exactly what caused the panic. You can then use your adult intellect and experience of the world to suggest ways of dealing with the cause of the panic. Very quickly your toddler will learn that even such seemingly terrifying emotions can be dealt with and that he has the power to do something to prevent and cure them. Many adults have never learned this lesson. They feel a negative emotion and panic because it feels bad and because they find themselves out of control, however temporarily. They can see no way of dealing with the panic, they have no other adult to turn to, and have never learned how to communicate in such circumstances even if there is an adult there who could help. The 33-year-old loses thirty years in a matter of minutes.

Many parents claim that their toddler simply couldn't express or communicate his reasons for feeling so badly about something yet this is rarely actually so. Children, once they can talk, can by a combination of even quite few words, gestures and other baby language make themselves perfectly well understood if only we are open to listening. Here again, though, we come up against our own poor training in communication skills and may feel terribly frustrated because we know he is trying to tell us something yet we don't seem to have the skill to interpret it. As adults we can use both intellect and intuition to learn what to look out for. By carefully observing our child we can quickly teach ourselves to pick up even very minor messages and then to act on them. It takes practice and patience but is an extraordinarily valuable investment for our future relationship with that child. In our relationship with any subsequent children we may need to modify our detailed thinking and behaviour because each child will communicate slightly differently and we will need to be flexible enough to make the adjustment. But much of this can be great fun and even a source of personal growth for us as parents. People say they learn a lot from their children and this is one thing we can learn – how to be much more perceptive and then to apply what we have learned not only to our children but to adults around us too.

We have seen how at this age the child can experience quite a lot of emotional turmoil as the world begins to present itself to him with a vengeance. However, to handle this properly the most important lessons are that even the worst of emotions can be communicated and handled and that however bad they appear to be they come to an end and the world returns to normal. This latter means that we as parents have to teach young children that it is possible to control our emotions and actions and that this is best done if we learn internal control. Most children get back to normal fairly quickly after such an upset but others will sulk and brood on it and will need to be encouraged to do something nice to show them that everything is back to normal as far as you are concerned and that things are OK again in your relationship. Once again the personality and the early learning of the parent will come powerfully into play. If he or she is still a toddler just beneath the surface then the parent may well be so negatively affected by the child's outburst that he or she will sulk or become moody and the child, learning from this, will think this is how one should behave after an emotional upset.

All of this calls for considerable insight and self-evaluation if we are to be effective parents, because if we persist in giving our child negative messages we can hardly be surprised if he builds them into himself only to exhibit them later, perhaps to our displeasure. How often it is that parents say that what annoys them most is seeing their own negative traits and characteristics in their children and many wonder whether it was all predestined in their genes. Genetic makeup does play its part, of course, but, having said this, young children are so flexible that a successful parent can discourage harmful or negative personality features and encourage positive ones. However, in order to do this you have to be able to recognize what is harmful and what is not.

The whole subject of how to express negative emotions is a vexed one. There is a widespread belief, and throughout the book I have tended to subscribe to it, that it is healthy to ventilate negative feelings. 'If only I could get it off my chest!' is what many people feel. However, giving vent to negative feelings can make matters better *or* worse, depending on circumstances. The important thing is not simply to 'discharge' the emotion but rather to do something that allows the individual to calm down and to achieve a more balanced perspective on the problem. So it is that a baby or young child expressing extreme negative feelings might, by simply 'getting it off its chest' as a form of relief, so alienate the parents that the net effect is a harmful one.

Just as in adult life, there are alternatives to negative emotions and destructive behaviour in childhood. How about channelling some of this energy into physical activity, for example? Let the child bring out his anger on his building blocks or by running around the garden. Once the worst is over you can cuddle him and comfort him to show him that everything is normal again and that *you* are normal again. We often get so wrapped up in what our toddler is doing that we don't realize the effect it is having on us. The child often does, however, and will need reassurance that his negative effects on you won't jeopardize his relationship with you permanently. Try to find out what alternative activity your child finds attractive in certain situations and then encourage him to bring them into play at first under your guidance and then on his own.

DEVELOPING A RELATIONSHIP

As your child grows into being a real person he will become very much more aware of you and the effect he is having on you. What he needs now, in addition to love and affection is a sense that he is valued and admired for what he can do and for who he is. Try to show a real delight in his achievements so that he feels appreciated. This can be much more difficult than it at first sounds because many parents so undervalue *themselves* that they cannot readily acknowledge the achievement of *others*, even their own young children. Some parents are even envious of their little children and this clearly inhibits their ability to take a delight in their achievements. A wonderful way of encouraging your child to feel valued is to let him take increasing control of your games together. He now expects you to follow *his* lead and will be thrilled when you do. All the time you are expanding his world and encouraging the links between love, security, learning, emotions and sensations. If ever you feel envious or frankly competitive with your child think through why this should be and perhaps talk things over with your parents, or brothers and sisters, to gain insight. If things are really bad you might benefit from seeing a professional. Some young mothers feel rather like a little girl themselves much of the time and, quite unconsciously, feel rivalrous towards the new little intruder who seems to get a lot more fun than they do. All of this is even more difficult for such a woman when sorting out rivalry between brothers and sisters who are her children because many a woman like this feels rivalrous too. (For more on sibling rivalry see page 254.)

As their toddler's personality becomes better formed many parents feel compelled to influence him in such a way as to become what they wish they had been. An intellectual mother may, for example, quite unconsciously, favour books and ideas rather than physical activity and constructive toys. Similarly, an outdoor type of father may completely misread his sensitive, artistic or musical child. Depending on their personality children will either go along with their parents' moulding or rebel. The latter can be exceptionally painful for all concerned so it's vital, even at this early stage in life to be sure that you aren't over-identifying with your child. You are you and your child is himself – he is not there to help you to fulfil *your* wishes and if you try to do this you will store up terrible troubles for the future. Most dangerous in the short term, and indeed the long term, is that it will become very clear to the child that he can't be what *he* feels he should be but that he will only be valid in your eyes if he is what *you* want. This kind of conditional love can lead to untold misery – which often persists into adult life to produce marital and other havoc. So if you think you are favouring one area of your child's life too much, and especially if it is an area that you yourself are keen on, beware. This may mean encouraging behaviour that is natural to him but not at all so to you. If you are quiet and gentle yet have a little boy who gets the greatest pleasure out of fighting, physical activity generally and banging loudly on his toy drum it can call for almost superhuman strength to curb your displeasure and encourage him.

In such circumstances it might well be that the traits you see in your child come from your partner, or someone on his side of the family. And this is just one of many examples where having another adult closely involved in child care is so valuable. You may be ill at ease, or even actually unable to cope with the situation but you can call upon your partner to back you up. Next week the roles could well be reversed. This is one of the many reasons that single parents and those whose partners are rarely around to help with parenting have such problems. They cannot cope with the different personality styles of the child, if only from time to time, and have no one else to turn to who can. Many single parents in fact cope very well with such difficulties. And in some families the absence, for whatever reason, of the father is a positive advantage.

This is a turbulent but exciting time in the emotional development of a child and it can raise all kinds of fears in parents. Some, especially mothers, begin to fear that their greatly loved 'toy' baby might now reject them as he becomes an independent little person. Some parents, now that they can see how their child is beginning to turn out, fear whether they will be capable of parenting and coping with all the problems they feel they can foresee.

Others fear being controlled by their child and see him or her as a tyrannical nuisance. Terrible power battles ensue, which soon cause the best of loving relationships to wither. Coupled with this is a fear of having to exert authority over the child. Some adults, especially if they were badly treated themselves as children, think they might in turn become over-controlling, physically and emotionally, of *their* children and so back off and all too easily set few or no limits. Then they are plagued later as the child runs out of control. Try to see the whole matter of authority for what it is – a stepping stone to teaching the child to become self-regulating. Working together with your partner you should be able, between you, to overcome this particular fear if only because with your sufficiently different personalities you will be able to make up for one another's deficiencies.

A fear that it will never end is also a common problem. Toddlerhood seems to go on and on and many a parent is frightened by their child's dependency needs. Unable to see a time when the child will be able to cope on its own, some at least go for hasty and premature separation perhaps in the form of the mother going back to work or, if the father is involved, by working more or spending more time in hobby activities. But these sorts of answers are exactly the opposite of what such a child needs. He needs more security if he is clinging and over-close – not less. Self-sufficient children are produced by very close and intimate loving, not by pushing them away at every opportunity.

7

MAKING SENSE OF EMOTIONS

The next eighteen months – until the age of three – is a time of increasing independence and the discovery of new skills, a time for curiosity and experimentation. Sometimes called 'the terrible twos' this need not mean that terrible behaviour is the norm. Rather, as with an early adolescent, a youngster of this age is riding two horses at once and that can be painful for all concerned. He is less and less like a baby, yet not really an independent young child, and discovering how to cope with the emotions this brings to the surface can be difficult for everyone. It is all to easy to be carried away with the concept of 'the terrible twos' and then act it out. This is a real pity because you can so easily condition your child into all kinds of negative behaviour patterns once you get locked in battle on a day-to-day basis. As with other periods of change it is only a temporary phase.

THINKING AND TALKING

At this age a child begins to create ideas which is when conceptual thinking starts. Before this age a toy, once out of sight, ceases to exist but the child can now remember what the toy looked like and can retain a memory of it sufficiently long to recall it when the object appears again. Soon the child applies this new capacity to people and relationships as well as to inanimate objects. So it is that he can commit to memory what Mummy is like and can picture her even when she isn't there. He can then call on his memory to reassure himself that she still exists even though she is not there in person. When she returns his world is physically complete again and he has learned that even things he can't see, touch, smell, or whatever can still exist and return to him. Being able to hold on to images or symbols of things and people within his mind is a major developmental milestone and the forerunner of imagination, creativity and fantasies. Once we can create for ourselves the idea of something or someone who isn't there all kinds of doors open to us. Of course there is also a potential for bad too because we

79

can create harmful images or just inappropriate erroneous ones.

Parallel with the development of conceptual thinking comes the use of play to create a pretend world. A little girl may now play with her dolls as if *she* were the mummy, reinforcing her ideas of what mummies are like. It is fascinating and instructive to watch such play – you learn a lot about your own mothering because it can become obvious what has made an impression on the child. If she is always yelling at her dolls, is very strict with them, keeps leaving them so that she can do little things, or whatever, it should be a guide to ways in which you could modify your parenting. Of course you will also see your child behaving well towards her dolls and toys, which will make you feel good. At this important stage children start to learn about interactions with others and play can be an ideal medium in which to teach. The trouble is that the aware child (and most are very aware at this age) will soon see the conflicts in the way you say she *should* behave towards her dolls and toys and the way you *actually* behave as a mother in real life. This is just the start of a long road of confusion in which our children see one thing but are told to do another. Your being aware of the hypocrisy of this sort of behaviour is half the battle. Again, it's an example of how we can learn so much about ourselves from our children, if only we are open enough. We all give mixed messages throughout our lives and they cause harm at work, at home and in our close interpersonal relationships. Now, when our children are so young that they tend to be transparently honest, can be a good time to re-examine the way we behave and see if it's really what we want.

Language too develops greatly during this time and many children really take off as soon as they can communicate verbally. What a joy it must be for the child to say 'Daddy get milk' even if the novelty soon wears off for Daddy! Now at least he can communicate with adults on their ground and he begins to make a real contribution to family life. The *child* is relieved of the previous frustrations of being unable to communicate his needs effectively but you may now find the endless chatter terribly wearing.

Slowly during this period emotions and ideas grow stronger to form complex concepts that make sense in the adult's world. But all this involves a lot of psychic work and some children, as they progress in leaps and bounds emotionally and intellectually, lose ground in areas in which they were once competent. So it is that a child who you thought was dry at night can suddenly start wetting the bed, having the two-year-old temper tantrums you thought he had left behind, or sleeping badly. This regression occurs because the new developments are threatening to him and he needs, unconsciously of course, to go back a stage or two to be a baby again and feel secure as he experiences them. One sees parallels to this in adult therapy. As an adult really begins to become involved in the psychotherapeutic relationship he or she often regresses, like a child, and for the same reasons. A good therapist can often use this process constructively.

As your child learns to grow emotionally and intellectually, then, he will need emotional support, just as he needs physical support when learning to walk or ride a bicycle. Express more love and affection and go out of your way to be sensitive to his moods and emotions thus helping him to cope with them. If your child who was previously independent becomes clinging don't push him aside and tell him he's babyish but give him more love and allow him to re-anchor again in the previous stage in which he felt safe.

The same technique is useful in marital counselling, where the parallels are similar, and can be used by any couple. When anything in life, from a sexual problem to a redundancy, hits us and knocks us off balance it makes sense to allow ourselves to regress from our current adult relationships to one of two stages. The first is to go back to courtship and to have a holiday from genital sexual activities. This lets the pressure off the couple to perform with all its implied threats (like the three-year-old) and enables them to enjoy one another unconditionally as they used to during their original courtship. This is often enough to tide the couple over the current

This two-year-old is really interested in where his missing ball has gone. He is starting to think creatively about the problem.

storm. Some, however, need to regress even further, back into childhood, even perhaps to being a 'baby' again. What's needed now is for the 'well' partner to be able to allow the unwell one to make this journey secure in their love and unconditional acceptance. In this haven of love a grown man can feel free to cry his heart out or a middle-aged woman revert to childlike behaviour in complete freedom knowing that they will be secure from criticism or censure. In this way the strong becomes weak and the weak strong which in itself can work wonders in a longstanding relationship.

But back to our 'real' toddler. Hand in hand with all this development he is now beginning to use ideas to guide his feelings and emotions. As he becomes more adept at using ideas he can start to come to terms with fears, guilt, insecurity, power battles, and so on. At this stage learning problems tend to become apparent and it always makes sense to seek professional help if a child isn't making the progress you think he should. Many a deaf or even partially deaf child, for example, is greatly held back both intellectually and emotionally because the condition isn't detected early enough.

Assuming all goes well, however, and it usually does, your child will now be experimenting increasingly with his new-found emotions using his growing intellect. He now tells off his teddy bear and lovingly cuddles a doll that has 'fallen over and hurt itself'. You need to encourage the whole range of emotions to be expressed through play or they will surface in

---

A time for sharing things with Teddy. Yesterday he told him off but this is all a part of learning to communicate at the developmental level he has reached.

other, more socially disruptive, forms such as aggression against adults or other children. This is especially important when it comes to expressing negative emotions such as frustration and anger because they seek an outlet somewhere. If your child sees you happily accepting them when he expresses them in the context of his make-believe world he will be more at ease with them and will see that his world – and your love for him – doesn't collapse when he feels like this.

COPING WITH FEAR

A common negative emotion, perhaps the commonest after aggression and anger, is fear. We are all afraid of at least some things and we see on page 107 that this could stem from the collective unconscious. But it's not just snakes, the dark, or dragons that frighten us – we frighten ourselves, often with our emotions. The main thing we can offer our children in this context is the ability to cope with their fears and the reassurance that it is normal and reasonable to be afraid. A parent who says, 'You can't be afraid of *that* belittles the child's experience which tells him in an all too real way that he *is* afraid whatever an adult might say. As with all emotions, both positive and negative, it is important for us as parents to acknowledge their existence and to take them seriously even if they don't seem serious to us. That we find this difficult to do is all too obvious in marital therapy. One partner will say something like 'It's crazy, she shouldn't be afraid of . . .' but she is and it is deeply affecting their lives together. His inability to put himself in her position debases her feelings and makes her wonder what she actually *is* experiencing if it isn't fear. Many of us tend to deny the reality of the feelings of others and the price we pay can be a heavy one. We also tend to 'project' our views, however unconsciously, on to our partner and then act as if they were truly theirs. (For more on the process of projection see page 110.) If someone we love, whether they are three or thirty-three, expresses a fear or concern then that becomes our concern, however silly or unimportant it appears to *us*. Many people in therapy say that most of all they want to be fully understood by someone and accepted for what they are, as they are. Alas, most of us have learned from very early in life that our fears, guilts, insecurities, or whatever, are not taken seriously and we then go through life behaving in the same way to others.

All of this points up a crucial lesson in the emotional development of children – that any and all of our children's emotions need to be taken seriously and dealt with. Just because a person is only three months or three years old doesn't make their emotions any less valid than ours as adults. On the contrary, because children have so little control over their own lives they should be afforded even greater love and care to offset the fact that they can't help themselves as we adults can. Before the age of five or six children can't really use their intellect to rationalize and cope with a situation (or indeed their parents' reaction to it) and so have even fewer tools with which to do the job.

If adverse circumstances such as divorce, separation, redundancy, marital trouble, or bereavement hit your family the children will almost certainly need more love and attention in order to cope with their fears. (See also page 223.) It would also be sensible to encourage them to play pretend games that will bring their fears to the surface so that you, and they, can deal with them. As with adults, submerged fears and worries often produce inappropriate and damaging behaviour yet most parents either cannot or will not see this. The little boy who, for example, is rough and even violent to his friends at play times, may simply be reacting to the new *au pair* or some other change in family life. His real fear may be that his mother is about to leave him completely – not just for most of the time as she now does to go to work – and he expresses his fear as aggression towards others. Such a child needs love, not punishment, and a chance to talk out or play out his fears.

As in the earliest phases of emotional development, the child needs help to return to a stable state after such disruptions. He should by now be well aware that such feelings don't last for ever and that the end of the world is not about to occur but most children need a lot of reassurance on these points, year after year; how much, depends on their character. What is different now, though, is that you can use the child's emerging intellect to communicate to you what produced the original stress. You can also, of course, employ reasoning to explain how to cope with it. While he is as young as three this can be slowly incorporated as a coping method but he will advance very patchily. Sometimes the rational, intellect-based approach will work just as if he were an adult and on other occasions it will fail dismally, just as if he were a baby. To some extent this depends on his current emotional and physical state. For example, an ill three-year-old will be much less amenable to the intellectual approach than he would usually be. It also depends, of course, on the parenting and personality style of the parents. If they react highly emotionally to any stress in life then they will be ill-equipped to take the intellectual approach. This has nothing at all to do with intelligence. What is needed is the ability to step back from simple emotional over-reaction and for the adults, at least, to be sufficiently rational to wheel out their brains and use them.

EVERY CHILD AN INDIVIDUAL

A useful and, indeed, for some parents, novel concept is that of the uniqueness of each child. With this in mind you can really get to know your child's personality and temperament so that when he or she reacts adversely (for them) you will pick it up and be able to do something about it. Almost every parent of several children says at some time or another how amazing it is that their children are so different, coming as they do, from the same pool of genetic material. And yet this very uniqueness puts all kinds of stresses on us as parents since it means that we must tailor our parenting to take all the differences into account.

These very individual facets of our children have profound effects on mothering – a fact that is often overlooked by 'Baby books'. Such authors often assume that once a mother has learned how to mother she can do it again and again with any of her children.

However, this is sometimes not so and there is little doubt that the personality of the baby greatly influences how any given mother mothers him or her. So it is that a particularly attractive child (to that mother) will be easier for her and will thus receive 'better' mothering than a less attractive child. And by 'attractive' I do not, of course, mean just physically attractive.

In other words, mothering is a two-way process which is deeply affected by the 'consumer' as well as the 'supplier'. This is a concept that I find helps even quite experienced mothers when they find things hard going with a particular child. They have, if only for a moment, forgotten his uniqueness and have started to blame themselves for their shortcomings as a mother. Often this is unnecessarily harsh.

Around the age of three or four most children's individual characteristics begin to show – although, of course, they will have been 'different' since birth. Now the main task for you as parents is to encourage this uniqueness by concentrating on what makes your child different from the other children, or even from yourselves as parents. Children of this age greatly benefit from being cherished and valued as unique individuals. We saw earlier how some parents see only what they want unconsciously to perceive – things that fit in with the stereotypical child that they thought they would have – and perhaps even deserved. The dangers of such a 'battle' are formidable and the bodies litter many a broken adult relationship. So at this age it is important to respect your child's unique style of play, speech, emotional development, physical skills, or whatever, and to enjoy them with him wholeheartedly. Unconditional love and respect are at the very heart of balanced human beings: children who have lacked such unconditional cherishing are plagued throughout life in one form or another.

Even limit-setting can be looked at positively from this standpoint; within the limits you set, the child can express his uniqueness. The danger we are all prey to as parents is of being so over-controlling that the child feels its individuality is being trampled underfoot. Quite different approaches to limit-setting in different children may be called for. Some children are, after all, much more self-policing than others and each child will need to be treated differently. This, in turn, teaches children the value of flexibility. Most children of this age are stubborn and create power battles over something or another and this is perfectly reasonable as a part of learning to cope with the world. We may not find the struggle easy (whoever said parenting would be easy?) but children must learn how to stand up for things they think are right for them, even if we disagree. This is the training ground for later assertiveness. What your three-year-old is saying is that from time to time he wants to be in charge. How much we can allow him to be in charge is up to us – and our own personality limitations.

The insecure, unyielding parent cannot allow their children any real control at all. He or she digs their heels in and prepares for battle which, needless to say, follows rapidly. But none of this is necessary and is certainly not desirable from anyone's point of view. Even a child of this age, assuming he is not actually in the middle of a tantrum at the time, will respect your ability to be flexible. In the context of his loving home he should be able to learn that there are times when his parents will give in and allow him to be assertive. Slowly, as he gets older, his parents will allow him increasing amounts of control over his life and in this way he sees the value of doing 'deals' rather than having endless battles and confrontations. Life is about being able to be flexible so as to accommodate the needs of others yet many of us are very inflexible when bringing up our children.

Managing power battles calls for skill and diplomacy – as in adult life.

Some children bitterly resent this and find ways of punishing us either there and then or later in life.

Power struggles are at the heart of many adult relationship problems. Those working with problem marriages often look for disorders and imbalances of power and usually find them. Much of the time those with problems in their adult relationships are behaving as if they were about three years old, and for the same reasons. They have too little warmth and unconditional love; they have too few opportunities to take control of their own lives and so feel unacceptably powerless; and finally they have difficulty, just like toddlers, in accepting the limits on their lives. It's a sad fact that millions of adults see their lives and marriages as if they were frozen at about the age of three. True, for much of the time they are play-acting at being adults and may even be quite successful at it but it takes very little to push them back to the old power struggles of the fourth year of life.

There's another interesting parallel too. Some three-year-olds, unable to sense the love, care and warmth they need by being good, go about trying to find it by being bad. One US expert in the field has called this 'love by irritation' and many an adult three-year-old does this much of the time. Such an individual is a permanent nuisance to his or her partner, or even to others around him, in an effort to be noticed *somehow*. They have tried every other method, usually unconsciously, and nothing seems to work. Such couples have stormy marriages and are often amazed to see their own three-year-old playing the same games. This occurs particularly with over-controlling parents. The child of such a parent says to himself unconscious-ly, 'If they won't let me control my life in this or that way I'll do so in another way.' This may appear to be unacceptably rebellious behaviour but it rarely is. It usually calls for more flexibility and a review of 'parental' control.

CHILDREN AND ADULTS

The reason it is useful to keep making comparisons between adult–adult relationships and parent–child ones is that the two overlap so much in family life. The husband who over-controls his wife and treats her as if she were a little girl much of the time sets an example for his children – one which, even if it were appropriate for his adult relationship, and it might be – would not work with them. Just because such a marriage style works for him and his partner does not mean that it will work for his children. On the contrary, they may, as they get older, misperceive the balance of control in the marriage and rebel against the model that in fact works well for their parents. It might not be until they are parents themselves that they are able to see that such a parent–child model can work well in many marriages.

For others it does not work and it is harmful to the man's partner – and indeed to him. Incidentally, the reverse is also often seen, a situation in which the woman is a perpetual bullying mother to her husband's 'little boy'. This too has severe consequences for their children's development. Either way around, the over-controlling adult all too easily finds him or herself over-controlling the whole family and trouble can brew very quickly. This is especially likely to occur with those children who have inherited some of the characteristics of the parent who over-controls them.

The most important lesson to come out of all of this is to work on your own relationship so as to obtain insights as to how you run it and so to try to see how this is affecting your children in the way you parent. If you find you tend to be over-controlling generally then give your children (not to mention your partner) some area of life that they *do* have control over. This helps them feel valid as individuals and, perhaps surprisingly, will make your life a lot easier as you have fewer rows and use less psychic energy on this area of your life.

As has been pointed out by many family therapists, there are no secrets in families. Even very young children know what's going on – or at least that *something* is going on. Battles over power, over how to bring up the children, and many other subjects are commonplace in most homes, if only from time to time, and even young children will pick them up and use them to their own ends. Sometimes we'll pick on our partner to have a row with when in reality the cause of the aggression is a child, and vice versa. But it's essential to be aware of the way our children manipulate us as parents. Even a three- or four-year-old will have learned how to manipulate a parent. This may seem a cynical or even callous thing to say but it happens all the time in families, usually quite unconsciously, of course. Again, and as always, insight and self-knowledge are invaluable in stopping these games but it might take a professional to get to the heart of the problem if things can't be sorted out between you as a couple.

When the going gets tough in marriages most people retreat to emotional, physical and sexual inactivity. They talk less, ignore emotions and deny feelings. Quite quickly this spills over on to the relationship with the children and the family becomes unfeeling, non-responsive and uncommunicative as a unit. It is interesting that a common feature of families in which the father sexually abuses one or more of the children is the denial of feelings and emotions. In such a family emotions that are there are not felt; what is seen is unseen, and so on.

It's important, if things are not going well between you as a couple, to make every effort to be aware of the children's needs, even if you don't feel disposed to do so for your partner. Their early development is so crucial and their modelling so powerful in those pre-school years that you could do them long-term harm if you were to get into the habit of living a life that denies or flattens emotions all the time. What we *can* do is to modify our own behaviour in a way which helps not only our children but us as individuals, and our relationship with one another.

Whilst it might not be obvious to most readers, we can actually use our children's growth to complete our own. Stages that might not have been well negotiated or even remain incomplete in our own inner child can, with effort and insight, be completed as an adult, perhaps with the help of our partner, a really close friend, or a professional therapist. We all embark on parenthood hurt, damaged, or incomplete in one way or another and it would be a very rare individual who could learn nothing from the growth of their children's emotions and personality. This is why a book such as this is, in my view, much more than simply a sort of 'baby-care' book and is why I have throughout the book jumped backwards and forwards in time.

8

GETTING TO GRIPS
WITH THE WORLD

Over the next year or so as he comes up to school age a child spends a lot of its time learning how the world works. Logical thinking becomes attractive to him and he grapples with the concept of cause-and-effect. At the simplest level he can now explain much of what he sees around him in the physical world and at the emotional level too he can see how his emotions and those of others have predictable effects. A baby learns the simplest lessons of cause-and-effect in terms of his behaviour: 'I scream and Mum comes to feed me', but now the child can relate cause-and-effect to his ideas and adult reactions to them.

Unfortunately, this doesn't always proceed smoothly because as adults we communicate so many things to our children directly from our unconscious minds to theirs. Children can get messages about things we may not have formally talked about and make cause-and-effect decisions based on such unconscious material which at times will be correct and appropriate and at others, not.

REALITY TESTING

Following on closely from this is the notion of unreliability. Some things in a child's emotional life seem to be governed by the laws of cause-and-effect but this doesn't happen every time. One day he behaves in exactly the way he knows he should yet, for some reason, Daddy is cross with him. The child is thrown into confusion because the response seems inappropriate – and indeed it may be. Every time he bangs a hammer on the table it makes a predictable noise but human responses seem to be much less predictable. This involves him increasingly in what is called reality testing where he has to learn to distinguish what is real from what is make-believe, a difficult task even for adults, especially when it comes to emotions. He now has to come to terms with the fact that what seems real may not be and vice versa and this can have profound implications for his emotional life. If he thinks, for example, that he will be told off for touching his penis he will feel guilty about it. Why he even thinks this should be so is that he has (accurately) picked up the unconscious messages his parents have put out which say 'touching genitals is wrong'. Consciously, however, they haven't said this and may even have indicated the opposite by, for example, walking around in the nude themselves and being physically (but not genitally) intimate in front of their children.

The child is now thoroughly confused. Reality tells him that his parents are sexual and at one with their bodies and that he doesn't *in fact* get told off for playing with himself *but* he senses some kind of hostility to the subject and has to weigh all this up. I have used a sexual example but there are scores of others. A common one is the slimming mother who eats next to nothing yet tells her children to eat up all their food. And so it goes on.

Trying to make some sort of sense out of all this can be hard work for a three- and four-year-old who's also at a stage where he has to learn to control his impulses. Even if his parents don't mind him touching his penis or even frankly masturbating, he now learns that they *do* mind if he does it on the bus or at tea with granny. This calls for quite sophisticated concepts of what is appropriate where and when and some children simply can't cope. A few retreat from all genital activity, to continue the example.

But the same happens with emotions too. There's a time and a place for anger, jealousy, and so on but learning when it's appropriate to express them is difficult, especially when the messages are mixed and many of them are at variance with reality, and, as we have seen, this is often the case.

MOOD SWINGS

Coupled with reality testing comes the need for greater stability of mood in the first three years of life. Superimposed on this stability of mood there are many peaks and troughs, of course, just as there are in adult life, but we owe it to our children to show them, preferably by example, that life becomes pretty unbearable if everyone in the family is always in a trough or on a peak. People will forgive babies and young children almost anything but a four-year-old who is still tyrannical and unstable is a real nuisance to all around him. Now he may retreat into moods of his own and it can be difficult to get him out of them. Adult mood-swing behaviour is very infectious to the unstable child who is liable to mimic adult behaviour. We do our children no favours by allowing them to learn to sulk, be moody or excessively over-stimulated and excited, if only because such behaviour is seriously disruptive and will later be a real trial in their adult relationships.

Some fascinating research in the United States has found that we tend to remember things best if we are in the mood in which we were at the time when we committed them to memory. So it is that we recall certain things when we are sad if we learned them when we were sad, and so on.

Unfortunately, if we have mood swings from an early age we will later be able to recall only a fraction of our available memory (and hence our learning how to cope with life) because we will be on some sort of high or low which will exclude all other emotions and hence the ability to recall things associated with them. At the four-year-old stage most children will not be able to recall into conscious memory their earliest memories of life. They cannot, for example, remember being born, sleeping in their pram or taking their first few steps. These pre-verbal (before one can talk) memories *are*, however, all stored away.

But just as we should encourage such mood stability in our children it's less than satisfactory to fail to do so in ourselves. It's all too easy to be self-indulgent and let moods wash over us, to have an adverse effect on our partner or the children. Even very young children pick up the unfairness of this sort of behaviour and are confused by it. Some people, perhaps women more than men, constantly over-react to their child's tantrums. The tiniest thing gets blown up into a major problem. Such people have a learned need to have a tragedy in life to cope with or they aren't truly happy. Life on an even keel has little or no attraction for them and if things are going smoothly they, quite unconsciously of course, seek to upset things. To those on the receiving end of such behaviour it all seems disruptive and tiresome and children of such mothers soon come to learn that emotions are an overwhelming business. Hardly surprisingly, some such children retire from the emotional scene on the grounds that it's all too much and then become very flat individuals who fear that any expression of emotion will end up in some kind of drama.

This kind of behaviour on the part of one parent can put a child off showing and expressing emotions – perhaps for life. Alternatively, it can dissuade him from displaying emotions to that parent even though he tries to relate to the other one normally. This raises the whole question of balance within the emotional relationship of a child and its parents.

THE PARENTAL BOND

In my view the emotional development of children is best served by having two parents. Most children find that they can cope better with their emotions if they have a choice of different adults with whom to relate. One parent, especially the one who is most like the child in terms of personality and emotional style, may well be almost unable to deal with that particular child because it is like dealing with themselves and this they may be unable to do. By the child taking the emotions to the other, differently reacting parent, the problem can usually be coped with.

Two parents can dilute the excesses of one or the other, excesses which need not necessarily be negative. It is possible to be too kind, too 'nice', too

Learning about 'triangular' relationships starts early.

indulgent, unable to set limits for one particular child in a family, and so on. In such circumstances the other parent can redress the imbalance and the child won't suffer. The triangular nature of child–parent relationships is also important because it teaches him that people often come in 'packages' – in this case a couple. Children have to learn that they cannot possess the individual with whom they want to relate, if only because that person is already bonded to someone else. Anyone who has had children will know of all the very real rivalry that can occur between babies, especially, and one parent. But both parents need to work together to show, with one voice, that they come as a couple, and that this bond is of importance to them and to the stability of the family. In other words, it is not in the child's best interests if he tries to drive a wedge between his parents.

Depending on their various backgrounds and personalities parents will react very differently to the triangular situation. A man who, for example, was kept short of love as a child himself and who was separated from his mother himself when she went into hospital or was depressed for some time could, quite unconsciously, become jealous of his child and might go to extreme lengths to unhitch the mother–child relationship. This could take the form of finding fault with her breast-feeding (perhaps by encouraging her to think that she has too little milk), putting subtle pressure on her to return to work, and so on. His personal equilibrium will not return to normal until she has stopped relating so intensely to the baby, and it may not do so even then.

Experiencing a triangular relationship not only offers more choices to the child but also gives him a better chance of learning the value of flexibility. If a child has only one parent he is limited by what that parent can offer and this will, by definition, be restricted. A second adult not only doubles the scope but more than doubles it because by example and negotiation the other partner can shift position which, in turn, teaches the child a lot.

Yet another emotional lesson involves the concept of shifting balances within relationships and this is of value for the whole of life. There are times when one parent's emotional abilities and skills will be more suited to a child's development than others and with two parents the child has the opportunity to jump from one to the other to get the best of both worlds. Of

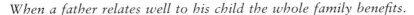

When a father relates well to his child the whole family benefits.

course, this is also open to abuse as any even very young child discovers because it is possible, by getting things just right, to play one parent off against the other and so manipulate the situation to suit himself. Many's the couple who don't see this subtly played game going on under their very noses, until it is pointed out. All they know is that things are going badly between them as parents, between them as a couple, or between them and their child. Being aware of this possibility is half the battle and often a good friend or close relative can help point to the areas that need changing.

The assumption so far is that the relationship between the parents is strong – and it may not be. Having young children is a trying time for most people today and unless the couple have a really good relationship the going can get very tough indeed. Cracks in the adult relationship are prised open by sleepless nights, temper tantrums in the child, disagreements about how to parent, intrusive in-laws, money problems, housing difficulties, the woman not working, and so on. Cracks that were successfully papered over before the children arrived can now assume massive proportions and for some at least it's a sign that they should demolish the whole building. Having a baby is the single most disruptive event in a woman's psychosexual life and most couples say that their relationship changes profoundly after the birth of their first baby. Sometimes it is a change for the better but often it is not.

A woman in such a situation may feel unloved, undervalued or under-benefited and so will invest increasing amounts of time in the activity that gives her most pleasure – caring for and loving her young children. This is considered a valuable pastime by many in our society so to herself and in the eyes of those who think like her she can feel worth while. Her husband though may see all this as evidence of further rejection whereupon he retreats to his work, the pub, or his hobbies. If you see this happening in your marriage try to turn the tables so that the father spends more time with his son or daughter; the child sees that it can't have a one-to-one exclusive relationship with its mother; and that there are actually advantages to relating to another adult.

At first the child may well blatantly reject the father's efforts but with practice things will change. Ironically, rather than harming the woman and her relationship with her baby, things can greatly improve. She now has some free time to spend on herself in the knowledge that the baby is happy with his father; she can take pleasure in seeing the child relate to the man she loves; and she is able to prepare herself for the reality that the baby is not *hers* but *theirs*. This last point is important as more children come along and pressures of time and energy mean that she has to share parenting pleasures and pains.

Even very young children should be brought up to see that their parents' bond is the most important alliance of the three involved in the triangular relationship. It is only by maintaining the bond that the child will have a happy and stable home life with its natural parents. This is a profound lesson for the future. Many people, having never learned this lesson in early childhood, or indeed later, behave as if everybody's love-bonded relationship were up for grabs. This can lead to disruptive and offensive social behaviour and to the destruction of perfectly good relationships. The child cannot be expected to see that what he perceives to be an alliance against him is in fact the best thing he has going for him, so we as adults have to be able to assert ourselves and act accordingly.

Single parents clearly have a potential problem here although it need not be insurmountable. It *is* possible for one, very together and highly aware adult to supply all the inputs that would normally have come from two but it is very difficult. Try to enlist the help of other adults, perhaps grandparents, or even in-laws. Friends too can be invaluable. As long as the child has more than one caring adult to refer and relate to things can still turn out very well.

But whatever your model, a single or two-parent family, it's vital to keep in touch with another adult who cares for you and about your child so that the inevitable temporary disappointments and setbacks that occur in all families don't get you down and spoil your parenting.

THE IMPORTANCE OF OTHER PEOPLE

Although there is little doubt that a child's parents are the most important individuals in his life, and especially in his early life, others are important too. None of us, however good we are as parents, can supply all our children's needs, if only because we all have personality failings and shortcomings. This means that our children will usually benefit from the company of others.

These 'others' include grandparents, friends, other relatives, mother-substitutes and play leaders. A chance encounter, say with a friendly shop assistant, can make a child's day and increase his self-esteem, just as a similar incident can do in an adult. Not all relationships with people other than the parents need to be 'meaningful' or deep to be valuable as a building block in a child's experience.

The problem with children having relationships with other adults is that we do not know how they will affect our children. Some of the influences will undoubtedly be good for the child but others may not be. In early childhood babies and young children very much want the security of their parents and especially their mothers and I believe that for most children this is the best. However, few would assert that children should come into contact *only* with their parents so the decision has to be made as to when

Children are more confident in social situations when they know they have a loving parent to go home to.

and with whom time should be spent. We have already seen that children gradually become more adventurous and feel increasingly at ease away from their mothers and I believe that it is pointless and harmful to try to rush this process. When a child is ready he or she will start to explore the world, including other people. This obviously means that sometimes a child will make a relationship with someone about whom we, as parents, are not happy. This might be another child, an adult, a relative, or perhaps a person in some sort of authority. The child may well take to the adult and will not understand, in the earliest years, what it is that we as parents are uneasy or frankly unhappy about.

We look at mother-substitutes on page 238. This has been dealt with as a separate topic because such women play so vital a part in a young child's life spending, as they do, so much time with a baby or young child. The potential for influence here is very great and few mothers, or fathers for that matter, can say that they are totally at ease with the beliefs and behaviours of their mother-substitute. It is inevitable that the unconscious beliefs of such an individual will profoundly affect the child she is caring for and the parent who leaves their child with someone for anything but the shortest of times must acknowledge that the child will be affected by the care-taker in many subtle ways. That some of these might be at odds with what the parents believe is almost inevitable and can, and does, cause heartache in many parents who find themselves in this position.

Once children start school their outside influences multiply enormously and we, as parents, whether we like it or not, relinquish our position as their main overall source of ideas, morals, and even teaching. Of course, parents still remain the most important single figures in the child's life but many other messages clamour for their attention and some of them will be different from ours. It takes a mature parent to come to terms with this (or otherwise one who doesn't much care what their children absorb from others) and on occasion it leads to jealousy as other adults assume an apparently greater importance than the parent in the child's life.

Of course, children gain enormously from mixing with others. After all, humans are social animals. But early on in life, and probably for much of the first year or two it is vital for the parents to be the core of the child's life to give him or her the confidence that someone somewhere cares, loves, and acts as a safe haven to return to when relationships with others go wrong.

CHILDREN – A STIMULUS FOR CHANGE

If you have a partner, and most parents do, then this is a time of life when you should be striving for more commitment and closeness, not less. Discussing the emotional issues I have described so far should open doors for you both, not only as individuals but as a couple and the reassurance you gain from a strengthening of your one-to-one bond will have profound effects on your ability to parent your child. If you find you are not getting anywhere, seek the help of a professional (see the list of helpful organizations on pages 262–3).

For some couples the arrival of children spells disaster for their relationship and for others it produces difficulties, some of which are never resolved. As I have tried to point out this need not be the way things go. Any couple who start off life together with goodwill, love and a degree of tolerance should, with a sharing, flexible attitude, be able to gain a great deal from the first few years of their child's life. What is so often seen as a drag of a time can then be used positively to enhance their communication as a couple and hence their ability to enjoy both parenting and one another better.

Much of this will come hard to some readers, especially those men who may never have thought much about emotions and find it difficult to express them. But if the thoughts expressed in this book have any value it must be in trying to prevent unhappiness and psychological disease which can only be achieved by all of us making an effort to change what can be changed and to accept with grace that which cannot.

Evidence from psychoanalysis and other sources suggests that it is during the very *first few years* of life that much of the real good or harm is done to a child's developing personality. We happily spend fortunes on caring for our children's bodies yet many of us resent spending anything approaching this sort of time and effort on their minds and their personalities. We *can* influence our children's future life, not only by our example in the early years but by the way we behave towards them. Clearly, we have a profound responsibility as parents to act in the best interests of our children, and especially in the early years as their personality and emotional life develop so critically. This often calls for a selflessness that has become somewhat unfashionable in a 'me-centred' culture such as ours in the West but the implications of the available alternatives are often far more difficult to live with.

Most of us now have only two children and have few concerns for their physical health in the early years. It seems logical and supreme common-sense, therefore, to make a serious investment in our children's future emotional and psychological wellbeing in these vital early years. If we do so we will know that we have done the best we could, irrespective of the intrinsic personality of the child. If we do not we cannot but blame ourselves in later life – and we all do it – when things go wrong. Even if in reality we could *not* have influenced things for the better, and this is rarely the case, we still punish ourselves for the way our children turn out, unless we have done all we could.

It's all too easy to look for a cop-out, as many parents do, with such excuses as 'My child is just not very lovable'; 'She's really a Daddy's girl and I don't get a look in'; 'He and I just don't hit it off'; 'I don't have the time/that kind of personality/intelligence'; or 'My own childhood was pretty awful and yet I've turned out all right'; but such excuses are just not good enough. Whatever the raw materials our children present us with we can, and I believe we have a duty to, do the very best we are able. This will mean considerable effort and even some small sacrifices on occasions but in parenting as in many other fields of endeavour, little that is worthwhile is achieved without at least some effort.

Many a critic of people such as myself claim that books like this make people feel guilty if things appear to go wrong. Clinical experience shows that parents feel guilty anyway when things go badly and that there is a good chance that they do not need to do so at all. Countless thousands of families raise well-balanced, healthy children who end up enjoying life and contributing to the society in which they live. It is by looking at how such families behave as well as those who go to professionals for help when things have not gone well that we can learn how best to approach this challenging subject.

PART III

UNDERSTANDING YOUR
CHILD'S MIND

9

CONSCIOUS AND UNCONSCIOUS

In this part of the book I want to look at the psychological features common to early childhood and to explore how we as parents can affect our children, albeit unconsciously much of the time, for good or ill.

Because there are very obvious limits to what experiments it is ethical to carry out on children it is almost impossible to be sure exactly what goes on inside a child's mind. There are many theories but most of them are too complex to cover in a book such as this. Nevertheless, it is possible to make use of theoretical speculations to attempt to gain insights into the processes at work so as to understand a child's behaviour and, perhaps more importantly, to be able to gauge the effect of various ways of bringing him or her up.

NATURE VERSUS NURTURE

As soon as we try to do anything in this area we are plunged straight into the old dilemma of Nature versus Nurture. This argument hinges on the relative parts played by a child's genetic 'blueprint' that is inherited from its parents, otherwise called Nature, on the one hand; and its life experience, Nurture, on the other.

Some of the most convincing evidence for the role of genetic factors comes from studies of twins, for which considerable claims have been made. Identical twins separated from birth and brought up in totally different homes by different families have been traced and, it is claimed, found to lead very similar lives. They may call their pets by the same names, drive the same type of car, marry very similar kinds of person, and so on. Such studies seem to support the view that genetics are not only crucial in a child's development but are in fact the major influence on us. However, this clearly is not the whole answer because, if we state it in an extreme way, everything that a child experiences would count for nothing, and this is clearly nonsense.

The available evidence suggests that a child's genes are the blueprint for both physical and mental development but that many factors can affect the outcome. For example, a child is born with a genetically set blueprint for intelligence. All things being equal it will reach this level but should adverse factors come into play it will be less intelligent. For example, it is known that children who are understimulated, ignored, institutionalized, or very malnourished will not achieve their full potential in terms of intelligence. Cigarette smoking by the mother during pregnancy has also been shown to have an adverse influence.

In emotional terms, the genes may not dictate that a child will be, say, a tense, anxious individual but rather at what threshold tension and anxiety will become apparent. If such a child is born into circumstances in which there is little or no tension or anxiety, then he or she might never become anxious or tense. On the other hand, such a child born to an anxious mother might well be highly anxious from birth, or even before birth, and this anxiety can become a way of life.

Although the concept of a 'blueprint' is a useful one it is important to remember that genetic factors often require very particular environments in order for their effects to become a reality. This means, for example, that some genetically determined disorders can be controlled, to a substantial extent, by changing the environment. For example, the use of a low phenylalanine diet in the disorder phenylketonuria detected in new-born infants largely (but not entirely) controls the manifestations of this single gene disorder. Also, genetic effects may sometimes work in opposite directions according to environmental circumstances. For example, the plant golden rod has two different genetic forms – one found in southern Sweden and the other in northern Norway. In high-intensity light conditions they grow to the same height, but in low-intensity conditions, the Norwegian variety is dwarfed whereas the Swedish one grows tall. It is not easy to find a human example quite as dramatic as this but the general point is still valid: namely, that one of the ways in which genetic effects work is by influencing responses to environmental conditions.

It is also undoubtedly true that genetically determined characteristics help shape people's environments – to some extent people 'choose' and select their surroundings. In this way a child with an outgoing temperament is likely to become involved in more social activities than his inward-looking sister. Clearly their experiences will be different as a result and these could thus be said to be genetically determined.

As we saw in Part I a baby's environment starts to affect it from the moment of conception and by fairly late on in pregnancy he or she is highly receptive to all kinds of physical, mental, and psychic stimuli in the mother. It could thus be that a baby's predispositions are being affected for good or evil, say by the mother's mood, long before he or she is born. This could explain why it is that some babies are already anxious or tense from birth. They have been trained to be so whilst still in the womb.

As we shall see later in this chapter there is a great deal of evidence to show that all experience is retained somewhere in the brain. We can consciously remember hardly any of our earliest experiences but this does not mean they are not having an influence on our later lives.

Few of us can recall our potty training. Did it start early or late? Was it lovingly or strictly carried out? Were we made to feel guilty about it? Few

What problems will this battle produce in the future?

people know the answers to such questions. Some experts question the effects of potty training on later life while many regard it as possibly having an effect on character formation, sexual preferences, attitudes to authority, sado-masochism, certain mental illnesses, and much more.

If this latter school of thought is correct – and the evidence is persuasive – then it serves as a good example of how experience can have profound effects on a child. The stage at which potty training starts for most children is before the time at which first memories can be easily recalled yet the impressions gained about the whole event clearly get into the mind somehow and stay there in a permanent form. Evidence suggests that they come to lie in the unconscious, which we shall discuss later.

So by potty training a child he or she appears to learn certain lessons. The first is that there is a need to control excretion. This is the main object of the exercise after all. However, it isn't this simple. More fateful lessons may also be learned. For example, the child may learn that excretion is a shameful subject calling for the utmost secrecy or that his stools are regarded with repulsion as a source of dirt or germs. Most subtly he sees his motions, his first gift to his mother, thrown away, often in disgust. Quite soon he realizes that he can effectively manipulate his mother by thwarting the progress of potty training because it obviously matters so much to her whether he performs or not. So a child who feels, for whatever reason, that he wants to punish his mother for something can withhold his stools and make her frustrated with him. This is probably the first time he realizes that he can exert power over another individual. I look at potty training in more detail in Chapter 14.

The subject of potty training is worth considering at length if only to show that everything we do to our children has effects over and above the obvious ones that we start out to achieve. Many, if not most, of the early memories are 'lost' to the unconscious but they never really disappear, as we have seen. They can be retrieved in psychoanalysis, dream work, regression hypnotherapy and using other psychological techniques.

THE UNCONSCIOUS

The concept of the unconscious is a difficult one to grasp, until, that is, an individual experiences how it works in his or her life. Put at its simplest it is that function of the mind that exerts a profound effect on our behaviour and mental health although we are unaware of it doing so. Everything we do or think originates in the mind but often the original trigger is quite unknown to us consciously. What makes things even more difficult is that the unconscious may give us perfectly plausible reasons for doing or thinking something which is false and yet we are not conscious of deceiving ourselves.

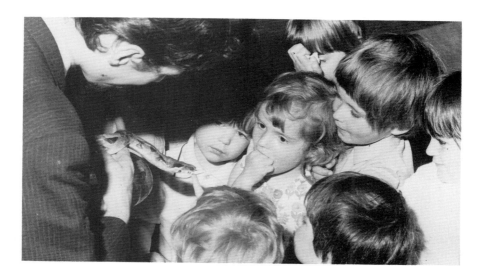

Each of these children has inherited an unconscious view of snakes.
Just look at the variety of expressions on their faces.

Our basic instincts such as sex come from and live in the unconscious and most of the contents of both the conscious and the unconscious are the result of experience. The psychologist C. G. Jung thought that these concepts could, and indeed should, be extended to include the idea of a collective unconscious, that is one that is shared by many, if not most, people in any given culture. In this way a child inherits very ancient unconscious notions, predispositions and potentialities which have been handed down from generation to generation. Examples of this are an almost universal fear of snakes, or the dark. A child does not have to learn these fears; they have been learned by our ancestors on our behalf and handed down to us. Some psychologists claim that there are other, more biologically based, explanations for such findings but if this is so they do little to explain commonly held beliefs and symbolism seen in many cultures across the ages. There are many theories as to how all this occurs but they are mostly somewhat academic and out of place here. What does seem to matter is that children are born with predispositions to certain emotions they have never experienced in their lives in the womb or subsequently.

The individual unconscious is a bit like a sponge. It soaks up messages, often quite unknown to the owner, and often directly from the unconscious of another person. Other things that get filed away in the unconscious are painful memories, ideas and feelings, especially from childhood, that have been shifted out of the conscious where they cause too much pain, to the unconscious where they can be 'forgotten'. Things that a child will put away, quite unconsciously of course, are those that produce frustration, criticism, rebuke, punishment and so on from others and especially from us, his parents. Other emotional issues, too, get stored away, especially those to do with jealousy, separation from loved ones, fights over potty training and many, many more.

But the unconscious does not just contain unpleasant emotions, it also holds our positive emotions and feelings. These good feelings seem to be much more readily available to the conscious and can easily be pulled out for inspection. This is in stark contrast to the unpleasant ones which tend to be difficult to find and are said to be 'repressed'.

The unfortunate thing about the unconscious is that it does not think rationally or logically, unlike the conscious. It easily confuses things as it tries to fulfil its wishes. If its needs cannot be met in the real world to compensate it suggests fantasies for the conscious mind. Dreams are thought to be such fantasies and dream analysis has, over many centuries, given considerable insights into the workings of the unconscious. This comes about because, when we are awake, our conscious mind censors out things we find painful or unacceptable but when asleep most, but not all, of the censor sleeps too and the unconscious takes over. Having said this, even during sleep our minds still play tricks on us and a dream may still not directly reflect the content of the unconscious. This might explain why we dream in symbols, especially about sexual matters.

Clinically the workings of the unconscious can be manifested, at least to some extent, as dreams, as slips of the tongue, jokes and people's behaviour. Subtle body language is especially valuable in making such an assessment. That the unconscious plays a vital part in the emotional and mental growth of children can hardly be disputed. Many of our emotions and feelings on almost every subject date back to childhood experiences, at least some of which will have been repressed and come to lie in the unconscious. These can be uncovered and as people do so, usually under the guidance of some kind of therapist, they start to see linkages that they never saw before. This bringing of matters from the unconscious to the conscious where they can be dealt with by the intellect is at the heart of most analytical types of psychotherapy.

If much of this so far, however interesting, appears to be somewhat academic then now is the time for an example of how the unconscious works in practice.

Some people are accident-prone. They are always dropping things, having small bumps in their cars, running out of petrol, damaging themselves in various ways, or whatever. All sorts of explanations have been put forward to explain this phenomenon: the accident-prone could be less intelligent, less dextrous, poor at learning from experience, or simply unlucky. However, the slightest investigation shows that those who are all of these (except the last) are not excessively accident-prone so there must be something else going on.

Closer inspection shows that some at least are unconsciously guilty about some aspect of themselves and are thus unconsciously seeking punishment. Their 'accidents' are not true accidents at all but neither are they self-inflicted. They are occasionally created to satisfy their unconscious need to be punished for their guilt. Once all this is brought into the conscious mind in therapy things often quite quickly resolve. The guilt is dealt with using the person's intellect and the accidents 'magically' stop.

Now that we have looked, albeit very briefly, at the workings of the unconscious let's look at some of the defence mechanisms that we all use. These are worth considering because we all use them from time to time and when we do so as parents they profoundly affect how we bring up our children.

DEFENCE MECHANISMS

Defence mechanisms are psychological (unconscious) processes that we use in order to deal with certain aspects of ourselves that, if confronted consciously, give rise to unacceptable psychic pain or anxiety. We all use such defence mechanisms from time to time and it is probably fair to say that we need at least some defences or life would be intolerable. A large part of psychotherapeutic work is aimed at stripping away these defences so that the individual can deal with the underlying matter that has caused their erection in the first place.

This stripping away has to be done gently and slowly within a trusting atmosphere or the individual can be left psychically 'naked' and unable to cope. A good therapist will help the individual construct more helpful and positive structures in the mind that remove, or nearly remove, the need for many of the defences that were present. This is helpful because maintaining these defensive structures is so costly of psychic energy, time, physical energy, emotions, and so on. Many's the individual who, having dealt with their main defensive structures and replaced them with insight, feels much more alive, vigorous and creative. Their energies are now being put to more constructive use.

We have seen already that *repression* commonly occurs. This is perhaps the commonest form of defence. Something is painful or unpleasant so our mind sorts it away into the unconscious where it lurks and acts, perhaps to our disadvantage.

Probably the next most common is *denial*. In this the mind unconsciously denies external, unpleasant events. Up to 40 per cent of widowed

An early example of projection. Who is really the more needy of the two – the care-giver or the receiver?

people experience the illusion that their loved one is actually present and 14 per cent say that they have actually seen or heard them. This is an example of unconscious denial of a painful loss. Similarly, a parent coming into a casualty department with a battered child may forget his or her name, address, and indeed much else. They have, unconsciously, to deny themselves their existence or they could not face the shame that would follow.

In a technique called *projection* we attribute to others, or even to objects, wishes or impulses of our own, especially in early life. First the aspect of the self, the wish or the impulse is desired and then it is asserted that someone

110

or something else possesses it. For example, a little boy in the process of growing up may develop feelings of hatred or rivalry towards his father – whilst at the same time loving him. He may then project the feelings on to the father and then react as if he, the boy, was hated. Another example from adult life is the woman who is afraid of her own sexuality. This is not at all uncommon. She then projects her own sexuality on to everyone else and accuses them of being preoccupied with sex. In this way she denies her own sexuality and can even feel virtuous.

In *reaction formation* we go to opposite extremes to obscure unacceptable feelings. For example, if we have a predisposition to be messy we might unconsciously overcompensate by being excessively tidy. Similarly, for example, someone who was excessively fascinated by the anal stage of development might later become preoccupied with cleanliness. In the same way over-generous people are sometimes found to be unconsciously mean. This obviously has profound implications for parenting, especially when it comes to being generous with time and emotions.

Displacement is another common defence mechanism. In this we are too afraid, for whatever reason, to express our feelings directly to the person to whom they should be expressed and then do so, quite unconsciously, to others. Perhaps the commonest example in the context of this book is the arguing couple. The woman, for example, may feel hostile to her husband yet cannot, for one of many reasons, express her hostility perhaps because she feels she will be criticized if she does so. Then, when her little girl knocks over the sugar bowl at the table, she goes wild and vents all her pent-up feelings from the marital situation on the child. The child sees the response as totally inappropriate but cannot, of course, explain it. This leads to confused and bad feelings in the child who cannot begin to understand what is going on. Clearly the answer is for the parents to be able to express their feelings to the appropriate person – in this case, one another.

In the unconscious process called *regression* we go back to a former stage of psychological development. We all do this as we take a childlike pleasure in things such as sports, nature, modelling, or whatever, and also when in situations we can't cope with, such as going into hospital. However, some parents regress to childlike behaviour a lot of the time and all too quickly both parent and four-year-old are behaving like four-year-olds. Clearly this is to the child's disadvantage because it needs a parent to relate to, not another child. In children and especially young ones, regression is common. The arrival of a new baby can make the older child regress to babyhood, and bedwetting, for example, again becomes a problem.

From all of this it is clear that the unconscious of both parent and child are crucial factors in the growth and development of children. We saw on page 25 that these influences start before birth and from now on a child

111

has no option but to accept the unconscious messages its parents put across. Given that we all have unconscious views and prejudices about so many things it is clear that our parenting style will be fundamentally governed by our unconscious minds.

This puts a considerable responsibility on us as parents to be critical of our own unconscious for the sake of our children so as to filter out some of the most damaging aspects before they reach the children. Alas, by definition, we cannot, unaided, have access to our own unconscious but we can, by revealing ourselves to our partner, learn a great deal. Rows over the bringing up of children are usually near the top of the causes of marital disharmony and it is often the unconscious mind of one parent getting at the unconscious of the other. By careful observation and discussion and perhaps by talking over the contents of a book such as this, many parents will be able to gain access to important material in their unconscious which, once brought into consciousness, can be dealt with to the advantage of the child. In this way, then, a loving couple who want to do the best for their children can caringly reveal their unconscious to one another and so undo the worst excesses that could damage their children and family life.

It is probably sensible to look through this section and re-read it making notes about things that seem to ring a bell. Then sit down one evening when you are not too tired and work carefully through things with your partner to see how he or she could help you. A good friend can also be invaluable. Fair-weather friends who will say only what they think you want to hear are useless in this context.

One of the traps that we all fall into, if only from time to time, is using our children as battlegrounds to solve our own unconscious problems as adults. Having children seems to lay naked the unconscious and almost all mothers are shot through with guilt. This makes it almost pathetically easy to pick fights over the children, many if not most of which are transferred directly to their unconscious minds. This is something well worth being aware of so that it can be avoided.

But the unconscious doesn't only work to hinder us and to produce problems for our children and the growth of their unconscious minds. There is, as we have seen, a considerable potential for good too. Most middle-class parents, however, over-intellectualize about their own and their children's physical experiences and miss out on the feelings side. Going with our unconscious drives for pleasure and parenting is vital. Many's the woman who wishes that she had listened to her own intuition and feelings about child care and not gone by the book when, say, breast-feeding, and it is all too easy to deny or ignore our feelings or those of our partner and so deny them to our child. Listen to your intuitive feelings and your unconscious and you will find that you usually benefit greatly, and so will your child.

10

THE GROWTH OF ATTITUDES

Few of us would deny that the attitudes our children have towards everything in life are vitally important to their future happiness and indeed to their ability to function in a complex world. We all have attitudes to most things, even if we are not consciously aware of them. It is because so many attitudes are ingrained into our personalities at the unconscious level that I have dealt with them here, after talking about the unconscious.

Few parents sit their children down and give them a lecture on racial prejudice, the sort of carpet that looks good in a bedroom, or why rugby football is a macho game. Attitudes to such matters, and thousands like them, seem to seep out of the plaster of the family home.

We all have attitudes then but why does it matter that we do?

The main reason that we should be aware of our own attitudes, and those of our children, is that many attitudes are positively harmful to us (or them) in daily life. When I talk about this with parents I speak of their 'tablets of stone' and they immediately know what I mean. We have all written various things on tablets of stone or, more accurately, they have been written for us in our childhood. We carry these stones around our necks for life and given that many of the negative ones are so harmful they serve to act as negative self-hypnotizers until we get rid of them. It is as though we are in a sort of hypnotic trance under their influence without realizing it.

If we as parents are aware of at least some of our *own* tablets of stone it helps greatly to relieve our children of *their* burden. Just one example will suffice to explain what I mean.

Many people believe that 'Anything that's worth having in life comes hard'. Children brought up with this particular tablet of stone believe that everything has to be fought for and toiled over and that nothing worthwhile is easily achieved. This is, in fact, clearly not so. A beautiful sunset, a stroke of luck on the football pools, a smile from a pretty girl in a shop, and so on have not been worked for yet are all valuable and make life more enjoyable.

Some children brought up to think in this way become depressed as adults when they achieve success. They feel unworthy or fraudulent if they perceive that the success has come too easily to them. For some the success turns to ashes in their mouths because they have not (sufficiently) 'paid' for it. And so it goes on.

It behoves us as parents to try to understand our own tablets of stone so that we can, whenever possible, save our own children the burdens these fixed attitudes have put on us.

There is little doubt that our children start to form attitudes very early in life. Inasmuch as the unconscious is working and soaking up messages from pregnancy onwards it could be argued that attitudes too are being formed from this early on.

Here, as throughout the rest of the book, I am deliberately avoiding milestones of emotional development because for the purposes of this book they are almost meaningless. As we have become more insightful and knowledgeable it is apparent that yesterday's 'little cabbage' is in fact a highly developed individual in many emotional and mental ways and we are clearly still only scratching the surface of the whole subject.

Attitudes are transmitted to our children daily via our unconscious. Few of us sit our children down and give them a lecture on friendliness, guilt, sex, success, race, money or whatever, yet as they grow they obtain, as if by magic, very clear views about such matters. They pick up these notions and attitudes unconsciously for the most part without us really knowing how or when they did so. Of course, children also learn attitudes from other people too but their parents are usually the most important source by far.

The first sobering thing when thinking about attitudes is that no matter how we see ourselves our children will see us differently, and possibly more accurately. Even if their view is *not* accurate we can do little about it because, as when we adults relate to others, we can only do so in relation to our perception of them. Clearly there is a considerable potential for misperceiving, for whatever reason. Because little children are relatively uncluttered with experience and knowledge I think they often perceive things rather more clearly than do we adults. Many's the child who can, well before school age, talk with some accuracy about the family relationships around him. Children sense moods and pick up body language very effectively and all of this, and doubtless much more, makes them exceptionally open to messages that we, as parents, put out.

We transmit messages about almost every subject much of the time but as some of these are rather difficult to exemplify let's take sex as an example because most readers will be able to identify with the subject fairly readily. Here are some of the commoner messages about sex that are found in adolescents and adults.

- Men are the natural sexual aggressors and should make the first move;

- Women are basically sexless and 'nice';
- 'Nice' women have sex only with a man they love;
- Sex is dirty, sinful and shameful;
- Men know what to do without being told;
- Sex is for having babies not for pleasure;
- Nice girls don't masturbate;
- Sex is bad for you.

There are obviously many more such messages on the subject of sex. In therapy many of these notions come up time and time again in a way that suggests that our culture teaches them, usually quite unconsciously.

This is when attitudes are learned. How long will it be before their unselfconscious delight in their bodies is marred by cultural inhibitions?

Whether we agree with such notions consciously or not is almost beside the point because we act in accordance with such unconscious beliefs and not according to our conscious minds. So it is that a mother, feeling terribly liberated, sees her baby son masturbating and doesn't make a song and dance about it. However, he perceives that her unconscious is ill at ease and registers it in his unconscious mind. This might or might not stop him masturbating at the time or even later but it will certainly have become part of his belief system that 'Mummy doesn't like masturbation'. Then it only takes the odd thoughtless remark about 'not touching yourself down there' on another occasion and the boy 'knows' that masturbation is wrong.

As parents try to instil attitudes about various matters consciously they use many ploys to impress the value of one attitude over another. One of the commoner negative behaviours, though, that has provably bad effects later in life is the parent who blackmails their child into doing or not doing something. Some of the emotional blackmails that are used are 'You'll make me ill'; 'You'll give your father a heart attack'; 'I'll kill myself if you do/don't do that'; or 'You'll make me leave if you do/don't do that.' These kinds of threat are very powerful indeed for a child of almost any age because he cannot control adult behaviour and is simply overwhelmed by it all. It is easy to see how such remarks, however thoughtlessly made and regretted within minutes, can create an attitude in the child that tells him that he stands to lose everything if his behaviour doesn't come up to scratch in his parents' view. This can then have exactly the opposite effect to that which the parents wanted. The child, seeing that his love bond is apparently so easily disposed of by his parents acts out the reality of his worst fears because he has nothing to lose. His behaviour may now become really bad, he may run away emotionally and become a sad, withdrawn or even truly depressed child. Children cannot stand any form of blackmail, they don't have the emotional and social apparatus to cope with it.

ATTITUDES TO SUCCESS AND FAILURE

Of all the attitudes one sees backfiring on children in later life perhaps one of the most dangerous is that of achievement. Many middle-class children are brought up from day one with the conscious, and unconscious, message that they had better do well at school, college, university or whatever if they are to be loved and valued. Often there is no direct pressure, the middle-class parent is too clever for that, but it is there all the same. 'One day you'll grow up and be a . . .' is the sort of thing that slips out quite easily, and all in all the message gets across loud and clear that to be really valued the child has to succeed in terms that the parents lay down.

Given that children, and especially girls, are so love-dependent this is positively cruel at the time and unwise for the future because many children do not stand a chance of living up to their parents' expectations for reasons that are completely outside their control. Often they know this and end up feeling a failure all their lives. Certainly it is reasonable to give a child some sort of expectations to aim for, provided they are realistically set, but to draw up any kind of deal, however unconsciously, in which love depends on their meeting these goals is terribly dangerous. Some such children, and especially girls, end up trying all their lives to drive themselves to a state of perfection in everything they do, unconsciously to try to meet the goals set by their parents and so win and retain their love. This is often seen in middle-class women and their daughters. Try as hard as she might the daughter can never satisfy her mother or rather the unconscious image of her mother that she carries around with her everywhere (even when the mother is dead) and this can lead to eating disorders that produce obesity or anorexia, and a lot of other problems related to poor self-esteem and even self-hate.

Rather than teaching our children the attitude that success is everything it would be more valuable to encourage them to learn how to cope with failure. In our culture winners get all the applause and few people love a loser. But ironically the vast majority of us must be failures, by definition. Surely the best approach is to applaud a child for trying, irrespective of the outcome. It even makes sense in my view to let children go in for things their parents know they will fail at. This at least gives them experience of failure in small things and lessons in dealing with it can be learned within the loving and caring base of the family. Many middle-class children are so hooked on success that when they first meet failure, much later as adults, they have no idea how to cope with it and often go to pieces or turn to crutches such as tobacco, food, sex, alcohol, tranquillizers, or even illegal drugs.

The best way to get the failure message across is probably to stress the fact that adversity is a good teacher. Very few successful people have got where they are in life without a good deal of failure. The reason that they are successful is that they have learned from their failures and have not reacted adversely by putting themselves down or fearing that the world will come to an end as a result. Such messages are all too often given to children, albeit unconsciously. The children then grow up to act in exactly this way later in life, failing to see that strengths can be developed through adversity.

So the best message by far is to praise the child for trying, helping him or her to understand why a failure occurred and then giving them the confidence to pick themselves up and start all over again. This does not mean that we should fall into the old trap of saying, 'Oh come on, it doesn't matter', because to the child it does and he or she knows that it matters to us as parents too. To say things like this is to deny the child its feelings and this can be very bad training indeed. Children know how they feel yet often their parents try to talk them out of the experience they know they are having.

It is vital to treat our children's emotions as valid and to deal with them as we would if they were coming from an adult. All too often in marital therapy one sees couples where this kind of denial of feelings is a daily occurrence, much to the annoyance of one or both. She, for example, tries to raise a subject of importance to her and he says, 'Oh you're not worried about that silly thing are you?' Or he teases her and she, feeling foolish now as well as concerned, backs off with the matter still unaired. A few occasions later and she simply stops discussing anything at all because she knows her feelings will be denied or ridiculed. This is the basis of many rows and broken marriages and it all starts early in life.

When trying to create attitudes about success in any field of endeavour for our children it is important to be realistic for that child. We cannot make the assumption that just because one of our children did something another will be able to do so too. And when setting goals the main thing is to be sure not to emotionalize them. Once the child feels that its whole worth is on the line and that his or her parents have a lot of emotion invested in the goal, he is in real trouble.

Success has been discussed at some length because it is such a common problem area in the world of attitudes – especially for the middle classes. But success really needs to be redefined on a much broader basis than is currently the case. A successful human being is not necessarily one who can, or even will, become the managing director of a multinational corporation but one who is kind, compassionate, empathetic, intuitive, insightful, contributes to society generally and not just in his or her job, gets a pleasure from life and shares it with others, and so on. We would do our children more good by encouraging attitudes that enabled them to get joy out of life and to make others happy than by winding them up to achieve unrealistic goals which are unconsciously aimed at fulfilling our own wishes or unattained ambitions.

Most parents want to instil attitudes of right and wrong in their children and many agonize about how best to do it. Obviously there are no hard-and-fast rules but there are a couple of guidelines that are worth remembering when doing this.

First, it is vital to remember that there are fashions in all things. Few matters remain static in any culture and any subject viewed one hundred years or one hundred miles away looks very different. The idea of what is right and what is wrong is constantly changing and as parents the best we can do for our children when forming attitudes in this area is to train them to keep an open mind. Closed minds break up marriages, homes and families and on a wider scale make for wars.

Second, there are few absolute rights or wrongs. In some cultures you are not a man until you have killed an enemy but such a concept seems crazy in our culture. Perhaps the only real guideline is not to tread on the toes of others. The age-old Christian precept of 'love thy neighbour as thyself' seems attractive at first but knowing, as I do, how little many people love themselves it loses much of its appeal. Most of us want our children to be able to assert their own rights yet to do so without infringing those of others. If they can run their life in accordance with this rule they will not go far wrong.

But we all make mistakes and deliberately, or for unconscious reasons, do wrong, and children are no exception. At this point many parents make the mistake of chastising the child and telling him or her that they are bad. This lays up considerable problems for the future and not a few for the present. No child is bad because it does wrong and he or she must never be made to think of themselves as bad. What they have done is bad, not them. As parents we have to make it clear that a wrong has been done but the overruling principle, it seems to me, must be to hate the sin but love the sinner. There is no evidence that this does anything but good yet in millions of homes the child who transgresses is treated harshly or even threatened with a withdrawal of love when what he or she most often needs is exactly the opposite – more love.

Attitudes abound on most things from religion to work, sexism, marriage and money, and frankly, one person's view is about as much good as another's on most things. Yet too many parents make *authoritative* statements as if they had all the answers when, of course, they don't. Most half-way intelligent children recognize this for the con-trick it is from a very early age and their parents lose in stature as a result. How much better it is to open up the subject to discussion so that the child can start to learn how to form attitudes rather than have them forced on him. Even very young children like to discuss things and are greatly flattered when their parents do so. This can, ironically, be a growth experience for the adults. Young children have such fresh views and are, as yet, so untainted by our culture that they come out with superb questions of which many a university professor would be proud. All of this makes the parents more aware of their attitudes and forces them to re-examine long-held and possibly fossilized beliefs. When asked 'Why?' the very worst answer is, 'Because I say so', as any child knows. Giving a seriously considered answer is all a part of according to children the dignity that we would any other member of society. Just because they are little they should not be trampled on. Perhaps the greatest single rule here might be the ancient Greek notion: 'Accept nothing in the unexamined state.'

It is not just attitudes to physical subjects that are important; a child has to learn to have attitudes to more abstruse concepts such as authority, discipline, his own body, his personal space, the legitimacy of his emotions, his attitudes to illness, and much much more. Let's look at how attitudes in one of these areas can affect life in general by way of an example.

ATTITUDES TO ILLNESS

Sickness behaviour has long been studied. The way we react to being ill varies greatly from culture to culture and with each individual's person-ality, and parents' patterns of behaviour will largely determine how their children will behave in later life.

Some people are stoical in the face of illness, some matter of fact, and yet others hypochondriacal. Some people go straight to the doctor with the most minor of symptoms and others go only when severely ill. Even the same person over a period of years behaves very differently.

Illness behaviour is part of a well-defined social pattern and we all have our views of how doctors (them) and patients (us) behave. It is widely held that many of those going to their doctors are quite unconsciously playing a role – the sick role. Studies suggest that only about four or five out of ten people going to a general practitioner have anything physically wrong with them and that about 80 per cent of all ailments are self-limiting. So what are we all playing at?

Illness behaviour (adopting the sick role) is a very effective way of being relieved from social expectations, an excuse for failure, a way of obtaining privileges and sympathy, and so on. For those who have few social ties, poor support and feel isolated, the medical system is a well-recognized and comfortable way of obtaining at least some of these. Thirty or more years ago perceptive doctors realized that what their patients came to them for was quite often unimportant but what it did was to establish a relationship with the doctor who would then confirm *them* in the sickness role. Doctors need people like this to make them feel wanted so that they, the doctors, can live out their role as health-givers. Unfortunately, many doctors do not understand this role-playing and so go along with their patients' endless demands for medical care. This results in numerous return visits, many if not most of which would be unnecessary if the patients' real problems and motivations had been perceived and adequately dealt with by the doctor at the first consultation.

Just as certain people unconsciously retreat into the sickness role because it is a release from unpleasant or unacceptable situations, others sacrifice their health to ambition, expediency, or the good of others. Young parents overwork in the full knowledge of what they are doing, sometimes also going without things 'because of the children' and so on. The health of general practitioners is perhaps a good example. British GPs have alarmingly high rates of alcoholism, drug abuse, broken marriages, coronary artery disease and suicide, yet they presumably 'know all the answers'. To some extent at least, they are choosing to sacrifice their own health in favour of that of their patients.

But closely allied to all this illness and sickness behaviour is society's concept of what is normal, and how it defines ill health. Mental illness for example, has been seen, at different times over the centuries, as demonic power, witchcraft and madness. The labels, the treatments and the social attitudes are all different and yet the 'reality' of the illness in question may well have been the same. Alcoholism is another example. When does social drinking become an illness? Sexual deviations, hypochondriasis and malingering are especially difficult to define yet somewhere along the line is a point beyond which sufferers could be said to be 'ill'. Certainly fashions and fads are all-important when trying to define behaviour of any kind, let alone illness behaviour. Forty years ago oral sex was a 'perversion' – today it is a fashionable pursuit that raises few eyebrows. Today we accept the fact that 30 per cent of the population have backache – it is 'normal' – and that thousands are killed on the roads every year. In developing countries parasitic diseases, infectious diseases, civil war, or poverty may be similarly accepted as 'normal'.

Clearly all of these attitudes start in childhood and are modified as the years pass but it is all too easy to see that the way we behave to children when they, or we, are ill can make all the difference as to how they subsequently behave when they are ill.

ATTITUDES TO ANXIETY

Attitudes to anxiety are another area that cause great concern, both during childhood and later on. As a culture ours makes far too great a use of anxiety as a controlling force when trying to instil attitudes into our children. Life and anxiety are inseparable yet we tend to create even more anxiety than is necessary. 'If you get top marks in your French exam I'll buy you a bike' is the sort of anxiety-producing comment I have in mind. The child now has considerable performance anxiety, quite unnecessarily. How much better it would be to encourage the child to achieve for his own self-esteem and for reasons that mean something to *him* or her and then to be generous, if you want to be, afterwards. Try to keep anxiety to a minimum by using it only where it's really necessary.

We all think it sensible to warn our children about the dangers of water or crossing the road and it is not unreasonable that they should be made to feel moderately anxious about such real hazards. But the sort of totally unnecessary anxiety that we all create, usually quite unthinkingly, can be exemplified by the father who is going away on business for a few days. 'Look after Mum for me while I'm away,' he says as he kisses his little boy goodbye. This might be virtually ignored by the child as a throw-away remark but it might not be and he may then, especially if he is susceptible to being anxious, worry all night about how he can possibly do this given that he has little or no control over what Mum does. Children worry themselves silly over the most amazing things, things that we parents would not dream of as important. Perhaps this kind of thoughtless and uninsightful behaviour is part of the reason that neurotic conditions tend to run in families.

SCRIPTS FOR LIFE

A knowledge of parental attitudes and social patterns, together with all the unconscious messages that our children soak up all the time come together to create what are called *scripts* and these form a statement of our attitudes. When a child goes to school, for example, he has a script, as in a play, which defines what he *has* to do and what he *may* do. At school it is assumed that there will be a teacher, a blackboard, other children, books and so on. It is also assumed that the child will look for a seat, quieten down, and apply himself to the work in hand. He doesn't have to re-learn all this every time he comes across it, his script enables him to carry out sequences of actions and interactions with people more or less automatically. It also enables him to predict the behaviour of others and of the world around him.

It was Shakespeare who told us that, 'All the world's a stage, and all the men and women merely players', and how right he was in psychological terms. Our unconscious scripts control our lives day by day so that we can function easily and without too much re-thinking and re-learning.

As with everything in the emotional and psychological life, however, this can have profound disadvantages because most of us would rather stick to our existing script than learn a new one. Unfortunately, a lot of life, especially today in a fast-moving world, calls for considerable flexibility and fairly frequent modifications to our scripts. Successful individuals can easily modify their scripts but those who have, perhaps because of parental attitudes, fossilized their scripts find change unacceptably difficult or even impossible. They battle with the real world, wishing that it were as they feel it should be and often become unhappy, anxious, or depressed as a result.

Children rehearse their scripts all the time when they play. Just listen to a little girl on the telephone to her dolls or her imaginary friends; a boy and girl playing doctor–patient games; the 'social chat' at dolls' tea parties; and you will see what I mean. Fantasy play like this helps children flesh out the scripts they receive from their parents and to some extent enables them to create new ones. Having said this they will usually act out the scripts we, their parents, have taught them and these will be in accord with our own unconscious attitudes.

A recent UK study asked parents what they considered to be the most

Now is the time for learning the 'scripts' that will influence a whole lifetime.

important qualities to encourage in their children. Honesty came out as by far the most important followed by courtesy (way behind); a sense of humour; the value of friendship; the importance of working hard; and then generosity. Clearly, such attributes will be encouraged by most families and built into their children's scripts.

When, later in life, the child grows up and looks for a partner what usually happens is that he or she seeks out someone whose life script matches his or hers as nearly as possible. This is usually done quite unconsciously, of course, as few people sit a potential partner down at their first date and ask them to fill out a questionnaire! Those potential partners whose scripts seem to be unacceptably different are rejected and, if the individual is lucky and careful, he or she will end up with someone who is what psychologists call homogamous. Such people have very similar life scripts and can thus co-exist on a daily basis with one another with the minimum of friction.

What therapists see all the time in marital practice, however, are those couples, some of whom may have been married 'happily' for years, who do not realize that their script is at odds with that of their partner. Each comes to the marriage with their own script, written in childhood, and they may indeed share a great deal in common. But the arrival of children, the possibility that the woman might go back to work, the onset of the menopause and a host of other things trigger ancient script material and both act out their lives from entirely different scripts, if only on the subject in question.

A great deal of marital therapy involves the therapist acting the part of the benevolent parent (not obviously so, of course) and helping the couple rewrite their scripts in certain details. This can be straightforward in many cases and incredibly difficult in others. The most difficult are those in which one or other individual's script is heavily dominated by the attitudes of their parents and when the material being dealt with in the current relationship dates back to babyhood or early childhood.

Most adults modify their scripts as they progress through life so that they are truly their own and happy to be so. However, many of those who seek therapy have not done this. They are still little children just beneath the surface acting out parental scripts. When all goes well this may not present a problem but when anything rocks the boat in their relationship they wheel out the old script and play life according to it. Very often such people know that they are their own worst enemies but can do little about it. Therapy makes the unconscious content of the script available to them and so enables them to deal with it and, if necessary, rewrite it. In this way change can occur in what looks like a desperate, or even hopeless situation.

But little of this kind of trouble need ever occur if we bring up our children to value flexibility rather than rigidity of thought. A child who is brought up to see the world as a positive place in which there are rewards and pleasures and in which it is unconditionally loved even when it feels bad will have the strength of personal worth to be able to alter its life scripts when necessary without feeling threatened or that something of great value has been lost. It is the most insecure of people who find themselves enslaved by their scripts and who end up in marital, work and other battles that damage them greatly. A sense of being secure and valued is the best gift that we can bestow on our children, not only at the time but as a preventive for the future. Not only is this worth while because it gives them the inner strength to be able to change their scripts as life requires but also because rather than losing anything they can see that they are gaining from the change.

This kind of security springs almost entirely from being loved and in the next chapter we will look at this subject in some detail.

11

LOVE IS ALL YOU NEED

There are few words in the language that are more difficult to define than love. This is hardly surprising when we look at things from a psychological point of view because love is largely a pre-verbal concept and clinical experience shows that we are rather bad at putting into words our thoughts about such concepts. Because of this I am not even going to attempt to define love except in somewhat scientific terms which might appear rather harsh to the reader. This approach does, however, have the advantage of simplicity in that we will all know exactly what we are talking about.

Scientists have come to use the word attachment when talking about love but whether attachment and love are exactly the same thing is impossible to say given that no one can truly define love anyway. By attachment is meant the need which is independent of the need to be fed by which a young animal forms social and emotional bonds with its mother. At first it was thought that babies loved their mothers because they needed them to supply food but animal work has shown that if you separate the need for food from that for attachment they are different things. Many studies have also found that new-born animals removed from their mothers fare very badly and may even die because the mother subsequently rejects them even if they are returned after only a few hours.

Clearly animals and humans are no different – both have a crucial need to be with their mother in the earliest hours and days of life. The length of this period varies greatly from species to species.

As a human baby grows up it produces in its mother another kind of love – a feeling called bonding. The mother bonds to her baby and loves it. This is probably biologically essential in humans because the length of time a human baby is dependent on its mother is great when compared with other animals and if the mother were not adequately rewarded by the giving and receiving of love she would probably find it an intolerable burden. It is at this early stage that the baby learns to give and receive love itself. Indeed, it would not be too dramatic to say that the seeds of all love for the future are sown in the very first few minutes and hours after birth. There is considerable debate as to just how important bonding actually is and it is

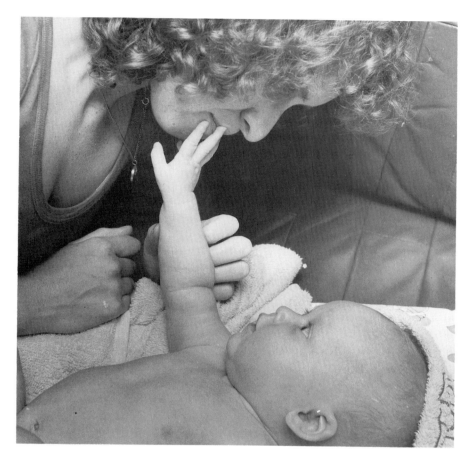

Love, attachment, bonding . . . all essential building blocks for future security and the ability to form relationships.

possible that the matter has, to some extent, been overemphasized in the past but there is absolutely no doubt that attachment is vital and that a child has a need to feel wanted and valued from very early on.

It is obvious to anyone who has had a baby or been involved with babies that there is a very special bond between mothers and babies. Just as with other animal species, human mothers are genetically programmed to respond to the needs of their infants and a baby continuously tries to attract the attention of its mother, and later its father, to make sure that its needs will be met. If they are not it could die, as we saw above, thus the process is of vital importance to the baby.

At around three months it is clear that the baby recognizes his mother. He has an extra special smile for her and within a few months will cry when she leaves him or her or if a stranger approaches. The baby is now 'attached' to the mother and obviously likes her more than anyone else. If the mother is not there to become attached to then the baby will become attached to whoever *is* the main care-giver in his or her life. Babies who are brought up in children's homes or by many care-givers become confused and even emotionally deprived, sometimes for life. This is why there is no doubt that the best way to bring up a baby is to have one loving, caring person to look after him on a consistent basis for most of the time.

Having said this, a baby can form multiple attachments. But however many people he is attached to there will always be one special favourite who is usually the mother. Although a granny, a father, a nanny or an *au pair* can be very important to a baby they are always 'second best' when the chips are down. For example, a working mother who usually leaves her child with a nanny is often upset when, if the child falls over, it runs to its nanny and not to her. She sees this as rejection, which is exactly what it is.

It takes a long time to become attached to someone whether the process occurs during adulthood or childhood. This is because it involves the formation of an interpersonal bond which is a long process. Most first-time mothers imagine that they will fall in love with their baby and he with them, at first sight, and many are bitterly disappointed when this doesn't occur. They shouldn't worry. Few women fall in love with their baby quickly and it certainly takes babies some time to form an attachment.

It is the emotional aspects of a baby's attachments that are so crucial, as with any love bond at any age. The people who wash him, feed him, and so on are certainly important but it is the person who interacts with him emotionally who really counts.

This first love bond, which we looked at earlier, sets the scene for all later attachment behaviour and can thus have fateful results. A child can still remain attached to someone even though he or she may mistreat them from time to time and the baby or young child who is physically or emotionally hurt by his main love-giver will still cling to her in preference to others. This shows just how important it is for a baby or young child to have someone that they can call their own.

Almost all attachment behaviour starts because babies rely on the person to whom they are attached not only to supply them with love but also to meet their many other needs. Such needs ought to be met lovingly, quickly and unconditionally so that the baby comes to think well of the world from very early on. Although there is little doubt that a lot of damage done at this time can be undone later in life there is every reason to suppose that the earlier this kind of behaviour starts the better it is for the baby.

Closely linked to loving is caring. One way to recognize love, even if we can't define it, is by watching people's behaviour. People tend to care for what they love. They are prepared to make sacrifices for it, jealously guard it when it is threatened and want the best for it. This is exactly what most mothers feel about their babies. No baby can articulate any of this, but even before he can express himself he knows that it is true.

All love experiences in life to some extent take us back to this first experience of love as a baby and it is easy to see that these later experiences could be coloured by our very first model. This is demonstrated in the everyday practice of sex and marital therapy.

But love doesn't stand still at this mother–baby stage. Like other complex emotions, it grows and changes. At first, as we have seen, a baby is totally self-centred. Quite quickly though it begins to give to its mother so that the two become a mutually rewarding loving unit.

In the Oedipal phase of childhood (see page 176) the young child now vests more of itself in the opposite-sex parent. Early in adolescence that love for the opposite-sex parent breaks off as teenagers begin to invest their love in themselves. This is followed later in the teens by a giving of love to others and eventually to one special 'other'. It is probably important to have gone through all these phases of learning to love if one is to be able fully to love someone else in an adult way. When dealing with those who have love problems later in life one sees that some, or even all, of these stages of love have not been adequately negotiated and that they are frozen at an earlier stage making it impossible to love another adult adequately.

LEARNING TO RELATE

Closely linked to these concepts of love is a line of psychological thought that is especially useful when thinking about the significance of the early days for relationships in later life. Called object relations theory it has a lot in it that is of practical value to modern parents.

Object relations theory is derived from Freud's ideas about psycho-analysis yet differs from them in that it proposes that personality is formed by the need for and availability of relationships with important figures early in life. Although our basic instincts are directed towards the objects needed to fulfil them – for example a man needs a woman to satisfy his sexual instincts – there is, according to object relations theory, a need to have a *relationship* with the object and not just to *use* it.

Object relation theorists consider that current, adult, relationships are influenced by a need to make them conform to the inner, 'blueprint' relationships first established in early life. Old deficiencies can be made good in the context of the present relationship and old pleasures continued. The individual is usually not aware of being influenced in this way but the influence is nevertheless there.

Object relations theory is valuable when thinking about adult relationships and particularly about sexual problems because it explains how we react to our partners. The very ambivalence (love–hate relationship) that was present in the first few months of life is there in every adult relationship. It is hardly surprising that a baby is influenced by frustrating or thoughtless behaviour in its mother, especially if its needs are ignored and it is left to cry. Mothers who have brought up several children using different methods say that the personality of those babies who are reared in a way that means they never, or almost never cry, is totally different from their other children. One does not need a degree in psychology to guess that such children will grow up to see the world as a friendlier place than would their brothers or sisters who were left to cry for hours.

All this is of profound importance for the man–woman relationship because so many adults behave towards one another in almost exactly the way they were treated in those early months of life. Many's the individual coming to psychosexual therapy who treats his or her partner like a screaming baby in a cot – ignoring the pleas for help. It is as though deep down in their unconscious they have put up the shutters.

In another way some people find it difficult to come to terms with the ambivalence they feel towards their partner and wonder why they can feel so hateful towards someone they love so much. Many marital and psychosexual problems and difficulties can be easily understood once a person can accept that loving goes hand in hand with hating and that in

This baby clearly perceives his mother as warm, loving and comforting.

some relationships the pendulum swings rapidly from one to the other. Object relations theory argues that how often the pendulum swings in any one direction depends greatly on whether the people looking after the individual when he or she was a baby were overall warm, loving and comforting or cold, unloving and frustrating.

ATTACHMENT

But back to attachment. Perhaps it should be said here that attachment is not the same as dependence. Dependence isn't specifically geared to the maintenance of closeness, is not directed towards a specific individual, doesn't necessarily last, and is not necessarily associated with strong feelings. Also, in dependence there are value implications. A person said to be dependent is not admired but to say that someone is attached to another is to speak approvingly of him or her. Certainly someone who is detached in their interpersonal relationships is not a person to admire.

Clearly a parent's main aim is a situation in which the child has a secure base from which to explore the real world knowing that he or she is loved and has that base to return to whatever happens. Much of the anger, frustration and upsets seen in young children reflects their uncertainty about whether their parents will continue to be available.

Research in the US and the UK suggests that about half the child population grows up with parents who provide this kind of secure base. Such children grow to be secure, self-reliant, trusting, co-operative and helpful to others. They have found that they are worthy of being helped and can, in fact, also help others. In contrast to this many children – perhaps as many as a third in certain populations – grow up with parents who don't produce this kind of stability. This leads to trouble later in life which can take the form of anxiety, over-dependence, immaturity and neuroses. When the behaviour of the parents of such children is examined in detail it transpires that several patterns are common.

- One or both parents are unresponsive to the child's needs or even reject him;
- There are many parenting figures in the child's life;
- The parents were absent for long periods (either emotionally or physically);
- The parents used threats of not loving the child as a way of controlling him;
- The parents threatened to abandon the family as a way of disciplining the child or bullying their partner;
- There were suicidal threats made by a parent, or the parents induced a feeling of guilt in the child by claiming that his behaviour was, or could be, responsible for parental illness or death.

Any of these experiences can lead a child, an adolescent or an adult to live in constant fear of losing his attachment figure. Such a person then becomes 'anxiously attached'. They make constant demands for love and care or may become a compulsive care-giver perhaps as a mother or as a health professional. They feel intense resentment when neither is appreciated nor reciprocated. As a parent they may be passionately jealous of the relationship of their children with the other parent. Prolonged deprivation of maternal care in the early years can turn a child into a delinquent, suicidal, affectionless and even pathetic individual. In other words, its first attachment bond colours its personality for the rest of its life.

People can also form attachments to animals as if they were people. Because the animal, especially a dog, is uncritical, loyal and ever-loving the bond can become so strong as to be pathological. Women, particularly, can become distressed and ill at the loss of a pet, which may indeed be their principal love-object in life. A very few even kill themselves after the loss of a pet. A few women perceive their dog as possessing the qualities their husband lacks, especially in that it 'loves' them. Some people, both men and women, as well as children, feel they can trust an animal to love them more than they can trust a human being. What does this say about their early attachment experiences?

Another, not uncommon, set of conditions occurs when an individual who has a history of a poor attachment is still exposed to a parent exerting pressure to be an attachment figure to her (it's usually the mother) thus turning the normal relationship on its head. Such children are encouraged to have a premature sense of responsibility for others, or are exposed to conscious and unconscious threats or behaviour that makes them feel guilty. Such children grow up to be over-conscientious, guilt-ridden and anxiously attached. Some experts think that school phobia and agoraphobia start in this way.

The behaviour outlined above that leads to poor attachment makes the child very angry but at the same time ensures that it doesn't show it. Much of the anger is carried forward into adult life where it is expressed, not towards the offending parent, but towards the individual him- or herself, the partner, or even their children. Such adults are also subject to strong unconscious yearnings for love and affection which commonly express themselves as inappropriate care-eliciting behaviour such as half-hearted suicide attempts, persistent and inexplicable bodily symptoms, anorexia nervosa, and hypochondria.

At the other end of the scale from anxious attachment is the person who is compulsively self-reliant. Such people have a 'stiff upper lip', considerable defences and do everything for themselves. They too crack under stress and are very susceptible to depression and psychosomatic symptoms. Such people have often had exactly similar experiences to those who show anxious attachment but have decided, perhaps unconsciously, that they will reject anyone who might give them love on the basis that they will probably be let down again, so why bother. Here too there is much underlying resentment and even anger that can often come out as bullying behaviour. Deep down though such people yearn for love and support.

A self-reliant person like this may also become a compulsive care-giver. They can only cope with relationships in which they are the givers. They are bad at receiving. Sometimes they will care for those who neither need nor want it and they can be a real nuisance to all concerned. Once again there is a lot of hidden anger at the parents for not having provided the love they so needed and wanted and again there is a burden of guilt and anxiety for having such feelings. Some such people develop a 'false self' as a result of not having received enough mothering as a child. They can be helped by recognizing their yearning for love, finding ways of receiving it in the here-and-now, and by getting them in touch with the anger they feel towards those who deprived them of it in the first place. People who are anxiously attached usually experience intense anger or self-reproach when their parent dies. They sometimes become depressed and their unhappiness persists for much longer than normal. In the case of the self-reliant, mourning may be delayed for months or even years.

Clearly, those who have poor attachment experiences as children will have a tendency to break down after a loss or separation in adult life but even these things are not the end of the story for them. They fare rather badly too when it comes to parenting. Such people make constant demands on their spouse, as we have seen. Some require their child to be a care-giver and others continue to overwhelm the child with love even when it is totally inappropriate. This has been called 'smother love'. A rivalrous situation may develop where a father becomes jealous of his wife's relationship with the children. He is caught up in sibling rivalry (see page 254).

Another problem occurs when a parent affected in this way sees a child of his as a replica of himself. He then attempts to stamp out the parts of himself he doesn't like in the child. Then, quite unconsciously of course, he uses the same kinds of discipline, being perhaps sarcastic, violent or guilt-inducing that were the cause of his own problem. Sometimes a husband will treat his wife in the same way. Of course, a woman might also treat her child or husband like this too.

What soon becomes clear when dealing with such people is that they seem destined, robot-like, to perpetuate the same model they had in their childhood and unconsciously seek out a partner or child to continue with the model even though they realize, even consciously sometimes, that it is all disastrous. Their biased perception of the world leads to strange behaviour and false expectations of the way the world will be. A woman, for example, who was repeatedly threatened (in reality or in fantasy) with abandonment as a child will then attribute such intentions to her husband. She then misinterprets things he does and says as if it were a fact and takes actions to cope with the situation that she believes exists. No wonder that such a marriage is plagued with misunderstandings. Throughout all this charade, unless she seeks the help of a therapist, she remains unaware of the realities of the situation and continues to run her life according to a set of beliefs that are totally mistaken. It is a no-win situation for both of them.

As a general principle it appears that in an adult relationship the more powerful the emotions in the here-and-now the further back in that person's childhood do they originate. They also tend to be less conscious in origin. Some of the most heart-rending stuff of marriage breakdown is when one or both individuals are relating to one another like hurt children or even babies. Needless to say, neither realizes that this is the case, they know only the pain they are suffering. The essence of marital therapy in such cases is not to focus on the present fights and discontents but to go right back to the painful and frightening times of childhood and to deal with the matters that lurk there. Many, if not most, of these involve some kind of disorder of attachment in the individual's development.

I hope that this section doesn't appear to be too dramatic to the reader but from my professional point of view it is impossible to over-state the case for more love, and especially for more unconditional, wholehearted love that is rarely, if ever, threatened. Clearly none of us have much control over having to go into hospital for a long time; some parents will be depressed for months and so be emotionally unavailable to their children; and yet others will have to fight in wars or work away from home for months at a time. But these situations should not, with luck, be the norm for most families. The vast majority of us, if we are aware of the dangers inherent in thoughtless and loveless behaviour, can make all the difference to the way our children grow up, and to the way they relate in their marriages both to their children and their partners.

To be born into the world loved and wanted is the best start any child can have. But even after such a good start there are many hazards to negotiate. None really threatens a child's development and future life more than a withdrawal or a loss of love. Love is the emotional food we crave from the cradle to the grave and without it we perish emotionally just as surely as we perish without food for our bodies. This doesn't mean that every child has to be loved in any Hollywood, roses-round-the-door sort of way or it will fare badly. This would indeed be an intimidating prospect because so few of us could hope to offer it. No. What children need is to be loved consistently, for themselves alone and not on the condition that they be something special or different from what they really are. This kind of love can withstand even quite bad parenting in other ways because it gives a child a sense of worth and stability that will last a lifetime.

12

'DISCIPLINE': LOVING GUIDANCE

Now that we have looked at love it is a good time to consider a subject linked to it. Discipline is essential in any group of people existing together. We cannot do whatever we like when we like or life would become anarchic and the quality of everyone's life would fall as a result.

The very word discipline raises many people's hackles. It suggests strict Victorian schoolmistresses who beat a child if it speaks out of turn. Unfortunately many parents, even today, still have this kind of approach to the subject, however unconsciously. They think of discipline in terms of punishment for wrongdoings. I hope to look at things slightly differently here because clinical experience shows that there are healthier and happier ways of ensuring that children grow up into sociable and self-controlling individuals.

First of all it is vital to state that disciplining a child should be aimed at one thing – making that child self-disciplined. It is not about forcing a child to conform to some sort of parental norm against its will. If we try to break our child's will we can almost certainly do it, if only because we have all the trump cards as adults and parents. However, this is a very short-sighted policy because the child will almost certainly get its own back on us later in life either directly or indirectly by its behaviour to us as parents, to society or to its own family later as a parent. This kind of mindless obedience – 'Because I say so' – is of no value to a child at all. It can usually only be enforced by stooping to behaviour of which we are less than proud.

Before we look in detail at some of the best practical ways of ensuring that discipline can be instilled into a young child, let's look at a couple of general points from research on the subject.

First, there is a growing body of evidence that suggests that much good discipline stems from an ability to head off trouble before it arises. Observational studies at first had difficulty in identifying what lay in the skills of good parenting because nothing seemed to happen. Recent work has found that this 'nothing' arose because skilled parents were good at picking up the signals of their young children and recognizing when things were about to go wrong. Distracting, restructuring, or consoling techniques (as appropriate) tended to be successful in avoiding confrontation. In other words, it is the avoidance of troubles, rather than what you do with them when they occur, that seems most important.

Second, there is increasing evidence that the old argument about 'strict' discipline and 'permissive' discipline was mistaken in its focus. Authoritarian parenting has mainly harmful effects but authoritative parenting tends to be beneficial. Authoritative parenting provides firm guidance, limit-setting, feedback on what is and what is not acceptable behaviour and so on, but in the context of an appreciation of the child's needs and sensitivities and an appropriate reaction to their individual differences.

The secret of good discipline is to encourage a child, by whatever means, to enjoy behaving well so that the rewards are very apparent to him. This also makes him a pleasure to be with and others will reward him for this too. The best principle is not to punish wrongdoings but rather to ignore them, if at all possible, and reward the good. The vast majority of us enjoy being rewarded and praised and this kind of reinforcement works wonders with children of all ages. If we ignore a child when it does something well but always yell at him when he doesn't behave himself he might just do naughty things in the hopes of getting at least some attention. Many parents who behave in this way interrelate very little with their children partly because they don't understand that good behaviour needs rewarding, only that bad behaviour should be punished. They are then annoyed when the child seems to get worse and worse when in fact what he might need is more attention.

Rewarding a child for good behaviour helps build his self-esteem slowly and subtly rather than punishing bad behaviour which tends to emphasize the bad and so make him think that this is all we care about.

But none of this is necessarily easy to do. We in the West, and particularly in Britain, are somewhat poor at praising people. We find it embarrassing to tell someone how much they have pleased or helped us, yet we all too easily complain. People of all ages thrive on praise and the world would be a much happier place if we were able to drop the little note of 'thank you' or praise to a friend, a helpful shopkeeper, a hotel manager, or our doctor, for example. This has quite profound implications for later life too. A child who is brought up to think of discipline as being about complaint and punishment rather than praise will have considerable problems when faced with 'discipline' problems in its marriage.

None of us behaves in exactly the way that we should to our partner and there are almost bound to be at least some grounds for complaint, if only from time to time. Many's the marriage that falters, or is even constantly on the rocks, because the couple don't know how to discipline one another. Often one or other yells and screams like an angry parent at a naughty child and the relationship suffers as a result because neither is really happy in the role that is cast for them. How much better to tend to ignore bad behaviour and richly reward the good, just as in childhood. Fights and battles then diminish and warmth returns to the relationship almost overnight. This kind of behaviour not only makes for happier couples but they become much better parents too. In this way the cycle of poor disciplinary methods can be broken in a single generation.

Yet bringing up children in a loving and warm way can bring criticisms from friends and relatives who say that you are weak or soft and that you will end up with delinquents later. There is no arguing with such people because their own rigid background makes them deaf to other approaches and incapable, without very considerable effort or professional help, of putting a more loving approach into practice. In order to accept that you might be right they have to admit that their method is wrong and this can be impossibly difficult for such rigid personalities. Also, one has to bear in mind that a person brought up in a rigid way simply does not have the flexibility of personality to be able to let children be themselves. Allowing children to be themselves is seen, usually unconsciously, as a threat to their own position, and people reared rigidly themselves cannot stand many such threats without becoming unacceptably anxious. They have to see things in black and white or they cannot cope. This can be especially trying for parents if the person expressing another view is a grandparent. The way to handle this is to be tough, if necessary, and make it clear that they had their chance to do things the way they wanted and now it is your turn.

Although the principles outlined here are practical and actually work there are times in the under-threes when temper tantrums need a special type of 'discipline'. A child of this age will sometimes react to being thwarted by having an outburst, usually in the worst public place such as the supermarket floor. He thrashes around uncontrollably, kicking and screaming. He is clearly very distressed because he cannot have whatever it is that he wants *now*. First time around this is not put on. He is simply reacting the only way he knows how to what seems to him to be unreasonable frustration and, not understanding time at this age, concepts such as waiting are alien to him. He now becomes very frightened and angry. What he most needs is love and reassurance but what does he usually receive? More anger and fright from the parent he is with. His or her reactions rather than cancelling out the harm the child is doing to himself actually add to them and they both panic and become angry together.

This understandably reinforces the child's behaviour. He learns that there is only one way to prevent himself from having these awful feelings and that is to force his mother to give in to what he kicks up about. And so he keeps on having the tantrums, much to her annoyance. He is now well

Things look grim for this pair, but soon he'll be calm again and will know that he is loved even if he does sometimes lose his temper.

on the way to becoming a bullying tyrant who gets his own way in life by yelling and screaming when things don't go just right. The mother has scarcely done the best she can for her child in such circumstances.

How much better for her to comfort the child and show him that at least one of them is in control and can make the world seem a better place once again. Soothing the initial outburst of rage shows him that even the most horrible of feelings can be coped with and that life returns to normal quite quickly afterwards. It also shows him that he can be angry and still be loved and wanted. In purely practical terms this approach works well, too, because although most onlookers in the supermarket hate to see a bad-tempered child manipulating its mother they *like* to see a mother comforting her child who is obviously having a hard time learning to cope with its feelings. So all ways round both mother and child come out better.

It was George Bernard Shaw who said 'Only ever smack a child in anger' and I believe he was right. Whatever the reader's views on corporal punishment it is difficult to make a case for smacking children of any age except when extremely provoked. Most children who are smacked, shouted at, shaken, or actually hit tend to use these forms of aggression when dealing with others. It is quite obvious that children brought up in such a way will tend to parent their children in the same way – and this is indeed what happens. Physical punishment also tends to make the child avoid that adult either by running away from home or by emotionally cutting off. Who can be said to be the winner here? Evidence shows that children unconsciously cause their parents' disciplinary behaviour to escalate by being defiant or persistently naughty. Such children also tend to go on to have trouble with other authority figures throughout their lives, being, for example, a perpetual nuisance at school or having repeated clashes with the law. Aggressive children tend to be punished more at school than do other children who commit exactly the same offence and boys, according to one study, are punished more for failure than are girls.

But any form of punishment, however gentle, is no substitute for good example by the parents. Children imitate their parents, often in quite alarmingly accurate ways. This is why the school essays of young children are so illuminating for parents to read. We may be verbally or subtly violent to our children yet claim to be loving and kind. They, however, when playing or writing about home life describe, in a very matter-of-fact way, a style of behaviour with which we would rather not be associated. Our children heavily identify with us and also imitate us and this can take them along paths that we might not consider to be healthy for them. This is just one of the reasons that having children is so tough, it highlights our own behaviour in ways that we sometimes find embarrassing. Several studies have found that children identify more strongly with warm parents than with cold ones and that they also tend to emulate the dominant parent in a relationship rather than the weak one. Interestingly, just as with all other parts of a child's emotional and psychological development, many of the lessons learned are stored away in the unconscious to be wheeled out much much later in their lives as parents and marriage partners. This is what makes these early few years so crucial when it comes to discipline.

THE CONCEPT OF CONTROL

Most marital problems that I see contain at least some element that has to do with power and control. In order to understand this and to see how it all starts in childhood let's look at the new-born baby again.

When a baby is born it seems sensible to assume that he or she is all love. It wants to be loved and tends to elicit loving behaviour from those around. As time passes, though, socialization requires that it act in certain ways, for example, by learning to open its bowels in a potty. As this control is applied the baby can all too easily see that even though such pursuits bring some rewards they also reduce its freedom to act in the way it wants. In short, it is controlled by someone else's rules, regulations and expectations.

As childhood progresses more and more control is added and it becomes all too easy for the child to perceive the control as crowding out the unconditional love the parent, teacher, or whoever, had for him. It now seems clear that one is an 'OK person' only if one adheres to certain social rules. Unless all this 'control' is applied with great care, love and warmth (which it often isn't) it is plain to see that the child will see the increasing level of control in his life as crowding out the love it once knew. Such a child now feels controlled by its parents' emotions, expectations and behaviour patterns.

When he or she grows up and meets someone to marry they come up against another person who has been similarly controlled, albeit in somewhat different ways. What I find is that very often people seem to choose one another on the unconscious basis of having almost exactly similar levels of 'control' built into their systems. Now the trouble begins. Both partners theoretically have all their love for one another available to invest in each other but much of it is masked by the control they feel has been imposed on their lives during childhood. Personality factors come into play and the stronger or more forceful partner will use the control element in his life, that he has learned is so 'vital' from his childhood, to control his partner. She, realizing that she has a large 'controlled' element within her, may be unconsciously seeking a controller to perpetuate the lifestyle she learned as a child. She may even 'need' a 'controller' because she fears that she will not be able to cope with the world if she takes control. All can be well with such a model for a while until, after some years, the controlled individual starts to realize that there is more to life than this and wants to have a measure of self-control. Once he or she actually experiences this heady brew the couple hits minefields all the way. The 'controller' no longer has anyone to control and the 'controlled' is often bitter and angry at both the parents and the partner for having put him or her in this position for so long. The bitten now bites back, often with terrible consequences for the marriage.

However, all need not be disastrous because quite often the 'controller' is delighted to be let off the hook and to share control of their joint lives – if only because the pressure on him to be in total command has been so great for so long. At this stage the relationship re-balances with both partners reshaping their behaviour so that neither feels 'controlled' or 'controller'.

Although this can happen spontaneously it often calls for the help of a professional to smooth the path. (I have gone on at some length about this because it is so common a story, especially today when women, who until recent times would have been content to have remained as the 'controlled' personality in the relationship are no longer able, or keen, to do so.)

With the battle resolved both partners take joint control of their lives and their marriage and the total amount of control in the relationship is reduced. The love that this struggle for control has masked for many years is now revealed. Such a couple now feel more in love with one another than ever and indeed have more love to give. They also have a lot more time and psychic energy to invest in one another and in other things because they are not having to act the roles of 'controller' and 'controlled' with all the power struggles and unconscious anger that these entail.

This is all worth thinking about here because it shows how vital it is that we discipline our children in a gentle, warm and loving way that doesn't make them feel that they are being controlled. If we raise them to experience discipline as control they will surely end up controlling others or being controlled, either of which can bring severe penalties in interpersonal relationships at home, at work and at play. Clearly in doing this we do our children a gross disservice.

So what then, in summary, are the main things to bear in mind when thinking of disciplining children of any age?

● *Be reasonable.* Don't expect too much too soon. Many parents,

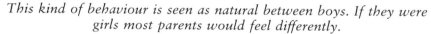

This kind of behaviour is seen as natural between boys. If they were girls most parents would feel differently.

especially first-timers, have quite unrealistic expectations of what a child can be expected to do, especially when very young. A young child simply doesn't remember the rules for long and anyway cannot see the sense in a lot of them. We adults have had many years to get used to the subtleties of rules and regulations but we need to put ourselves in the child's shoes to be able to see why certain things seem so unreasonable to a child. One thing that he is encouraged to play with, for example, looks much like another that he is told off even for touching, and so on. All this is confusing and means that as parents we need to be patient.

Exploration is essential in early childhood: be careful not to be so cautious and negative that you kill this essential learning phase in a child. If things are really valuable then remove them from the child's area of exploration rather than having endless battles about not touching them. Slowly, as he becomes more able to understand the adult value of things, you will be able to reintroduce objects and situations that can help him learn to deal with more difficult concepts of what is and is not acceptable.

● *Never tell a child he is bad*. 'You are a bad boy doing that' is a common rebuke in many homes. But the child isn't bad at all. First, he probably didn't know that what he did was considered to be 'bad' and second, even if he did, *he* still isn't bad. What he *did* was bad perhaps but not *him*. It is completely unreasonable to expect a child under the mid-teens to be as unselfish as is an adult. He or she will act in what they consider to be their best interests, and what else could they be expected to do? If you want to tell your child off for doing something that is inappropriate then tell him or her why it is wrong but ensure that they feel that they are still loved and wanted afterwards.

● *Don't sulk*. Many a parent, upset about the way their child behaves and yet, for whatever reason, feeling impotent or unable to control its behaviour, sulks and makes the whole family unhappy. 'That child will be the death of me' is the sort of comment that goes hand in hand with these sulks. Obviously bad behaviour, and especially if it is repeatedly bad, does make parents feel they have failed or are failing in some way. However, the answer is always to lavish more love on the child and to seek out the underlying causes of the naughtiness rather than to punish yourself by sulking about it. If you can't find a reason for a child's persistent wrongdoing then seek professional help. An outsider can often put their finger on the trouble right away.

No child wants its behaviour to damage its parents – at least not consciously so. Quite often, going against the rules is a way that children of all ages test the boundaries of what is acceptable and what is not and to have a parent who throws in the towel and sulks at the slightest provocation is no way to learn these lessons. If you find that battles over discipline are too much for you enlist the help of your partner and if this fails seek the help of a professional to look at *your* life. Perhaps your inability to discipline your child has little to do with the child and everything to do with you. If, for example, you feel, however unconsciously, that you were unloved as a child you will fall over backwards to spoil your child by way of compensating for your own poor experience of loving. This might well mean that you are incapable of setting limits and ensuring that they are adhered to, if only because you fear that your child will withdraw his or her love from you as your own parent(s) did. Given that you are so sensitive to love-withdrawal because of your childhood you will go to any lengths to keep the peace and the child will become unmanageable. It is not *he* but *you* who needs the help, if this is the case.

● *Don't use the children as a battleground between you as parents.* Many couples, often quite unconsciously, use the matter of disciplining the children to score points off one another in their marriage. Few of us have exactly the same ideas about discipline – which rules are worth setting and enforcing and which aren't. This makes the disciplining of children a potential minefield for all but the most aware of couples. It's best to sort out your positions on various important matters in private, not in front of the children. If you don't, they are usually so aware of what's happening that they will soon learn how to divide and rule your relationship. A halfway clever child will learn how to play the power battle to its advantage but this is a dangerous game because the prime rule, in my view, must be that the parents' relationship is central to successful parenting. Whatever a child thinks it can do it should not be able to drive a wedge between its parents or in the long term it will be the loser.

Agree on how you are going to handle matters of discipline and then:

● *Be consistent.* This follows on from the last point because children crave consistency. They pick up inconsistencies very quickly and are confused by them. They don't understand the subtleties of any particular situation and so need carefully considered guidelines that are usually adhered to. Of course, this does not mean that you have to be totally inflexible. Clearly the guidelines will need changing from time to time but it does mean that for a reasonable length of time the child can run its life according to rules that it knows are fixed and agreed on by you both.

By about eight or nine children will be old enough to realize that life is, in fact, a mass of greys, not blacks and whites, and now is the time to introduce more discussion about limit-setting. Up until about this age it is probably cruel to make a child have to worry about such things. This is our responsibility as parents. Consistency is also important when it comes to threats of punishment you make. If you say you will do something (or won't) as a form of punishment, then be sure to do so or you will lose all credibility. Empty threats are demeaning to a parent and reduce the respect the child has for the parent.

● *Reward good behaviour with warm emotions.* This is the cardinal rule of successful discipline at every age. If you also choose to reward the child in other ways, that is up to you but they should never take the place of emotional rewards. A new bike, a packet of sweets or an outing to the zoo is no substitute for knowing that he or she is loved, valued and wanted. Be on the lookout for even little signs of good behaviour and praise them when they occur. Make it a rule to find something good about your child to compliment him or her on every day. If you don't consciously try to do this it will go by default and you will hardly ever do it. Get into the habit of doing it. You will also find that once you behave in this way to the children it becomes a way of life with your partner too and as a result your relationship will grow. This can only be of value to your whole family life.

● *Ignore bad behaviour whenever possible.* Try, whenever you can, unless the behaviour is frankly dangerous, of course, to bite on your tongue when you see something naughty going on. Ask yourself if it really is that bad before letting into the child. Bear in mind that here, as in all human relationships, bad memories outlive good ones. Is it worth making a fuss about this particular piece of 'bad' behaviour or could you possibly, without having lost much, ignore or overlook it on the basis that one more negative input could well overshadow several positives that you are working so hard to achieve? It is easy to get into the habit of criticizing just for the sake of it. Many, mothers especially, would be shocked if they could see a video of themselves with their children. All too often it's an endless tirade of 'Don'ts', threats and prohibitions. They don't even realize what they are doing; it has become second nature to them to complain and whine at the children. Much of it goes straight over the child's head but the effect is nevertheless insidious and sets a pattern for negativity. A lot of this can be overcome simply by the parent taking control of themselves and thinking before they speak.

If you cannot ignore 'bad' behaviour distract your child from what he is doing to something you think is more acceptable. This teaches him that good can come out of the situation. He ends up being rewarded by something and not feeling bad that you have stopped him doing the thing that he was enjoying but which obviously upset you.

Perhaps a few additional points are worth mentioning here. First, much supposedly disciplinary criticism of children is simply an expression of the parents' negative mood rather than a form of feedback to the child on what he or she is doing. This behaviour is unhelpful both because it doesn't give a clear message to the child and because it creates a negative atmosphere that is generally counterproductive. Second, some naughty disruptive behaviour either has, or comes to have, an attention-seeking purpose. If, as parents, we pay excessive attention to behaviour that is designed to get a rise out of us it will serve only to encourage the very behaviour that we wish to discourage. Third, however (and this is a point that seems to me to get overlooked), it is important that parents give clear feedback to children on what they want them to do and what they *do not* want them to do. It is important that this is done as far as possible in terms of encouraging socially acceptable behaviour rather than the reverse. There is evidence that it is easier for children to respond if they know what alternative behaviour is expected of them rather than if they are simply told to stop whatever it is that they are doing.

● *Don't make generalizations.* 'You're all the same, you boys', and similar remarks can be very damaging. Try to keep silly generalizations such as these to a minimum. Don't make so much of simple things that they get blown up into a big problem. For example, if a little boy is playing with his penis in front of a friend of yours as you sit having tea don't discipline him along with the comment, 'They're all the same aren't they?' or suddenly a perfectly harmless piece of self-pleasuring takes on a whole new meaning as you generalize about the sexuality of the whole male population who are, according to your remark, all sex-mad. Such remarks don't go unnoticed by children and are filed away in the unconscious for future misuse.

● *Never blackmail.* 'If you do that you'll be the death of me'; 'I'll never love you again if you do that'; 'Stop doing that or it'll make me ill' and so on are all common types of blackmail remark that hit very hard at children. They usually take the comments exactly as they are said rather than as they were meant. Few parents would really do what they say in such circumstances but the child is not to know this. Such parents threaten to leave their children or their spouse, threaten suicide and a host of other things in an effort to gain, regain or keep control when they feel things are getting out of hand. Other parents threaten or blackmail by saying that something will happen to them, the children – perhaps that the child will be sent away to a home, sent to the police, or whatever. Clearly this is very harmful.

All such blackmail is profoundly dangerous as it threatens the child's love bond very greatly. He or she interprets such remarks at face value and acts accordingly, often to be more naughty because they are so afraid. A golden rule should be never, ever, to say or do anything that threatens the love bond between you and your child. They cannot take much of this and it can, as we have already seen, have the most awful effects later in life. No such remark is ever truly forgotten, in my opinion.

● *Show that you are self-disciplined.* Example is, as with most things with children, the best way to teach discipline. There are millions of parents around who are personally highly *un*disciplined, behave like louts and then complain that their children are badly behaved. This kind of double-think is all too apparent to most children who are affronted by the hypocrisy of it. 'Do what I say, not what I do' is the way that countless families run their lives but it cannot work for long. Almost all children respect their parents for showing self-discipline. Just ask any child whose father has given up smoking and see how thrilled he or she is. Even quite young children admire such qualities in their parents and will naturally try to emulate them. Once more, as with so many of these matters, it behoves us as parents to look into ourselves before we lash out at our children for their poor behaviour.

● *If you do lash out don't feel guilty about it.* Even the most saintly of parents will reach the end of their tether at some stage and might end up by lashing out and smacking the child. The main thing here is not to brood over it or go too deeply into it as a sign that you are about to go in for child battering as a way of life, or that you are about to break down and be unable to carry on life as a parent. None of these is likely to be true, at least not if the lashing out is an isolated incident. Be gentle on yourself and accept that no long-term harm has been done. At some stage later in the day tell the child that you are sorry you hit him and have a cuddle and a kiss. Get him or her to help you in the future by letting him know what it is that so provoked you so that the child can take some responsibility for preventing the same thing happening in the future. It is no bad thing for a child to see that his parents are humans who have deeply felt emotions and that they can even lose control from time to time. As long as control is regained fairly quickly all will be well and the child will have learned that this is possible.

Perhaps you too could learn something from the episode. If you know in your heart that you lashed out too readily perhaps it would make sense to talk it over with someone. It could be that you are under more stress than you thought or that you are displacing anger or frustration from somewhere else in your life on to the children. This can be a valuable starting point for learning more about yourself, if you let it be.

● *Don't go to sleep without having made peace.* If you have had a row with your child or have had to discipline him, for whatever reason, be sure to make things up before going to bed. Children become easily upset about things that would not give an adult a moment's thought and a lot of children's negative thinking and worrying takes place at night. Many's the individual who tells of how they used to lie awake at night as a child worrying about things that had happened in the day. Try, whenever possible, to make peace and show that all is forgiven well in advance of going to bed so that the child can sleep soundly rather than brood on things.

Forgiveness is a little-used word today but it is a simple concept that everyone understands. If a child has upset you let him know that you forgive him for what he has done and that tomorrow the slate is clean to start another day. Also, have the humility to ask forgiveness of your child if you have wronged him. Remember the old saying, 'He who cannot forgive breaks the bridge over which he himself must pass' and you won't go far wrong.

13

FOOD, GLORIOUS FOOD

From the time that a baby is in the womb until it is old enough to feed itself its mother is a vital source of food. The baby in the womb can be nourished only by its mother and in this sense depends entirely upon her to stay alive. What she eats not only nourishes the baby, it also influences him or her in other ways. Many foods have effects on the body that go way beyond simple growth and repair and it is now known that some have profound influences on brain hormones and indeed on other hormone systems of the body. So it is that what a pregnant women eats can affect the mood, level of physical and mental activity, and many other things in her unborn baby.

Once a baby is born it has to continue obtaining nutrients at a very fast rate because it has so recently been 'feeding' almost continuously via the placenta and is still growing very fast. The brain in particular calls for large amounts of energy in these early few weeks. It is hardly any surprise therefore that human babies need to feed very often in the earliest days. This life-or-death requirement for food drives a baby to seek out its mother's breast, or breast substitute, and to lay great stress on its presence or absence.

Although there is no doubt that touch and indeed many other senses are important to new-born babies, there can be no dispute that a baby's mouth is central to its survival in the early part of its life. Whether it is feeding from breast or bottle it will crave oral satisfaction for its overwhelming sense of hunger. In any human system a bodily craving or biological need creates a tension in both the mind and body of the individual who experiences it. So it is that when we feel hungry, want to have intercourse, want to empty our bladder, or whatever, we experience a building up of *tension*, some small amount of *anxiety* and a *hope* that our need will be fulfilled. Sometimes the need requires the presence of another person, if it is to be fulfilled. This is the case with both intercourse and breast-feeding, but often we can satisfy ourselves such as when opening our bowels or emptying our bladder.

The build-up of this anxiety, craving or whatever we choose to call it, is vital because it drives us to seek an answer to satisfy the need. When we obtain satisfaction we feel happy again, our anxiety is defused, we regain a

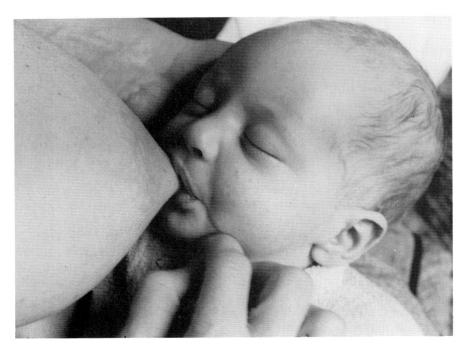

This baby isn't breast-feeding – he is blissfully content using the nipple as another would a dummy.

sense of stability in the world and believe once more that our needs will be answered in the future.

In a new-born baby the mouth is undoubtedly of vital importance. Because it is central to its survival it is not hard to see that nature has made everything to do with feeding pleasurable. If it were not, the human race would have long since died out from starvation.

But at this stage of a baby's development it is not just food that is being obtained when he or she feeds. All babies seem to need to be loved and cared for. Indeed, there is evidence that if they are not, they do not thrive physically or mentally, let alone emotionally. Nature seems to have so ordained things that the very business of breast-feeding a baby ensures that the mother spends time with it, cuddles it closely to her body, and in so doing continues the relationship she had with him or her in the womb. For this reason some perceptive experts in the field of baby care have called this 'the second nine months of pregnancy', so vital is it.

Loving and feeding then are very closely linked in human beings. A baby who cries because it is empty and needs food feels loved and reassured if its mother feeds it as soon as possible. The child very early learns to reward its mother with smiles and other appealing behaviour so that she, in turn, obtains pleasure from the feeding. In this way the baby's need for nourishment becomes inextricably tied up with the mutual reward system that builds between mother and child. This is why so many women find that their relationship with their baby takes a leap forward when he or she starts to smile. Suddenly the mother finds the whole thing much more rewarding. Before this stage the baby is simply not mature enough to be able to recognize that its mother is different from itself, or indeed her breast. Very early on it is likely that the very young baby thinks of the mother as *being* a breast. As he or she matures the mother becomes attached to the breast in the baby's mind and then the breast attached to the mother, in the baby's eyes. Once a baby can smile he can acknowledge visibly his mother's love and she can feel that what she is doing is worth while. She *knows* intellectually that her baby needs love but now it becomes obvious to her.

All of this is extremely important in human babies because they are extraordinarily dependent for a long time. The young of many other species are able to seek out food for themselves but mammals, and the higher primates in particular, are quite unable to support themselves nutritionally for a very long time. This means that the mother is tied to them every bit as much as they are tied to her. For this reason breast-feeding has had to be enjoyable for women or they would not have done it and the race would have died out.

It is not too fanciful to suggest that a baby whose mother feeds it fairly soon after it expresses a need for food and who does so lovingly will create in her child a sense of the world being a good place. Tensions and anxieties are relatively short-lived and satisfaction comes with love and physical closeness. However, this does not always occur, even in the best of mother–baby relationships. Think, for example, of the mother–baby duo who are normally happy with one another. The baby is fed when it wants to be and the mother is happy to do so. Then one day, for a reason beyond the control of either of them, she does not respond when the baby wants to be fed. The baby now experiences growing tension, anxiety and frustration until its normal cries for attention become angry screams for its food. One can never know what goes on in a baby's mind but it makes sense to suppose that such a baby could actually believe that it will not be fed and that this could be the end of its life. After all, unlike an adult it cannot seek out its own food, it is totally dependent on the mother. Now, what was a mild and happy baby is an angry and frustrated one worried about survival. It starts to hate its mother for abandoning it.

After she has finished her phone call, or whatever it was that she was doing when the baby started to cry for food, she feeds him or her only to find that the child is still furious with her and may even bite the breast or hit her. He is punishing her for her absence.

At the same time the baby knows that it cannot go over the top with this punishing behaviour because it still needs the mother to survive. And so he or she calms down, modifies the anger and settles down to a feed.

After such a first episode life is never quite the same again. The baby now has to contend with the knowledge that he can both love and hate his mother and that the feelings are very different. He is exceptionally worried about hating her just in case she gives him up altogether and this is a chance he cannot take. So as not to drive his mother away such a baby now projects his or her hostility on to things in the environment. Now he feels safer because he can give vent to his emotions yet not run the risk of losing his mother.

Another way that babies cope in this situation is to turn their anger inwards on themselves. In this way they can explain to themselves why it is that their mother is so loath to feed them when they want to be fed. It is not unreasonable to suggest that such a baby thinks, Could there be something wrong with *me* that she doesn't feed me when I'm hungry? Many a psychoanalyst claims to be able to trace feelings of inadequacy in later life to such early feelings of unworthiness and rejection, and indeed it is suggested that many of those who become depressed in later life have learned on their mother's knee, or more often, off it, that they are not worthy of such love and attention. This subsequently colours the way they view the world.

The psychosexual implications of all of this are discussed in Part IV but here let's go on to look at the connection with food in more depth.

Given that feeding and caring are so inextricably linked in early babyhood it is hardly surprising that food, and everything to do with it, is at the heart of many human activities through life. Almost all cultures use food as a social catalyst and food has always had a far greater significance than simply being a source of nutritional sustenance. Food is, in short, so deeply connected to the whole concept and practice of love that few of us consciously give this link a second thought in our daily lives. A 'good' mother in our culture feeds her children and her husband and one of the key roles of women in most cultures is the gathering and preparation of food. For many women these activities connected with food form a large part of their day and food, in one form or another, is never very far from their minds. So it is that food takes on an importance that is out of all proportion to its nutritional significance. And this is why mothers battle with children who are faddy eaters, or who don't like what they have cooked. As many a woman has said to me, 'It's not the food they are rejecting, it's me.' One has only to work with mothers whose babies reject the breast to see how real this all is. But it is not confined to breast-feeding mums – it can be seen in homes all over the country and with children of all ages. Even an adult's dislike of a food can have profound emotional effects in some families, so great is the importance placed on food by the woman of the house.

Against this background it is not difficult to see why it is that feeding times at all ages and stages of family life can be fraught with problems. The woman has invested not only time and money but also her love in the preparation and serving of the food and her expectations are correspondingly high. Anything that then denies her the rewards for all this trouble is seen by her as unloving or even frankly rejecting.

It is no accident that those working with people who have eating disorders – anorexia nervosa (self-starvation) or bulimia, compulsive overeating – can so easily draw out the most awful stories of attitudes to food in their families. Indeed, many women, currently fat or with some other eating disorder, tell of being made to eat up all their food; of the electric atmosphere at the family table; of the crestfallen look on their mother's face if any negative views were expressed about food she had so lovingly prepared; of the power struggles in the family that took place over mealtimes; and so on. Food in our culture is so heavily invested with emotion at almost every stage of life that it is hardly surprising that so many people have eating disorders of one form or another.

For many women, especially those who have a poor self-esteem, think poorly of themselves as mothers, have a poor relationship with their spouse, or all three, food is the main way that they show their love to their family. Such a woman may be somewhat insecure as a mother and not really know what to do for the best in many situations. What she *does* know is that feeding the family well will always bring rewards. So it is that such a woman will project many of her own fears, guilts, insecurities and so on on to her children and then seek to find solutions by feeding them more than they need. It is as if her unconscious is saying, 'Food is love: I cannot give you the love you need in other ways, so I'll give you more food.' In this way a child starts to eat more food than it knows it really wants, just to please its mother and so satisfy her needs for the giving of love. Such a child, and girls, because of their greater dependency needs and desire to be loved, are more at risk than are boys, soon becomes fat and starts to have a poor body image. Studies have found that by the age of four young children already view fat people as less attractive and less valuable than thin people. This sort of behaviour then is the basis of many a fat girl, or boy, and indeed many a fat adult.

Those who see problems resulting from eating disorders find that many such women crave food almost entirely as a source of comfort when things get tough in adult life. Such women are, in a sense, masturbating their mouths. They are 'making love' to the biscuit tin: seeking, in adult life, a source of gratification that properly belongs to the oral stage of babyhood.

At the first sign (real or imagined) of the withdrawal of love in the adult world they retreat to babyhood, quite unconsciously, of course, and to the pleasures of the mouth. Often such women realize that they are driven by this destructive behaviour and yet can do nothing about it. Their need for love in the here-and-now cannot be satisfied, for whatever reason, so they return to the last stage of their psychological and emotional development when they felt securely loved. Alas, for many this was in the very first few weeks of life. Not infrequently such a woman is insecure in her adult genital situation – she does not see herself as a real woman and easily retreats to becoming a baby. Such a woman is thus a mother and a baby at the same time. She may even, on occasions, see herself as a better mother to herself than she is to her children so she continues to 'baby' herself even though the rewards are a plump (babylike) body that in our culture is a turn-off sexually to most men. Women such as this often find that they produce a self-fulfilling prophecy in this regard. 'My man doesn't love me/understand me therefore I'll eat to console myself,' her unconscious tells her. And sure enough once she *is* fat he goes off her, unconsciously walking into the trap she laid.

Unfortunately, for many women in our culture eating is the only thing in their lives that is anywhere near as nice as sex so when sex goes wrong, and I don't just mean genital sex, they turn to food as their reward system. Clearly this whole subject is enormous and cannot be dealt with here except in the briefest way. What we can do though is to look at ways of making food less likely to become a source of emotional distress and putting it back where it belongs as a source of nourishment and a part of social intercourse.

Helping children to have a balanced and healthy view of food starts in the cradle. The best possible start is to breast-feed from day one on the basis that you do it whenever the baby or you feels like it. A baby who is immediately satisfied will grow in confidence that he is wanted, worth bothering with, and loved. He or she will be able to tolerate a degree of frustration from time to time secure in the knowledge that the norm is that food comes fairly soon and predictably after he or she expresses a need for it.

Breast-feeding is, arguably, the best way of achieving this loving bond of mutual satisfaction between a mother and her baby though it is nearly as good to bottle-feed, particularly from an emotional and psychological point of view. Of course, there is no comparison when it comes to pure nutrition; breast-feeding wins hands down.

As a baby is weaned off the breast and on to solid foods the key to success is to take things gently, at the baby's pace and to be guided by what he or she likes to eat. Keep up the breast-feeding alongside the solids for as long as the baby wants or until you feel that you can no longer cope with breast-

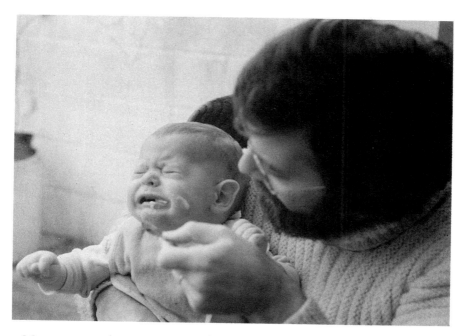

Most parents have experienced this. Keep the 'battle' to a minimum and remain flexible. The way you handle mealtimes could influence your child's views on food for a lifetime.

feeding too. For many a mother–baby partnership the answer is to stop day-time feeds and replace them with solids but to keep night-time feeds going for a while. This can be slowly reduced to a feed at bed-time and then the breast withdrawn altogether. On this basis some women go on feeding their children for three years or so though the vast majority of the child's *nutritional* needs will have long since been replaced by solids.

When it comes to toddler mealtimes, battles are the order of the day in many homes. Whether it is because the mother is insecure about her mothering, as we saw above, or because she simply doesn't realize that her child may not like the foods she, the mother, does, many a mother forces food down her toddler when he clearly doesn't want or need it. Increasingly it is becoming clear that toddlers 'know' that they are allergic to certain foods and so automatically reject them. The mothers of such children usually plough ahead though and force things down them only to find that the child becomes irritable, hyperactive, has multiple food allergic symptoms that baffle doctors, and so on. The only rule worth enforcing at this stage is to let the child eat what it wants and to stop fussing. No toddler ever starved itself to death so don't worry. Obviously if a child goes off its food uncharacteristically for a day or two there could be something physically or emotionally wrong and this will need looking into but this is very different from what I am talking about here, as any parent will know.

In some families battles about food between mother and child are simply symptoms of other dis-ease or disorder in the mother–child relationship and have nothing whatever to do with food itself. Such an embattled child knows that food is a subject on which its mother is vulnerable to a loss of love and it manipulates the situation accordingly. At last he or she has power – a rare event for most children who feel pretty powerless most of the time. Whenever battles (as opposed simply to dislikes) occur over food it's sensible to look much wider at what the real battle is. Such a child is usually unhappy about something in life, may be jealous of a brother or sister, might be unhappy about school, worried about the parents' relationship, or one of many other things. If you can't sort out the problem easily seek professional help before things become too entrenched.

Some children like to eat only a very restricted number of foods. This can lead to extreme frustration in the mother who battles to impose her ideas of a balanced diet. By and large it's fair to say that we eat too much in the West. And the trouble starts at this stage of life. Many's the child who knows very young that he or she can do perfectly well on very little food yet the mother strives to stuff more into him than he needs. This conditions the child to feeling overfull at mealtimes yet satisfied that he or she has answered its parents' needs for him or her to eat, as we saw on page 150. If adults behaved in this way to one another life would become unbearable yet this is what many of us do to our children.

Much more important than the amount of food we give our children is its nutritional value and its attractiveness. If you want a child to eat healthily the best way to really make it happen is to learn how to dress up the food and the occasions surrounding food, to be attractive to him. There are many books about healthy eating for children, several of which have helpful hints about how to encourage them to eat well on a daily basis.

As children grow it makes sense to ensure that mealtimes are as peaceful and as unemotional as possible. No one at any age should be made to feel bad about not eating something they don't like and it is best to make every effort to defuse emotional situations at mealtimes so that the atmosphere is calm and relaxing. Sharing the responsibility for the preparation of food as the family grows takes the pressure off the mother and spreads the pleasures with the other members of the family. Once this starts to occur it's interesting how attitudes to food change for the better. No longer is there such a one-sided investment by the mother as she puts herself on the line every mealtime.

Hand in hand with this it is helpful to have a broad and tolerant view about food in general. Many a middle-class family today is so set into 'the healthy life' that they have become obsessed with healthy eating and their children are made to suffer. There is no harm in having the odd ice-cream, piece of white bread, sweets, or even a food containing artificial colourings and flavourings (assuming that no one in the family is allergic to them of course). Children of all ages, from seven to seventy rebel against too harsh a regime of healthy eating so it makes sense to go gently and to be reasonable. Allow, and even encourage, children to choose their own foods within reason and get them to take a pleasure in preparing them as soon as they are old enough. If a child is going through a patch of eating faddily and poorly simply supplement his diet with a good multi-mineral/multi-vitamin supplement so that his basic nutritional needs are met. Many a child who eats few or no foods containing the trace element zinc, for example, will tend to lose their appetite for most other foods. Zinc is a good supplement that will boost the appetite and soon the 'problem eater' is a problem no more.

But it's not just the way we handle our children's food and eating that affects their views on the subject. What we as their parents *do* and *think* affects them profoundly too. The woman who is always on a diet, and failing; the mother who loses weight and gains it in a yo-yo fashion; and many other psychological influences are all obviously affecting their children's attitudes to food.

Many women today are near-obsessed with slimming and are almost permanently involved in it in one way or another. Just think what effect this has on their children as they try to come to terms with the illogicality of their mother's body image and its continual changes. Her dissatisfactions are usually all too obvious and very often there's an underlying hypocrisy of 'Do as I say, not as I do' as such a mother tries in vain to make her children eat 'properly' while she herself binges and slims in cycles.

Any woman who finds herself in this situation owes it, not only to herself as a mother but also as a wife and a woman, to get something sorted out, perhaps with the help of a professional counsellor of some kind.

Fat families produce fat children not solely because their genetic make-up somehow magically makes cornflakes or whatever attractive, but because the eating habits of parents are learned by their children. True, there can be underlying personality factors that are shared by both parents and children, factors that tend to make them turn to food at the slightest provocation, but these, once made conscious, can be addressed and modified in many people. Attitudes to food, however, run in families. In the opinion of many, it is the effects of these attitudes that make people fat, not the food itself.

Parents who follow these broad guidelines in their children's early days will almost certainly have no problems with faddy eaters; will have few, if any, battles at mealtimes; will have children who grow up slim and who don't turn to food for solace in any crisis; and will produce a generation of tomorrow's parents who will, in turn, have food in perspective for their children. For many of us food is a subject on which we are vulnerable so it makes sense to do all we can to understand this in ourselves when bringing up our children.

14

MOTIONS AND EMOTIONS

A lot of nonsense is talked and written about potty training but the truth is that every normal child naturally develops control over his bladder and bowels with or without training. The only thing he really has to learn is where to do it. Given that children learn by imitation it makes sense to suggest that the average child seeing other children going to the lavatory or sitting on a potty will do the same in time. This is indeed what happens in certain African cultures. So even if the parents do nothing a child will become self-trained in his own time.

In our culture we put children in nappies which can't be pulled up or down easily by the child in times of need. This means that he will give up in frustration if not helped in some way. A very few parents are content to allow their child to go without a nappy and put up with some puddles and messes as it learns to control its bowels and bladder but the vast majority opt for some sort of positive act of training.

Up until this stage of life a baby's mother is his care-giver, source of food, and love, and provider of everything he needs. Now she takes on a new role – that of teacher and trainer. And she's trying to train him in an exceptionally difficult task, the voluntary control of an involuntary, reflex process. It *is* possible to train a baby under a year old to use a potty, especially if you sit him down just after a feed but this is often ineffective because he isn't making any conscious decisions about the process, his body is reacting in a reflex way.

Because so many parents have heard about the harm done by too early or too strict potty training most now wait until the child is about 18 months before starting such training seriously. This has, to be fair, been made a lot easier with the coming of disposable nappies, making long-term nappy care less of a chore for parents. At this age a child seems to be about ready, in developmental terms, to sit up comfortably; to have enough nervous control of his bowel and bladder; and to have sufficient understanding and powers to communicate to enable the whole process to mean something to him. Additionally, by this age most children must be rather less than delighted with the constant feel of soggy, cold or dirty nappies which, in its turn, makes potty training appealing to them. Only when a child has most of these things going for him does potty training really stand a chance of success without too much effort or even without long-term harm being done.

There are many ways of potty training a child but the following method works well in most families. First introduce the potty as a toy from about 18 months. Put water in it, play with it or use it as a hat or a train. This accustoms him to the potty and its name. The next stage involves putting a doll or a teddy on it and letting him do a 'wee-wee' or a 'pooh' or whatever you call these things in your family. If your child sees other members of the family on the lavatory this will help because you can then have a dolly on the potty alongside you and show how the doll does its 'wee' as you do yours. Watching other children using a potty is a good idea too because children of this age are keen to imitate. One day, without any fuss, you could suggest that your child has a go on the potty. This has enormous appeal to the child that is near two because he will probably be only too delighted to see that there is a way out of nappy–wearing.

How ready are these three for potty training? The girls are still pleasing themselves 'orally' and the boy is seeking reassurance (by reassuring them) as he holds them.

Once the child has done something on the potty the combination of your praise and his pleasure will mean that he will want to repeat the procedure and you are well on the way. This early training is best done with the child undressed at bathtime or in the summer when he can run around naked in the garden.

Quite quickly a child at this stage will come to you during the day to ask for his potty but the watchful parent will soon become aware of the tell-tale signs such as a sudden stillness, holding the crutch, a certain facial discomfort, or signs of actual discomfort if the nappy is soiled. If the potty is close at hand it can quickly be popped into place and the child will learn once more to link early signs of impending evacuation with the potty.

Repeated and patient suggestions combined with a friendly, optimistic and encouraging approach are the order of the day when starting potty training. Don't show disapproval when he does it in his pants, simply clean it up in a relaxed way. Always praise him when he is clean and dry and when he gives you warning about wanting to go.

Many children are not potty trained well into their third year. This applies especially to boys and some have insufficient bladder control well after this. Only one child in a hundred is dry at night at a year old and it is not unusual for a four- or five-year-old to still be wearing nappies at night. Clearly the range of normality is great, so don't be put off by other mothers and their tales of their instantly trained children. They might have achieved it at a price that is unacceptable to you.

But potty training isn't only about becoming dry and clean or I would not be devoting so much space to it. As we saw in Chapter 9, although most of us can remember little or nothing about these very early years, the lessons learned then will have been absorbed into the unconscious and never really disappear. Potty training is about control: control over one's own body and the influence of others in insisting on that control. Once a child can control its bowel and bladder it has a power over its parents because it can produce, or not produce, what they want. The child's stools thus become its first gift that it can bestow – and some choose not to do so for one of many reasons.

When we think about all this carefully it is rather strange that something that the child produces from its body is taken away from it and thrown away, often with considerable disgust. Many a mother says things about germs and dirt as she disposes of her child's excrement and this possibly has lasting effects on him. From then on he sees all excretion as dirty and unacceptable. Some boys brought up in this way end up becoming impotent in later life, especially with women they love because they unconsciously think of semen as being a form of excrement and cannot bring themselves to soil the woman. Some women too have such problems and do not want to have semen on their bodies or even in their vagina.

During this, the anal stage, of a child's psychosexual development, the child obtains considerable pleasure from evacuating his bowels and bladder. (I look further at the stages of psychosexual development in Chapter 16.) Indeed, most adults too find these sensations pleasurable, at least to some degree. The release of the pressure that has built up in a hollow organ of the body is almost always pleasurable and emptying one's bowel and bladder are just two such sensations.

But research shows that because of the obvious, or even unconscious, pleasure that babies get from their excrement and its control and the concepts of dirt and mess that go hand in hand with potty training, the subject is far from a neutral one in terms of psychological and emotional development. It has been found, for example, that women who are generally severe and punitive with their children are likely to be harsh in potty training too. Such women have been found, in studies, to be severe and controlling about obedience, masturbation and sex play.

From a knowledge of learning theory one would expect trouble with early, harsh, rigid, over-controlled potty training, and this is what appears to happen. Such training produces a sense of anxiety in the child who is keen to please, in fact desperately so on occasions. This can easily lead to feelings of aggression towards the parents. This is especially likely to occur if the mother has been cold and rejecting in the first year or so of life. A child treated like this will often kick, scream, bite and refuse to be trained yet even so some parents make the whole thing into a battle of wills, to the child's detriment, as we shall see.

Temper tantrums, irritability, and temporary loss of control are common in such children and these can persist into later childhood. Chronic bedwetting, especially among boys, has been found in studies to be more common in those who were trained energetically and too early or too late. Traumatic training can have other deleterious effects too. In one study, over half of the children referred to a child guidance clinic for a variety of emotional problems (restlessness, tics, speech disturbances, psychosomatic disturbances, or school failure) had been bowel trained too early or by coercive methods. A majority of the children also reacted to their potty training immediately with one or more of the following: continuation of wetting, fear of the lavatory, tantrums, defiance, anger, or an over-concern with cleanliness. Nearly two-thirds were still wetting themselves at three. In another study children trained early and harshly became highly compulsive, aggressive, negativistic and fearful in later childhood.

Excessive potty training makes some children generally timid and over-conforming. They so fear making the wrong response that they do only that which they feel sure will bring approval and success.

But this is not the whole story even yet. If the anal stage of development progresses well it is an impetus towards creativity and productivity. Frustrations at this stage can, it is thought, lead to character traits such as obstinacy, compulsiveness, and an over-concern with cleanliness and orderliness. These are probably a defence (see page 109) against returning to the anal stage which, it was impressed on the tiny child, was unacceptably dirty and messy. Some people who end up becoming highly obsessional are probably at the extreme end of this spectrum of behaviour. On the other hand anal frustrations can end up producing untidiness, disorderliness and even destructiveness. Psychoanalytical work suggests that some people who remain 'fixed' at the anal stage, and they are many, hold things to themselves, just as they used to withhold their stools from their mother, or have learned that to retain things (keep stools inside them) is good. They become hoarders; are mean with their time, their money and even with their semen, in the case of men. To be fair, the whole concept of the anal stage is somewhat culture-dependent – but having said this, it seems to be valid for our western culture.

Other more obvious ways that anality can persist, according to Freudian psychoanalysts, are as an on-going interest in anal matters. Such a person might be exceptionally keen on anal sex, on women's bottoms, on smacking people's bottoms, or have fantasies of such things whilst masturbating or making love. Some people of either sex greatly enjoy having their anus stimulated during sex and many a prostitute knows that some men get pleasure from having a finger in their anus to stimulate their G-spot (prostate gland) during intercourse or masturbation.

All of this makes the anal stage a very important one in the psychosexual development of children. It can have several potential ill effects, as we have seen, and the reasons for this are many. It is the first time that the parents, and especially the mother, change their role from pleasure-giver to trainer; it has profound effects on how a child learns about the control of its own body and about how others seek to control it; it learns for the first time that it has real power over its mother; it starts to think for the first time that something it produces could be negative and 'dirty'; it associates the functioning of its body with sensations of pleasure – a pleasure that other people have negative feelings about; it is the first time that the child's own will and desires come up against those of its mother's unconscious notions about what is 'right' and 'wrong' – and all this in a child not yet two years old!

For this reason the stage of potty training is of vital importance to psychosexualists. Many a problem in later life starts here, though to be fair there is no single model of potty training that works to the exclusion of others. What *is* certain is that harsh, punitive, early and unloving potty training produces problems, some of which persist into adulthood and even into old age. Indeed, some elderly people, once their interest in genital sex has waned return to the anal stage and once again become fascinated with excretion, just like a developing child.

This has been dealt with at some length because potty training is just one, albeit important, form of training that we foist on our children. However, the lessons learned from this area can, and should be applied to other areas of their development. For example, in any form of training pleasure should outweigh pain and negativity; it should not start until the child is ready physiologically and psychologically or it is more likely to fail or to produce long-term harm; it should be consistent in its application; it should be done with love and patience; it should take into account the fact that all children develop at their own unique rate and that children are all different even within any one family; it should favour rewards for desired behaviours and ignore inappropriate behaviours; it should use play and symbols to encourage the child; it should involve imitation of both parents and other children; and it should be taken gently, at the pace of the child, not that of the parent.

Lastly perhaps, it would make sense for the reader of this book to think ahead to the potential after-effects of training a child harshly or prematurely in anything. Reactions against the training itself and the subject matter of the training are very common. We are all guilty of this to some extent and for some of the time. We imagine that because *we* are interested in or gifted at something, that our children could, or indeed even should be too. We then go over the top to 'encourage' them often with disastrous results. One of these can be a frank rejection of the whole subject either there and then or later in life, often to the detriment of the child or even his or her own children.

15

IS IT WORTH BOTHERING?

The first psychoanalysts believed that an in-depth understanding of an individual's childhood would reveal the origins of all their adult psychological, emotional and even psychiatric problems. This simple hope has not been substantiated over the last century and even major contributors to the art and science of psychoanalysis now think that there is much more to the matter.

This is not, of course, to say that what happens during childhood is unimportant but rather that it has to be put in its proper perspective. For example, there is no reason to believe that a particular personality feature of a child will necessarily be manifest in that individual as an adult, although sometimes this will be true. That early influences are important cannot be denied but what recent research has found is that they are not necessarily permanent or irreversible. Children are much more resilient in the face of adverse influences than was previously thought and changes occur that can add to or diminish the influences of early childhood both later in childhood and even right into adolescence. Even in adult life change is still possible and those of us who work with adults are often amazed at what can change if the person is motivated and co-operative.

Whilst it is true that isolated events in early childhood have an effect on the child it is much more true that the body and the mind heal themselves with time and that negative starting points do not by any means always predict a negative outcome in adulthood.

All this is very heartening for parents who feel that they might have got things 'wrong' when bringing up their children. Whilst there is little doubt that it is better to get things as 'right' as possible from the start there is also no doubt that even fairly major setbacks can be redressed by caring and loving parents.

This book is not about psychiatric illness, mainly because this is a subject for professionals and not parents, but nevertheless it is interesting to look very briefly at a few psychiatric conditions that seem to be linked to childhood psychological and emotional development.

Schizophrenia, for example, is a very common condition that fills more mental hospital beds than any other except depression. About half of all those who become schizophrenic in adult life have clearly shown abnormal patterns of behaviour in childhood. Over the last 25 years a great deal of research has been done to try to find out what these predictors might be. But what seems to emerge is the fact that what at first looked like antecedents for schizophrenia were in fact vulnerability factors for mental illness in general. Several studies have found that children who later go on to become schizophrenic were socially incompetent during their school years. Having said this a 30-year follow-up study found that children who were shy, withdrawn or hypersensitive were *not* more likely to suffer from the disease in adulthood. Poor family communication combined with hostile or critical patterns of behaviour seem to favour the development of schizophrenia.

Overall, research suggests that there are three main things that predispose a child to becoming schizophrenic later in life; the first is an abnormality in interpersonal relationships accompanied by odd, unpredictable behaviour, social isolation and rejection by their peer group; the second is any form of verbal impairment, any clumsiness or trouble with co-ordination between the eyes and body movement; and the third is a poor ability to concentrate. Having said this, only about half of all schizophrenics have this kind of childhood story.

As we see on page 219 depression is not uncommon in children but it often takes unusual forms compared with the adult condition. Before puberty depression is much more common in boys but afterwards girls take over and then throughout life women outnumber men very greatly. Very little is known about the effects of childhood depression on adulthood. It seems reasonable to suggest that a child who is depressed will tend to learn such behaviour and then resort to it in times of trouble as an adult but no trials have been done to prove this. Some are under way at the moment. Certain experts in attachment theory have always claimed that parental loss in childhood makes a child more likely to become depressed later in life not because of the actual loss itself but rather because it creates a vulnerability to stress later on. Such children have learned that they cannot control the 'bad' events in life and are used to feeling helpless, to having a low self-esteem and so on all of which leads them to interpret downbeat events in life as yet another example of their worthlessness.

Recent research suggests that it is a serious lack of parental affection and loving care in childhood that predispose to depression. In this sense the death or absence of a parent has adverse effects because such a parent cannot supply that love.

Emotional disorders are much more complex to research into partly because they are so difficult to define accurately and because they often don't get to the medical profession to be studied. There can be no doubt that both genetic and environmental factors play a part in how we all turn out in life. A child brought up in an obsessional household will undoubtedly tend to show obsessional forms of behaviour, even if he rebels against them later in life either consciously or unconsciously. Even from the very earliest days in the cradle parents say that they can tell the nature of their child's personality and emotional characteristics.

Having said this many children with quite severe emotional problems go on to become perfectly normally functioning adults and many anxious adults first started to have problems in adulthood after a normal childhood. Things can also vary very greatly from child to child within any one family if a particular child is, for example, victimized or unwanted, compared with the others.

When it comes to looking at antisocial behaviour in adulthood there is almost always a story of such behaviour in childhood. Antisocial behaviour is commoner in children than in adults anyway and only a minority of antisocial children go on to become troublesome adults. However, antisocial behaviour in adulthood is almost always preceded by such behaviour in childhood.

What about experiences in early childhood? Could they or do they create permanent changes that affect the individual as an adult? Animal studies of various kinds have found that stresses can produce lasting changes in the system of the body that copes with stress, changes that are accompanied by an enhanced resistance to later stress. Other experiments have found that infants exposed to few visual stimuli have structural changes in those parts of the brain that deal with vision. A severe lack of sensory inputs can also lead to measurable changes in brain chemistry and structures.

But all these experiments tend to affect only one sensory system. When it comes to emotional and psychological development things are more complex because many interlocking systems are involved and one probably makes good the deficit in another. For example, although there is almost certainly a 'sensitive period' during which a mother can best bond with her new-born baby all is not lost if this bonding doesn't occur at this critical period. A longer period of learning might be needed to achieve the same effects later but they usually *can* be obtained, so flexible is the human infant.

So the lesson from all this is that babies and young children are much more resilient than was previously thought and that even quite negative events and behaviours in early childhood can be redressed and the damage minimized or totally reversed by loving, caring parenting.

What children cannot stand, without coming to emotional and psychological harm, is an environment in which they are not loved and cared for. The more consistent and unconditional that love is the better, but none of us is a robot and we are bound to have good days and bad days even if we are very aware of what we should be doing as parents and are trying our best for much of the time. Children, it seems, remember and are affected by overall impressions rather than even quite long-term disruptions. Against a background of unconditional love and care most children can tolerate a lot of physical disruption (such as moving house several times, emigrating, deaths in the family, and so on). Such events arguably affect the parents more than they do their children.

The other thing that has to be said is that a couple's marital relationship is probably far more vital to the emotional growth and future of their children than most realize. In many a household today the whole aura is one of emotional upheaval as the parents live in disharmony or near divorce, not to mention the problems of those adults who are actually divorced or separated. Much of the volcanic ash from such an eruption lands on the children and parents who are in such a state themselves often find it difficult to care for their children in the way they would like. Their ability to love is impaired too as their main love bond in life is thrown into jeopardy. It is not difficult for such a couple to sink into despair and to find it increasingly difficult to relate normally to their children. In some cases the children are seriously ignored or shunted from pillar to post to become semi-institutionalized without ever having been in an institution. On the other hand a parent may invest an unhealthy amount of love and attention in a particular child instead of in an unsatisfactory and unsatisfying adult. This can put quite unreasonable pressure on the child to become a mini-adult in the crisis and some never stop behaving in this way for the rest of their lives.

It is beyond doubt that children of divorced parents are themselves more likely to be divorced – there are numerous studies which show this to be true. Just how this arises is not known for sure but some of the ways in which it occurs have just been mentioned. If we as a society think that marriage is worth preserving as an institution then we owe it to ourselves to do everything we can to prevent divorce today on the basis that our children will be less likely to resort to it themselves. For this reason I feel that marital therapy should be much more widely available than it currently is. With help from outside parents can be enabled to stay together, and to provide a loving relationship on which their children can model themselves. From the security of a good marriage parents can create a stable model of loving and caring for their children and this, as I hope I have shown, is the foundation of that emotional and psychological stability which forms the basis of healthy and creative living. At the back of the book you will find a list of organizations from which such professional help may be sought.

PART IV

THE GROWTH OF
SEXUALITY IN YOUNG
CHILDREN

16

THE FOUNDATIONS OF
PLEASURE AND PAIN

There are few subjects involving a child's psychological and emotional growth that cause more concern to parents than does the growth of sexuality. It is clear to most parents that from very early on children have a personal sexuality that both children and parents must come to terms with, yet because the whole area of personal sexuality is so tense in our culture this is something especially difficult to deal with in children.

We saw in Chapter 10 how it is that we communicate attitudes to our children about every subject in our lives but nowhere, it seems, is this more obvious than when it comes to matters to do with sex. I have devoted a whole section of the book to the subject because it is such a good and easily understood model for thinking about how we deal with our children and their unconscious attitudes in general. Quite a lot of what follows could be translated into other spheres of life, for example our attitudes to food, but few people are either so interested in the subject or deeply affected by it as they are by sexuality in all its manifestations.

The trouble with even talking about childhood sexuality, as I have found from giving numerous lectures and discussion groups on the subject, is that many adults find the idea totally unwholesome and even somewhat disgusting. This is because most people think that sexuality is all about genitality, which, of course, it is not. This is not true of adult sexuality and is much less true of that of a child.

But babies and children *are* sexual, as anyone who has experience of children will confirm. Who has never seen a baby boy with an erection, perhaps when breast-feeding? Who can deny the fact that even babies masturbate? Who would be able to ignore the powerful feelings of a child towards his opposite-sex parent in the years just before he or she starts school? In most cultures worldwide where sexuality is taken for granted as a normal part of everyday life these things are commonplace and wholesome. In the West, however, we have come to regard much about sex as dirty, sinful or generally unacceptable and as a result *childhood* sexuality is an even more unacceptable topic for discussion.

Many of our attitudes in this area stem from the fact that in our culture children are supposed to be 'innocents' in such matters. This then puts a burden of responsibility on adults, it is argued, to protect them from such material. Of course children do need protecting but to protect them from sex, a basic and natural human instinct, is much like saying that we should protect our children from coming into contact with food, our other basic need in life. In those cultures where sex is treated openly and where there is no unreasonable preoccupation with it, as there is in our culture, people seem to be relaxed about the whole subject and perversions and deviations appear to be uncommon.

The development of sexuality undoubtedly starts, like everything else, in the womb and there is evidence that hormones, especially male hormones, play a role in the pre-natal sexual development of a child. There is little doubt in my mind that a fetus will have experienced some sort of sexual feelings even before birth, although it is, of course, impossible to detect them. Certainly immediately after birth babies quite quickly develop genital responses and even new-born baby boys have been found to have an erection. From this rather 'primitive' sexuality in the uterus a baby grows into an adult with all the range of psychological, physical and emotional sexual responses that are a part of human sexuality. Without the majority of us achieving this kind of maturity there is no future for the human race. Sex is vital for the survival of the species just as food is vital for the survival of the individual.

Clearly it is nonsense to suggest, as some of the more repressive, 'moralist' elements of society do, that children are innocent until their wedding night when they magically become sexually mature and experienced. Any parent knows only too well that things start long, long before this and that they have to be dealt with whether they find it easy or not. When it comes to the subject of sex and their children the burden on parents today is greater than ever before because sex is now more openly discussed and because children are exposed to more sexual stimuli than even their parents were at the same age, let alone their grandparents.

The trouble with talking about sex and children is deciding how to construct a theoretical model that seems to have explanatory value not only on the matter of genital sex, but on other facets of sexuality too.

Perhaps the best model that has so far been constructed is that of Freud even if, in the light of empirical evidence, it needs re-working. Unfortunately, few people, even those who consider themselves quite well informed, have ever read Freud in the original. Many, indeed, if not most, think that he wrote only about sex and that the whole of his life's work was centred around the subject. Nothing could be further from the truth. His writings and theories span a vast range of psychological subjects and when reading large tracts of his work there is hardly a mention of sex at all.

What Freud did do, and which no one else has been able to do, not even a century later, was look at the growth of sexuality in children in a way that explains all kinds of things in adult life. And this is part of the purpose of this book. None of us who spend our days listening to our patients for hour after hour can help but be impressed by the long-term effects of things going wrong with the earliest lessons about love and sexuality. Indeed, there are few areas of life that present more minefields to the average adult. The subject is a vital one and yet many adults, and a lot of them parents, try, however unconsciously, to side-step the issues and hope that they will somehow go away.

It is obvious that a pattern for sexual behaviour is present in every new-born baby. Just as there is a blueprint for its physical, emotional and personality development so there is also for its sexual development. As we have seen on page 103, the blueprint is only half the story because a child's environment can also profoundly affect how its sexuality develops, just as it can affect its physical and emotional growth. The prime influences on this growth, or failure to grow, as the case may be, as in most other areas of life, are the child's parents.

So highly charged in our culture is the whole area of sexuality that we parents are, for the most part, unaware of what lies in our unconscious and thus unable to do much about how this affects the emerging sexuality of our children. So it is that we, usually quite unconsciously, dump our old prejudices about sexuality on our children so that they end up with all our 'messages' written into their life scripts, without their knowledge. It is because so much of the learning and communication about sex goes on at this unconscious-to-unconscious level that the whole area is so vexed. If we ourselves do not really understand our own sexuality it is easy to see that it would be very difficult, if not impossible, to come to terms with our children's. And this is why so many parents have such strong emotions about their children's sexuality. As with so many things to do with parenting children unwittingly open up old wounds and reactivate old emotional circuits we took for dead.

THE MOUTH STAGE OF PSYCHOSEXUAL DEVELOPMENT

The first of Freud's stages of psychosexual development is the oral stage. Clearly this is instinctual so as to ensure that a baby will suck from the breast and thus survive. But the oral stage does not start at birth: babies have been seen, on X-rays and ultrasonic scans, to suck their thumbs *in utero*. Most people can readily see that a little baby gets considerable pleasure from its mouth and lips. Anyone who has watched a new baby feeding at the breast will know that the bliss on its face says more than simply 'what a nice drink this is'. The mother comforts the baby, soothes it, looks at it and smiles a lot. The baby is very close to her, and her body's warmth and even her heartbeat make him feel secure, wanted and happy.

This building up of trust and confidence is the foundation for the future of any child who is to think of himself as loved and valued. A baby treated thus will tend to become someone with a sense of optimism, self-assurance and even self-esteem. Clearly he is worth something to his mother if she takes all this 'trouble' over him and the feelings of emotional warmth that accompany these experiences have a profound influence on the future.

More to the point perhaps is the baby who is left to scream. He is more likely to end up with a poor view of the world, to have notions of self-doubt and distrust and even perhaps, eventually depression. It is quite possible to see that a baby whose oral needs are not satisfied at this stage of his development could end up later in life unconsciously trying to make up for what he never had. Such drives are indeed seen in the two main areas of life where orality commonly persists: sex and food. It is the view of many who work in the field that a baby whose oral needs are frustrated at this stage is more likely to become addicted to food (especially at times of stress), oral sex, or other oral substitutes such as smoking, later in life than is someone who negotiated this developmental stage well.

Although sucking at the bottle or breast produces food for a baby it quite plainly supplies other needs too, as we have seen. And given that obtaining food is so vital to a baby's very existence it is easy to see that the pleasurable sensations associated with it are locked into the baby's ways of thinking and feeling at a vital developmental level. Which is why, later in life, those who did not come through this stage well return, almost automatically, to the oral pleasures they so craved but did not get. Anyone who makes for the biscuits as soon as the going gets tough knows exactly what I mean.

As a baby grows and matures it can suck not only its thumb but also other objects that come within its reach. This is not only a way of learning about the world (by finding out what things feel like via the mouth) but invests the mouth with further value as a source of pleasure and discovery. That thumb-sucking clearly has a deeper meaning and value to a baby than its parents wish it did is plain to see by the opposition, however unconscious, that there is to the practice. Although clinical studies show that thumb-sucking causes no damage to the teeth, even some of those parents who know this are still concerned.

This takes us on to another closely linked point about oral, or indeed other drives. When we need to satisfy a pleasure drive we usually find a way of doing so that is culturally sanctioned for our age. A baby is allowed to suck at the breast but an adult is not, at least not in public. A man cannot suck his thumb but our culture 'allows' him to suck on his pipe. This is a form of displacement, which we looked at in more detail on page 111. But however we do it we all tend to find ways of satisfying these 'primitive' pleasure drives in one way or another. In my clinical experience babies who are totally breast-fed whenever they or their mothers want to tend not to suck their thumbs or need comfort blankets. However, empirical studies do not support this view, perhaps because they look at babies breast-fed as if they were bottle-fed – to a schedule. I maintain that all the pleasure needs of such children in the oral stage are wholeheartedly supplied and that the hours they spend comfort-suckling at the breast make them feel secure and orally gratified in a way that a schedule-fed baby can never be. It would be interesting to follow up such children to see how they fared later in life with obesity and smoking as just two examples.

So far we have looked at sucking only as a form of physical pleasure but it is clearly part of a much deeper relationship between a mother and her baby because the breast is attached to a woman – usually the child's mother. At first a baby must think that a breast is simply a sort of milk supplier but fairly soon he realizes that it belongs to his mother and as a result he now invests her as a person with pleasant feelings when she supplies milk and thinks badly of her when he is made to wait and cry. For the first time in his life he now links another person with the experience of his personal pleasure and pain and he looks to his mother as his supplier of food and his way of answering his very basic need for oral gratification.

Many a mother says that she notices that her baby boy has an erection as he feeds, be it at breast or bottle. This is perfectly normal and is, without a doubt, a part of the loving and close experience he shares with his mother. Some little girls roll their thighs and, according to some mothers, lubricate vaginally too. Over my many years working with breast-feeding mothers I have heard on numerous occasions that mothers themselves become sexually aroused when breast-feeding both boys and girls. There is nothing sexual in this in the usual adult sense of the word but there is little doubt that such pleasant feelings help make the whole business pleasant for women and so encourage them to want to go on doing it.

But back to the baby. Even if a baby becomes sexually aroused during feeding this is almost certainly secondary to its mouth pleasure, which is the main centre of attraction at this age. The mouth ensures the baby's personal survival and it expresses its love for its mother through its mouth.

THE POTTY TRAINING STAGE (THE ANAL STAGE)

Assuming that things go well with the oral stage the child progresses to the next, anal, stage at around the middle of the second year. Now, the baby focuses not on taking in but on putting out. It is now the production of urine and feces that gives the main pleasure. During the second or third year a child learns to control its bowels and bladder and can obtain pleasure from producing or withholding its waste products. We looked at potty training in Chapter 14 so all that remains here is to remind the reader that harsh, inconsistent, over-fast potty training almost certainly has adverse effects on later life. These are detailed in the section on page 160.

THE CLITORIS/PENIS STAGE (THE PHALLIC STAGE)

Now that the child has negotiated, hopefully successfully, the oral and the anal stages, these pleasures become secondary to phallic pleasures around the age of three.

This stage is characterized by a new-found pleasure in the clitoris or penis, depending on the sex of the child. Masturbation starts about this time of life, many coming across it quite by accident. Most parents say that their children of this age did not masturbate but, on discussing the matter with adults when obtaining details of their sexual histories, this appears to be wrong. In other words, parents often do not really know whether their children masturbate or not. This is partly because, of the stages of psychosexual development to date, this is the first that enables the child to step away from its parents and experience pleasures over which they have no direct control. Very few parents are so at ease with their own sexuality that they can, with impunity, watch their child masturbate so they distract him or her or tell them off for touching their genitals. All the child knows is that, as with the mouth and the control of excretion they have discovered something else that is pleasant and want to explore it. However, parents have other views and so start to lay their sexual messages on the child, usually quite unconsciously.

For example, many families have no name for the genitals. This is odd to the child because every other part of the body has a name. This can lead to 'unmentionable sex' in later life. Other similar concepts can lead to 'dirty', 'sinful', 'fearful', 'unhealthy' or 'shameful' sex according to the belief systems of the parents.

Almost all these messages are put across unconsciously by the parents who then, quite honestly, deny that they have ever put their children down on sexual matters. In this way what our parents taught us goes straight into the next generation and explains why it is that changes are so slow to take place in the areas of sexual education and understanding.

As a culture we tend to suppress the sexuality of girls more than that of boys and certainly it is a fact that mothers are more tolerant of the sexuality of their boys than they are of their girls. There are several possible reasons for this. First, it could be that women are more fascinated by their little boys' emerging sexuality and so, however unconsciously, discourage its development less. Second, on the basis of 'set a thief to catch a thief' women know more about female sexuality than they do about that of the male and so realize how important it is to keep it in control, which could be why so many women are harsh to their daughters, especially as they get older. Third, there is, even today, in our so-called egalitarian society, still a double standard when it comes to sex and parents of both sexes will think of male sexuality as being more acceptable than that of the female. So it is that we still tend to encourage our older boys to be 'lads' but strongly discourage our girls from becoming 'tarty'.

But whatever the reason for the differences there is no doubt that girls end up being more sexually repressed than are boys and that this very early stage in life has fateful, and often negative, effects on adult female sexuality. Sexual and marital therapists see the harvest of this every day in their work.

At this stage then the little boy or girl begins to derive real pleasure from genital stimulation. Whether or not their 'orgasms' are the same as adult climaxes is anyone's guess because we cannot ask them and anyway could not make comparisons even if we could. But there is little doubt that young children of this age masturbate, however covertly in the form of rocking, thigh-rubbing, or whatever. Quite quickly children learn to pick up their parents' adverse body language and so stop doing it in public but there is little doubt that they continue to do it nevertheless. Children of this age do not have the full-blown sexual response of an adult and boys do not ejaculate but to them such experiences must be every bit as powerful as they are to us as adults, which is why they want to carry on with it. Clinical experience suggests, for example, that about a third of all women when asked, cannot remember a time when they haven't masturbated since childhood, so clearly it is commonplace, and with good reason.

Children soon become interested in other people's bodies, in those of their parents, and in genital difference. It is now that boys start to wonder why it is that girls don't have a penis and on the basis that the penis is something rather definite and fairly obvious, imagine that girls must, for some reason and in some inexplicable way, have lost theirs. Some little boys actually say unprompted that girls' penises were removed because they were naughty and touched them and others fear a similar punishment for themselves. Some girls think they have a secret penis and others blame their mothers or have the most bizarre and complex of explanations as to why they don't have one.

From now onwards children start to develop ideas about being of one sex or another. This leads on to the next psychosexual stage, that of relating to the opposite sex.

17

FIRST LESSONS IN LOVE

THE OEDIPAL STAGE

Discovering that you are a boy or a girl proceeds slowly and erratically. Clearly children identify with their same-sex parent and this is a good start. For example, many a three-year-old girl is already like a miniature woman and possesses social skills that many a young man would envy. In fact, girls seem to be able to progress in this area of life more quickly than do boys. They can certainly discern the sex of others sooner than can boys.

Around the age of three or four, though, many parents notice a marked change in the behaviour of their children towards them. In this phase of their development the child becomes more attached to the opposite-sex parent than was the case previously. A little girl, for example, tries to be of service to her father, flirts with him, wants him to be interested in what she is doing, wants him to cuddle her and may even want to get into bed between him and her mother. Quite a lot of girls of this age say that they want to marry their father and it takes very little by way of a rebuke from him to make her upset for a long time.

All of this, and its male counterpart towards a boy's mother, is perfectly natural and can be observed by any parent who keeps their eyes open. It is a vital part of learning how to love the opposite sex and starts within the safety of the family home. But sometimes real problems can be produced if the other parent takes the behaviour amiss and finds, however unconsciously, that it stirs up old notions of sibling rivalry (see page 254) or jealousy (see page 233) that had lain dormant for years.

The balance, as with all matters to do with sex, is a fine one because there is indeed a possibility that the relationship can become over-close in some families. Without implying true incest it is simply that the adult all too easily becomes dependent on the child and so comes to look to him or her to provide emotional or other sustenance that an adult should not rely on a child to supply. This is especially likely to happen if the marital relationship within the family is not good. The parent then looks to the child to be the kind of partner he or she should ideally have had in the adult world which, for the child, can have disastrous effects later in life when he

176

or she finds it difficult or even impossible to relate to the opposite sex in a mature way. At one end of the spectrum are those children who, from this age onwards, are brought up to be miniature adults to their opposite-sex parent in such a way that they never actually become children at all. When they grow up they cannot act in a child-like way, are very adult and serious and cannot see the fun in life. They may also be so fixed on the psychosexuality of the opposite-sex parent that they cannot ever truly free themselves to look for and make an investment in someone else of the opposite sex.

Clearly a parent who has produced such a child has done him or her little good. Unfortunately, at least some such parents have behaved in the way they have in an unconscious bid to answer their, the parents', needs and not those of the child. As with everything in the rearing of children this is a bad state of affairs. Children are not given to us to answer *our* needs as parents or to make up for the deficits in life that we cannot ourselves remedy. If we try to make them fill these roles we usually do them nothing but harm.

Seeing the effect that her behaviour has on her father a little girl, at the same time, senses her mother's hostility and a girl of this age may say that she wishes her mother would go away and leave the father to herself. As she feels this she also wonders if her mother might retaliate and try to harm her for trying to take her man away from her. However, she also realizes that her mother is important in the family and so has to live with the ambivalence of it all. She then may try to placate her mother and to divert her attention from the deed in hand by being especially nice to her. It is thought that women's greater capacity for empathy and their ability to conceal feelings starts at this stage of psychosexual development.

A boy is already involved in a love bond with his mother right from birth and so does not have the same switch to make. However, his feelings about his mother and his father are exactly like those felt by his sister in reverse. Physical contact with the mother may produce an erection and his interest in her body intensifies. It is, for example, suggested that most men find partly dressed women more arousing than naked ones because at this stage in life they see their mothers partly clad, perhaps in underwear only and that this is such a formative time that the link between emerging sexual feelings and such dress is forged for ever.

Whatever the truth on this matter it is vital that the mother should not act seductively towards her son for the reasons we saw above. This is helped to some extent by the boy's fear of his father's retaliation should he try to get too close to the mother.

From the point of view of future problems two main areas seem to be important here. First, is the notion of female sexlessness. Girls are 'nice' and boys are 'naughty, dirty little things' for being interested in sex. The second is that boys enter the world of men as they avoid girls. As he so obviously cannot possess his mother he turns emphatically to men and their pursuits and identifies with his father in an effort to achieve this. Earlier he had his role as a male outlined by his mother. Later the culture rewards boys for masculine behaviour and puts them down for having feminine interests. The balance at which this all settles out varies considerably from child to child and we all end up as adults with a mixture of masculine and feminine personality characteristics in differing degrees. Indeed, some men are more 'feminine' than are some women, and vice versa. This in itself is of considerable importance for the future because it is often the opposite-sex characteristics in our partner that are at one and the same time attractive and a source of difficulty in our relationships. None of this has anything to do with homosexuality in either sex. A man who is caring, nurturing, emotionally sensitive and so on is not necessarily homosexual – simply a man with a larger than normal feminine component to his personality. The same could be said of women who are assertive, stubborn and have other masculine traits.

I think the answer here must be to encourage a certain amount of masculinity in girls and some femininity in boys. In this way they come to be rounded human beings and not cultural stereotypes with all that this entails. A woman with a strong masculine side to her personality can be assertive, sexually aggressive, positive and make things happen in the world. Similarly, a man with a feminine side can be caring, nurturing and loving, rather like a woman, but still be a true man in every other way.

At the end of this stage some boys stop masturbating and then rediscover it at puberty. Interestingly, boys often forget pre-puberty masturbation and think that it all started at puberty. Some girls, on the other hand, as pointed out above, often see masturbation as having been an ever-present part of their lives since babyhood.

Boys at this stage then, dismiss mother and firmly and usually quite quickly get into the world of men. For girls the process of separation is not usually so clear-cut or speedy. Their interest in the father continues, albeit in a weaker form, for some years.

THE LATENCY STAGE

Although some people dispute its existence inasmuch as children continue to have an interest in sex throughout their development, the next stage that most children seem to go through is one of relatively little heterosexual activity or pleasure. This lasts until puberty. At this stage a child's early preoccupations with its parents widen out to include other adults and it takes an increasing interest in the world around it. Curiosity about sex may now lead to the study of dictionaries, newspaper articles and so on and sex

These little girls in the latency phase of development are more concerned with their female and feminine roles than with boys. All this will change as puberty begins.

becomes of interest outside the family rather than something that exists only within it.

Some children start to play doctors and nurses at about the age of three and this can continue into the latency stage (which starts at about seven or so). Sex play with brothers and sisters up to and including the latency stage is innocuous but after this age, if continued, it can impair the ability of the child to relate to others of the opposite sex. This latency stage lasts until the hormonal changes of puberty force a new sort of interest in sex on to a child.

THE PRE-ADOLESCENT STAGE

As puberty approaches the sex hormones get going and girls who stopped masturbating at the end of the phallic stage now re-start at about nine or ten years old. Although it is still an 'innocent' activity this is soon to change. The girl now becomes interested in men and their bodies and starts to have sexual fantasies and dreams. Her father, once welcomed in the bathroom, is now banned and sex games become increasingly popular with other girls. Girls, unlike boys, rarely teach one another to masturbate and their homosexual phase of development is less obvious than that of boys. This is probably because girls have innate sexual skills whereas in boys, and indeed in all male primates, there is a much larger learned component to sex. Just before puberty girls seem to become very interested in sex generally and often in sex between animals too.

Boys gang together even more strongly at this age when usually they denigrate women and regress to the anal stage. They become near-obsessed with talking about excretion, breaking wind, and telling endless lavatory jokes. They will teach one another to masturbate and many experience group sexual activities such as seeing how far they can urinate, ejaculate, or who has the most pubic hairs.

At the end of latency and as adolescence beckons the first half of a child's sexual development, that which takes place at home, is completed. Any harm done by the parents now begins to become increasingly apparent. In later life, perhaps in therapy of some kind, the old memories, the long-forgotten events and the host of material that found its way directly into the unconscious, can all be re-discovered, albeit with some difficulty. In this way it is possible to piece together with considerable certainty an accurate picture of what any given individual's childhood was like.

Naturally, we are all unique but there are three patterns that come up time and time again at this stage in life as a result of having negotiated these stages poorly. The first is that many people arrive at adolescence with a poor view of themselves. They already have notions of self-hate, blame, self-consciousness and depression, for which the main reasons are poor parental relationships; the child realizing that he or she was not wanted; and poor child spacing. The second is the suppression of sexuality resulting in the child being frozen at a particular stage outlined above, perhaps making him or her regress to an earlier stage or somehow turning him or her away from normal development.

The third commonest problem is the persistent attachment to the opposite-sex parent which can arise if the parent was over-close or, indeed, over-rejecting.

Clearly all sexual development has considerable importance for the future of the child both in the one-to-one relationship and also for other relationships in general. How we as parents handle this changes too from child to child as we ourselves mature and gain in sexual knowledge and confidence. So it is that we can, quite inadvertently, bring up two children five years apart very differently simply because *we* are so different and because our one-to-one relationship has changed.

GENDER IDENTITY

Although I have so far focused on the Freudian psychoanalytic model with respect to the development of childhood sexuality, and although it is a very useful concept, especially in day-to-day practice with both adults and children, there are other matters that are worth looking at, however

A delightfully natural way of learning about genital difference.

briefly, if we are to approach a balanced overview of childhood sexuality.

Children learn very early whether they are boys or girls. Two-thirds of three-year-olds, according to one study, know their sex and most experts agree that the majority of children know which sex they are by the age of four. Soon after this children start to be able to recognize other people's sex and by the age of between four and six most children will not only know that they will grow up to be a 'mummy' or a 'daddy' but will also see that this is a pre-set pattern that will not change.

Most young children think that the way to differentiate between the sexes is by things such as clothing and hairstyles and not until about the age of eleven do they realize that the major difference is genital. Interestingly, the average girl is ahead of the average boy on this. She also knows which sex she is well before she has any true appreciation of sex differences generally.

Most pre-pubertal children think of genital difference as natural but about a third of both boys and girls think that girls have a penis that has been lost, has grown small, or was cut off.

As early as three most children show a preference for the same sex, be it another child or an adult, and as they get older this preference seems to increase in strength, especially for boys. As with so many things to do with gender and sex it is paradoxical that in western culture more girls want to be boys than the other way round but this is hardly surprising given that males are seen to be so advantaged in our society.

Boys and girls differ considerably in their behaviour and there is, especially in very young children, a large overlap between so-called 'masculine' and so-called 'feminine' behaviour. There are, however, very real differences in gesture and play. One study found that limp wrist, arm flutter and flexed elbow were much commoner in girls than boys and that girls tended to put their hands on their hips in a different way from boys. By the age of three or four boys show mainly masculine preferences in toys and play and it is claimed that such sex differences can be observed as early as a year old. From watching children at play it is clear that by the age of two or three most children already know a lot about what is expected of them, as judged by the standards of the adult world. Boys tend to advance quickly in this model, much quicker than do girls, and it is clear that boys are more concerned that they act only within the bounds of the stereotype.

As we have seen, genital play is extremely common in children. Studies have found that about a third of mothers of one-year-olds report genital play in their children and that such play is commoner in boys than in girls. Little boys do not ejaculate before puberty and because there is no rest period required between orgasms they can re-stimulate themselves repeatedly over a short time.

Between the ages of two and five such activity increases with about half of all children of this age playing with their genitals. Games that involve some sort of sexual exploration are common by the age of four and exhibitionism and voyeurism, both with other children and adults, is a characteristic of this age. Some children at this age clearly find urination 'sexual' in some way and other children like to handle their mother's breasts.

During the latency period of a child's development his or her *overt* interest in sex goes down, as we have seen. It is, however, still very much there (however covertly) and may be expressed in terms of same-sex interests rather than heterosexual interests. Masturbation goes up during this time from about one in ten boys at age seven, to eight out of ten at age thirteen. Two-thirds of 13-year-olds also indulge in heterosexual play.

Ideas of romantic love begin in the pre-teens with the majority of ten- to twelve-year-olds claiming to have a sweetheart, according to one survey. This same study found that by the age of ten two-thirds of them had been kissed and that by the age of twelve five out of six had been. Another study found that two-thirds of both boys and girls reported having been 'in love' by the age of eleven. Clearly by this age children already know that sex is about personal relationships and love and not simply procreation, which is what they tend to think in the earlier stages.

Many parents worry that their children might grow up to be abnormal sexually in some way. Some are concerned that a boy who is a bit of a 'wimp' might turn out to be homosexual or that a tomboyish girl who doesn't seem to like boys much might become a lesbian. Evidence on all this is confusing but there is some good research which can be called upon. There are many well-conducted studies that show that there is a link between childhood sexuality and subsequent adult sexuality in any one child. One study of more than 200 male homosexuals, for example, found that two-fifths reported having been more interested in girls' toys and interests when a child; a similar proportion had liked dressing up in women's clothing; and that over a quarter had been thought of as 'cissies'. Nearly half the homosexuals reported four out of six signs of female-type sexuality compared with none of the heterosexual men studied.

Other studies have found that about half of adult male transsexuals had dressed in female clothing as children and that more than half had preferred girls' toys to boys'. Half of all cross-dressers remember cross-dressing as children and other studies have found that about half of all 'feminine' boys grow up to have some sort of psychosexual abnormality as adults.

Just why these things should occur is uncertain. But what is becoming more clear is that most of us, whether as children or adults, have the facility or predisposition to be more or less masculine or feminine whichever genital sex we are. Some men are feminine in certain of their personality characteristics and some women are similarly masculine. In all of us there is a balance between the two and often this balance shifts quite a lot. For example, a somewhat macho man on becoming a father for the first time can sometimes discover areas of femininity in his personality that he never realized he had. Just how such balances of masculinity and femininity arise in any one child is not known but it certainly isn't anything to do with what the parents contribute by being present or absent. For example, most boys who have been brought up without fathers turn out to be perfectly 'masculine' and children raised in lesbian households appear to be just as well balanced sexually as those brought up in heterosexual households, according to one major study on the subject. Children raised by homosexual fathers usually turn out to be heterosexual and it is only fair to point out that the vast majority of those with sexual identity or, indeed, other sexual problems come from 'normal', heterosexual homes.

What can be said in summary then about this highly complex and emotive area? Before birth a child's emerging sexuality will be affected to an unknown extent by its mother's sex hormones and, if animal studies are anything to go by, it is possible that other hormones could affect matters too. For example, a study in Germany found that rats, if severely stressed when pregnant, gave birth to a larger than expected proportion of homosexual offspring. We simply cannot and would not wish to do such research in humans and so will probably never know the final answer on this type of animal finding.

At birth a child's genitals are what determine in the main how he or she is subsequently treated. After this a child will come to see him or herself as a boy or a girl according to which sex they are assigned and how they are brought up. Although this gender identity is established at about the age of four and remains fixed from then on it can be considerably modified by cultural stereotyping and by family influences.

Clearly, whatever is happening during a child's psychosexual development, and whatever theoretical model is used to help understand what is going on, matters will be greatly influenced by the child's social and emotional development. Difficulties with interpersonal relationships are likely to affect psychosexual development adversely and vice versa.

But sex in the family is not just a subject on which there are elegant theories, however valid; it is also a very practical matter and needs to be handled in a way that produces the least possible trouble for all concerned. I shall explore that aspect of children's sexual development in the next chapter.

18

SEX AND THE FAMILY

Not long ago people did not talk about sex and many of today's older parents, those brought up in the forties and fifties, claim that they received no formal education on the matter at all. Many, if not most, say that their parents, too, told them little if anything about the subject though this could be a false perception of what actually took place. For example, most mothers claim to have told their daughters about the basics of menstruation yet the majority of daughters say that they were told nothing. Neither is lying, they are both telling the truth as they perceive it. Since in our culture mothers in general and our own mothers in particular are portrayed as being sexless, most daughters quite unconsciously disregard what their mothers tell them on such personal sexual matters as boys and menstruation. In this way the information that was given never really reaches the girl's conscious mind and so, to her, doesn't exist.

Today's generation of parents is much more open about sex although this does not mean that any more of the facts they give their children will necessarily be accepted, just as has been the case in previous generations. It is now common practice to discuss subjects such as divorce, abortion, contraception and pregnancy in a family setting; at least this is so in many middle-class families. Today's parents also know that a child is absorbing messages about sexual matters all its life and that what they, as parents, do and say has a profound effect on what the children grow up to believe.

Most people find talking about sex difficult, even to other adults, let alone to their children. This is especially so when it comes to talking about pleasure. Most aware parents today are happy enough to give 'practical' information but few are at ease with discussing what makes sex so specially exciting and pleasurable for them.

Most of today's parents say that they are happy that the whole subject is more open than used to be the case when they were children, but few are at ease with the fact that more knowledge seems to open up more choice. Many parents worry that their children might know more about the 'plumbing' yet really not be that much better able to cope with the

185

emotional aftermath of physical sex than they, the parents, were 25 years before.

When bringing up young children there are certain recurring themes to do with sexuality so let's look at each in turn, albeit very briefly.

WHO, HOW, WHAT AND WHEN?

A pregnancy in the mother or a friend the child knows is often a good starting point for talking about sex. As with all such discussions there are problems of knowing what to tell, how much to tell and who should best tell it.

In reality, knowing what and how much to tell is usually not much of a problem. Any parent who knows his or her child will know how much he or she can absorb at any given age or stage of development. The error many middle-class parents make is trying to say too much. They deliver a Nobel prize-winning lecture when all that was required was a one-line answer. This reflects the parent's unconscious concerns about the subject and means that he or she overdoes things in an effort to be informative and neutral rather than playing it straight emotionally and psychologically.

In this sort of family pregnancy and birth are pleasures and the children learn to be at ease with the whole reproductive area of life.

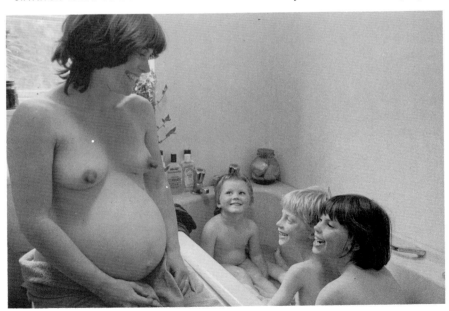

Who should tell is also a matter of little importance in practice. Most young children spend more time with their mothers than they do with their fathers in our culture so it is understandable that most such questions are aimed at mothers. This is probably no bad thing since women are, on average, more feelings-centred and are, after all, deeply involved in the day-to-day business of sex and its results as a part of their ongoing responsibility for pregnancy, childbirth and caring for the young. Whilst some children will naturally feel closer to their fathers on such matters many young children are totally spontaneous in their desire for knowledge and it is the person who is around most who will tend to have to handle them. Older and teenage children will have more considered subjects to tackle, many of which can be dealt with at leisure by either parent, according to whom the child feels closest. It might seem ironic but some girls would rather talk about periods with their fathers than their mothers, for example. In most families, however, girls find it easier to talk to their mothers about female things and boys to their fathers about male things. A father, for example, can't hope to tell his daughter what it's like to have a period, a baby, or an orgasm, though to be fair her mother can speak only from her personal experience which could be, and arguably is on occasions, of no more value than what the father could say.

Some parents are so nervous about the whole matter that they set up a 'meeting' to talk about sex and try to 'get it over with' at one sitting. They then consider that the painful deed is done and that they have done their duty for good. Almost certainly a better approach is to be available for the child to make its needs and interests known at almost any time. Then you can deal with such matters just as you would with any others in the child's life. Sex has for too long been treated as a taboo subject but is really just a subject about which parents are exceptionally reticent and ill informed.

This latter point is of considerable importance. It never ceases to amaze me how little the average person knows about sex. Most parents of today have had very few sexual partners and know precious little about the sexuality of others. All they can talk about is their personal sexuality which is, understandably, somewhat embarrassing and, by definition, limited. This is why, in my view, many parents find sex difficult to talk about with their children – they know so little that as soon as the child asks anything other than the simplest of questions they fall into a pit of ignorance and, rather than admit that they don't know, bluff their way out of the situation or shut the child up. Either way the child realizes, usually quite consciously, let alone unconsciously, that all is not well and sex starts to take on an aura of oddness that other subjects do not. In my view parents ought to make a serious effort to become better informed about sex so that they can give well-thought-out answers to sensible questions which children need to ask, answers that are not frivolous, and not just top-of-the-head prejudiced remarks that could, and do, taint the child's view of sexuality for ever. There are few areas of life in which most intelligent parents behave in this way yet they do so in the sexual arena almost every day of their lives.

Just waiting for a child to ask may not be the only way of handling things. As children get older and menstruation, wet dreams, erections and so on become realities they need information *at that time* to help them understand what is happening to their bodies. This might mean actually raising the subject from cold. Although most parents say that ideally they would like to share the giving of sex information, in fact what happens is that mothers do most of it whether it is given spontaneously or formally.

The setting of limits to what is discussed and how far to go is a major problem today for many parents. Some worry, and rightly, that the child might be overstimulated by too much information, especially of graphic details, and many of the questions that could arise might also raise issues about which the parents themselves disagree. Telling, though, does not necessarily mean telling *everything*. It is, for example, probably not wise to regale young children with too many details of stillbirths, miscarriages and abortions when talking about where babies come from and pregnancy in general.

WHERE DO BABIES COME FROM?

Given that many adults find the merging of sperm and an egg to give rise to a new life inside a woman little short of a miracle it is hardly surprising that children find it almost incomprehensible.

This is often the first question that children ask, partly because they have a personal experience of a woman, sometimes their mother, becoming pregnant. Often, in a young child, the question is of little significance or no more than 'Why are tomatoes red?' and under about the age of five it can be treated in the same way when answering. Every parent will have to find their own ways of describing what happens but most settle for something about 'Daddy putting a seed in Mummy's tummy' or words to that effect. This may or may not lead on to a discussion of sexual anatomy because any half-way intelligent child will want to know how such things happen and where the seeds come from.

Quite quickly any discussion of sex organs leads on to concerns about genital differences. Boys often wonder why girls don't have a penis. Indeed, it seems that they are more concerned that girls have lost a penis than they, the boys, might have lost a vulva. Many young boys feel that they are being fooled in some way and that really somewhere, somehow, girls do have a penis that is hidden or that it was cut off for some (possibly sexual) misdemeanour. Some boys just cannot believe what they are seeing, so amazed are they that there is a part of the body that girls just don't seem to have though they have feet, arms and so on just like them.

Partly as a result of this, young children are somewhat inquisitive about one another's sexual anatomy and games of doctors and nurses and mummies and daddies are both consciously and unconsciously aimed at finding out what the position really is on this vexed question. Sometimes parents are asked by their children if they can see their parents' genitals but most agree that this is unwise. I feel that it is always unwise for a parent to involve his or her personal sexuality with their children for fear that the situation could be mis-read by the child, or indeed the parent.

In most families the matter of where babies come from is an on-going slowly revealed matter that evolves over many years and well into the teenage years. Many young children have misconceptions, which are perfectly understandable, that babies are somehow eaten, perhaps in seed form. But from this somewhat 'primitive' start children become interested in a more scientific way in the whole subject as their knowledge of the world generally increases in complexity.

As children approach puberty their needs for information change greatly and much more specific issues become the focus of attention. This can present problems for many parents who have neither the knowledge nor the will to go into things in any depth. There is a very good psychosexual argument for neutral outsiders giving this sort of information anyway, in my view, if only because most parents cannot easily deal with their personal sexuality (and probably *should* not do so with their children) and because the children, as we have seen, may not be able to deal with what they are told by a parent.

Given that sex is so intimately linked with procreation, at least biologically, it is hardly surprising that it is this that gets most discussed within families. It is, after all the 'legitimate' function of sex for which we have to make no apologies if only because without it the species would cease to exist.

Much more difficult is the whole matter of sex and pleasure. Young children rarely need to be told much about this because they do not, as yet, see sex as having a non-procreative function. As children get older, though, it is all too clear that men and women like cuddling, kissing and so on, and many parents feel that the discussion of such matters can easily lead on to talk about the pleasures of sex.

This is a minefield for most because they fear that by communicating to their children even a hint of how lovely the whole thing is they will have them out and about trying things for themselves in no time. This could, of course, occur but it rarely does. The secret is to get across to the child that sex is pleasurable but at the same time pointing out that it isn't until he or she is older that they will be able to cope with the powerful feelings it

Children are naturally fascinated by their bodies and those of others.

produces; for this reason they should be very careful about getting involved in sex. This will, of course, not stop the average 14-year-old from experimenting with petting but, carefully discussed, it should be possible to make the child realize that intercourse itself is not to be undertaken lightly if only because of the emotional after-effects if the child is too young to deal with them.

The trouble is that there are no hard-and-fast rules about any of this. Some 14-year-old girls are perfectly capable of dealing with a quite serious man–woman relationship while other girls of the same age are still children and it would be cruel to make them go through it. Boys on balance are much less mature than girls of the same age and as a result don't get nearly so deeply involved with girls and sex, at least not early in their teens.

The answer seems to be to try to make a judgement about each of your children separately, based on your knowledge of their personality and their sexuality. Some children are, after all, simply much more interested in sex than are others. Problems arise, of course, as the sexuality of the parents starts to influence the situation. So it is that a woman who herself was fairly open about her sexuality as a young teenager now comes to be somewhat strict with her own daughters because she cannot trust them to 'be as sensible' as she was. Here, as with almost everything to do with child rearing, the answer must be to give children the benefit of the doubt until proven otherwise. If you clearly tell children that you trust them not to do things of which you disapprove and then leave them to police themselves the chances are that they will behave well. Treat a child as if it were an idiot and it will probably oblige you by behaving like one.

It is my belief that it is best to err on the side of telling children more at any age rather than less. Given that we are unconsciously reticent on the subject of sex we will always tend to say too little and so short-change the child in one way or another. Most of the people professionals see complain that their parents told them little or nothing and it is all too obvious to me, and to them, that this has harmed them as adults many years later. Such people, and they account for most of us in a culture such as ours which perceives sex so negatively, grow into adults who have strange and erroneous ideas about sex. Most of us are pathetically ill-prepared for what is so central an issue in our lives.

But although procreation is at the heart of sex there is so much more to the subject that we should just touch on a few common areas of concern within families.

NUDITY

Until their first child comes along many parents give no thought whatsoever to the matter of nudity. Most middle-class parents today are happy to be naked in front of one another and to leave the bedroom door open. But as children are added they become in some sense 'outsiders' to the man–woman relationship and many parents now start to have qualms about their previously free-and-easy attitudes. Young children have no concepts of privacy and so barge in as a woman is inserting her tampon, while the parents are making love, or while they are bathing.

It is almost impossible for people occupying a small space with one another to live in a way that totally precludes seeing one another nude, if only from time to time. Most families share a bathroom, for example. Juggling the multiple needs of the many members of any one family can be a difficult job for today's parents. They themselves may be quite at ease with nudity but their children may not be. An emerging teenage daughter is probably not best served by seeing her father naked, for example. If nudity is accepted by the children's peers then it appears to do no harm. It is when they feel freaky because of the way their parents behave that trouble starts for them. If everyone else at their school accepts nudity around the home, then all is usually well.

Having said this, we all have a right to privacy, especially the privacy of our own bodies. As a child grows up, and this occurs much younger in girls than in boys, he or she will come to a stage quite naturally when they want more privacy. This should, of course, be respected by the parents and others in the house. Very often it is the child who leads the way in increasing personal modesty and this should be respected and not ridiculed.

We parents all have different needs for privacy, mainly based on the way we ourselves were brought up and also on our unconscious inhibitions. Both of these are, of course, closely linked. So it is that one woman will be totally at ease bathing in front of her even quite old children whilst she will feel shy about inserting a tampon in front of anyone at all, including her husband. The danger for the very *un*inhibited woman is in believing that her children *should* in some way be the same as she is. This calls for being very sensitive about things. For example, just because you as a parent feel at ease doing a particular thing it does not necessarily mean that your child will.

Some parents are unwilling to let their children see them nude because they, the parents, are less than happy about their body image or because they have some kind of blemish such as a birthmark or a scar. Another common reason is that the woman feels that she is overweight and that the child will think she is ugly compared with other women it sees.

But the main question that parents have on this subject is whether or not nudity at home actually harms the child in any way. There is no answer to this. One school of psychoanalytic thought claims that no child over the age of two should see an opposite-sex parent naked. This thinking came about as the result of analysing children (and indeed adults) and seeing what they had to say about the adverse effects of parental nudity.

Most people today find this somewhat difficult to accept and certainly do not run their lives as though they believed it to be true.

What certainly can be said is that it is harmful to bring children up to think of the human body, theirs or anyone else's, as something of which to be ashamed. I have patients who are so confused and up-tight about their bodies that they are disaster areas in their marriages many years later. One such woman had never seen herself naked until she was 18; she always bathed under a towel.

Somewhere in between the two extremes outlined here there is a sensible middle path that most middle-class people follow. I repeatedly say 'middle-class' in this section of the book because attitudes to sex differ so greatly by social class in most western cultures. For example, it is not uncommon in urban northern areas in the United Kingdom for a man to have been married for 20 years and never to have seen his *wife* totally naked.

But as well as simply being naked there is also the matter of provocative nudity within the family and this probably does have ill effects. For example, it makes sense to me that a man with an early morning erection should not parade it around the house as he goes to the bathroom. Some parents are concerned that this might make their little boy feel inadequate about his own much smaller penis but it is simply bad manners apart from any far-reaching psychological damage that might or might not be done.

Closely linked with nudity is the matter of female underwear. It is held by some psychosexualists that the reason that most men are so turned on by women partly clad is that it unconsciously takes them back to their own childhood, possibly during the Oedipal stage as we saw on page 176, when their mother, realizing that it was inappropriate to go around totally naked, started to cover up with underwear. This, on the basis that 'the best bits are hidden', probably then excited the boy in a way that total nudity did not, it is argued. Certainly, many women say that they realize that they are actually *more* provocative to men when dressed in bra and panties than they are when totally naked.

TALKING ABOUT PERIODS

Almost all mothers claim to have told their daughters about periods, as we saw on page 185. That many of the girls did not consciously 'hear' what they were told is all too obvious. To many women having periods is much more personal than passing water or defecating and for many inserting a tampon or changing a sanitary towel requires the utmost privacy. They themselves still unconsciously regard periods as a sort of loss of control which takes them back to their pre-potty-training days when to be messy was to be like a baby without control over her bodily functions. Many young girls starting to menstruate say that this is what they fear about it.

Suddenly after many years of being in control of one's body things start to get out of control again.

Menstruation is a difficult subject for parents to tackle and most women would rather not do so until absolutely necessary as a part of preparing their daughter for what is to come. Don't forget too that this very daughter will have been watching her mother's reactions to her periods for years and will, by the time she is about to start, have a very good idea about what periods mean to a woman. If Mum is always bad-tempered pre-menstrually and makes downbeat remarks about the 'curse' the daughter is already unconsciously brainwashed into expecting pain, mess and other lifestyle disadvantages to menstruation. So against this backdrop whatever her mother or her teachers say she will believe that menstruation is pretty bad news and will behave accordingly.

Many mothers feel ill at ease explaining in any detail exactly how to use a tampon, for example, partly because it means that the child begins to get far too accurate an idea of female anatomy. Children often seek out sanitary products (partly because they are often secreted which only makes them more interesting) and then ask questions about them. They seem to have a radar system that can seek out sanitary products and sex toys a mile away! But the very fact that such things are hidden away just goes to show how strong many a woman's feelings are about her periods. Some are ashamed, as we have seen, others are downbeat about the subject, seeing it as a terrible liability of being a woman; and others just wish it would all go away. No wonder then that girls often get a raw deal when it comes to learning about periods and that they too come to believe that it is an unwholesome subject to be avoided or medicalized if the mother is always 'ill' each month.

Most parents seem to agree that the best things to discuss when talking about periods are their positive connection with health and potential pregnancy. The main things that most children need to understand is that blood loss on this occasion does not mean death or injury. Once a young child gets this message it is usually satisfied.

PARENTAL SEXUALITY

Although most parents are happy enough for their children to see them holding hands or even kissing the vast majority draw the line somewhere about this level in the personal expression of their sexuality. This is partly because sex is a private matter between them and partly because they think that it might, in some way, harm their children or encourage them to do likewise outside the family. Affectionate touching then is all right for most of us but sexual touching isn't, at least not in front of the children. Some children are very badly affected by their parents showing even quite simple forms of affection partly because they are jealous and partly because they think of the activities as very 'private' and not to be indulged in front of anybody. Most parents then draw the line at what they consider to be affection and leave it at that in front of their children.

But what if children happen to see more than was intended? There is probably very little harm done but it is best to say something about wanting to be private to cuddle, make love or whatever the child observed. It is certainly unwise to get cross and behave harshly towards the child or he or she could think that something awful was going on that they shouldn't see at any cost. It can be infuriating to be interrupted while making love, as any parent to whom it has happened will know, but the answer is to be as gentle about it to the child as possible. A simple answer is never to start making love without locking the door. This at least gives some time in which to think and come back to the realities of the outside world as represented by the child's intrusion.

It is highly unlikely that children will come to any harm seeing their parents making love in this way and the odd accidental encounter probably does no damage. The harm is probably done in the way that it is handled.

A few children when being told about the facts of life actually ask to be present when their parents 'do it'. Needless to say this isn't on for most parents and it is my belief that no children should see their parents actually making love. It is difficult to be certain why I feel this way because there is little enough evidence that definitely proves it to be harmful, but clinical experience of those who claim to have been harmed, and an intuitive feeling about the subject, suggest that this is so. This is rather surprising when we think about it because we show our children everything else and they learn by demonstration in most areas of life. Yet few cultures around the world have ever encouraged children actually to learn about intercourse in the parental bed. It seems sensible to abide by this ancient wisdom and assume that it is right.

PARENTS TOUCHING CHILDREN

If it is difficult for parents to know where to draw the line when it comes to touching one another in front of their children, thinking about parents touching their children can be even more difficult.

Although many parents say that they know intuitively how much touching is permissible, others are not so sure. For example, the young girl playing 'horses' on her father's knee who begins to get aroused and flushed and seems to be getting more out of it than he intended can raise all kinds of uneasy feelings in the father. Should he stop at once for fear of increasing what is so obviously a kind of sexual excitement, or what?

Whilst most of us would admit that some sort of personal and even genital touching is permissible at certain stages and ages of a child's development there are limits. For example, few people would condemn the mother who kissed her baby boy's penis as she dressed him but the same act at the age of five or ten would be seen by most as quite unacceptable. Mothers have all kinds of culturally sanctioned ways of being physically close with their children (and indeed with the bodies of others) and this could be why it is that so few women are ever involved in child sexual abuse. The vast majority of such abuse occurs with a man known to the

Horseplay gives a culturally sanctioned opportunity to be physical in a way that is usually frowned upon.

child, often a father or father-substitute. But given the current interest in the subject of child sexual abuse it is hardly surprising that many fathers, especially, are extremely wary of doing anything that could be misconstrued as being abuse by either the child or anyone else.

Unfortunately, so great is the hue and cry at the moment that there are signs that fathers, especially, are being less physically close to their children for fear of overstepping the mark. Such a fear is usually unfounded because men who actually abuse children are usually of certain broad types. This problem is discussed in more detail on page 251.

The only guidelines that can be made to work when it comes to touching a child is that if the child feels bad about it it must stop at once whoever the person that is responsible. This could mean that what, to an adult, seems quite trivial, touching or other intimacies, would have to stop because it makes the child feel ill at ease or scared.

CHILDREN TOUCHING PARENTS

Most parents find it unacceptable for a child to touch a 'private' part of *their* bodies partly because it is seen as provocative and potentially dangerous. The main reason though is that such touching by a child is an intrusion into the parent's personal space and as such is annoying and unacceptable just as such unwelcome touching would be if done by an outsider.

But all such discussions about personal touching are difficult because within loving relationships it is hard to say 'No' and much easier to say 'Yes'. This means that most parents find themselves being somewhat flexible on the subject and not adhering to absolute limits about touching if the child seemed innocent in what it was doing. Many young children, for example, want to touch their mother's breasts well after breast-feeding is over. If the contact seems playful rather than sexual it would be an unwise parent who'd make a fuss about it.

TOUCHING OTHER CHILDREN

There is little doubt that children explore one another's bodies and especially 'forbidden' parts of them as a part of learning about the world. This means that whether we parents know about it or not it is probably going on. 'Mummies and daddies' and 'doctors and nurses' are games that have gone on for centuries between young children of the opposite sex. There are two different ways that parents can choose to handle this. The first is very 'cool'. They set no limits and see it as a need for exploration and a way of satisfying natural curiosity. The second group place restrictions on their children before the fact or afterwards by the way they react or punish them. Those who do not set limits say that it is fruitless to do so because they cannot possibly be with their children all the time and they want to bring their children up to trust their own sense of what feels right, safe, healthy and appropriate.

I feel that it is probably sensible to set no limits – at least not consciously. After all, as we have seen throughout the book, we will have been setting such limits quite unconsciously for years and these will, in their way, determine what the child will or will not do, even if we say nothing specific on the subject. There is no evidence, of which I am aware, that any genital play between children of approximately the same age does any harm at all provided, of course, that they don't do any physical harm. Even such contact between brothers and sisters before puberty seems to produce no long-term effects worth talking about. Children are intensely curious by nature and are likely to be even more so about things that their parents are secretive about so it is inevitable that some experimentation and discovery will take place whatever we as parents do about it. Children's natural caution and good sense usually prevails and more harm is done by parental over-reacting than by anything else.

MASTURBATION

Most parents say that they are happy to see their children touching their bodies – until, that is, they touch their genitals. Few of us are so at ease with sex that we are happy to watch others touch their genitals unless they are our lovers – and some people cannot even manage that. Though most middle-class parents feel that they ought to be more at ease with the subject of masturbation they mostly say that they are not and that even talking about it upsets them to some degree. As a result it is a matter that is often left untouched when discussing sex with children.

Mothers of boys and fathers of girls say that they don't know enough about how it feels for the opposite sex to be able to tell their children anything very helpful anyway but this is probably a cop-out because we happily talk to our children about things that we have no personal experience of in many other spheres of life.

All of this means that many parents avoid the subject like the plague and only say something when absolutely necessary such as when a child masturbates in public.

First, let it be said that masturbation is totally harmless and is a natural expression of human sexuality at all ages. Babies of a few months old have been observed to masturbate and the practice gives pleasure until very late into old age. Because it is a private pastime it is only reasonable to stop children from doing it in public but other than that there is no reason to put further restrictions on the practice.

Almost all children masturbate at some stage in their development and some do so from very early in life and never stop. Although many children masturbate openly some do so covertly either in private or in company. Becoming giggly in the bath, going red in the face when rocking back and forth in the cot, a certain tension in the air when a parent walks into an older child's bedroom, and so on are all tell-tale signs that the child is enjoying some sort of auto-erotic experience.

Of course, many parents do not see such things as masturbation and then claim that their children do not masturbate. On questioning, they often claim not to have masturbated until puberty themselves but again this is because they perceive that masturbation has to be like the adult model or it isn't occurring at all. This simply is not so. Many young children masturbate yet of course no boy of this age ejaculates even though he goes red in the face and huffs and puffs.

It appears that most parents can come to terms with masturbation in their children if they look upon it as some sort of simple, pleasure-seeking device rather like scratching their head, or rubbing their arm. Most say that as children are so 'innocent' it cannot possibly have any sexual content, whatever this means. Many, when asked, say that it is an unavoidable aspect of growing up and to listen to them one could be forgiven for thinking that this was just one more nasty business to have to endure, rather like having periods.

A few, very 'liberated' parents see masturbation as a valuable learning experience even very early on. This it certainly is. After all, we all have to learn what pleasures us from personal experience if we are to be able to guide our lovers to do what we best enjoy. There is little doubt that in older children masturbation is to intercourse what learning to talk is to becoming a successful debater. Having said this, even the most tolerant of parents are bothered if a child gets too absorbed in masturbation and seems to be becoming obsessed with it. It is, however, rather 'moreish' and some children naturally want to overdo it. Though few people can say that they know with any certainty what *is* excessive in this context it is fairly obvious if the child is always at it and it is making him socially isolated and non-communicative.

Many fathers find masturbation acceptable in their boys but not in their girls. Girls tend anyway to be more secretive about masturbation so boys will usually tend to come to the notice of their parents and others but girls masturbate every bit as much as boys do, if in more subtle ways.

Parents today claim that they tell their children few or none of the negative myths about masturbation that they themselves were brought up to believe. On the contrary, the pendulum has probably swung the other way in middle-class homes with an apparently very tolerant attitude to the subject.

SEX EDUCATION FOR THE YOUNG CHILD

There is little doubt that most children learn nearly all of what they come to know about sex directly from the unconscious of their parents. All other forms of sex education pale into insignificance by comparison.

The next most common source is the conscious minds of the parents. This takes the form of conversations overheard by the children; relationships observed in the household; sexual and other intimate acts observed; what parents actually say to their children; things they leave around for children to see, and so on.

But today, children also learn a lot about sex from other sources too. Siblings, peers at school, the media, the churches, advertising, formal school courses on the subject, and so on. It is probably impossible ever to pin down exactly where and how a child learned about a particular thing to do with sex.

Some of these non-parental sources are more or less within a parent's control. They can, for example, choose their children's reading matter to some extent (though they must acknowledge the fact that children will also seek out the parents' reading matter too as they get older); they can switch off the television; and they can control the discussion of sexual matters in the family setting. To some extent they can also control what their children are taught at school.

Many parents feel helpless at what their children are picking up about sex, often in rather subtle ways from soap operas on television, for example. Whilst none of these is frankly pornographic they all extol the 'virtues' of adultery, extra-marital sex, greed, lust and power which all affects the way a child comes to view its own emerging personal sexuality. Given that such material mirrors the world in which we live it could be said to be just another part of life that the child will have to confront sooner or later. Alternatively, it could be argued that 'sufficient unto the day is the evil thereof' and the child forbidden to have access to such material. Which path is chosen will be decided quite unconsciously by the parents.

Most parents, when asked, say that the best thing they can do for their children in the matter of sex education is to be there and to be accessible and open so that the child feels it can ask anything and receive a reasonable answer. This, many say, is especially important once children start really to be influenced by outside forces such as churches, schools and the media. Handing a child a book about the facts of life is never enough and most parents realize this only too well.

But today's complex world is changing so fast that many parents find it difficult to keep up with what they themselves believe and understand about sexual matters and this, in turn, makes it difficult to give definitive information to their children on many subjects. How many of us have, for example, a really well-formulated and intelligent view on homosexuality?

We know what we *feel* about it and we don't want our children to become 'one of *them*' but that's about as far as it goes for most of us. Is it surprising then that we cannot talk about even the most simple of concepts to do with the subject without becoming insecure, anxious and as a result dismissive? Here again I feel that we owe it to our children as their parents to acquaint ourselves with what the facts actually are on the more common sexual matters likely to come up so that we can do them a real service instead of trotting out all our old prejudices unprocessed.

Around puberty the sexes become 'homosexual' in their interests inasmuch as they take an interest in same-sex pursuits. This is much more marked in boys. Girls may talk a lot about men and sex but usually keep it all at arm's length personally. But whatever is actually 'done', there's little doubt that girls and boys from about eight or nine onwards start to take a much more intelligent interest in sex and have conversations with their parents on the subject. This includes all kinds of personal 'revelations' about the sexual life of their family, including discussions of their mother's periods, father's penis, the noises the parents make when making love and much more. In this way a youngster starts to build up a view of what sex might be about for him or her. When taking place between girls such information is often quite useful but between boys it can become coarse or giggly, put women down as 'silly', exaggerate their personal prowess or attractiveness, and so on. Boys of this age are, in short, already on the road to impress rather than to inform and the battle to obtain a woman is begun. Some give the impression that they are enormous experts on sexual matters and, according to their different personalities, are either believed or ridiculed by their peers.

Obviously there is much more that could be said about this subject but this short résumé will, I hope, have given the reader a taste of the main areas of concern and difficulty. As with other areas of child development any individual child will have very different needs, levels of interest, appetite, and so on. With one child sex is an ever-present matter that needs careful handling from very early on yet for another, even within the same family, the subject never raises its head overtly until well into the early teens. This latter child may be no less sexual than its more 'obvious' brother or sister but may simply be less extrovert about such matters or indeed about life in general. Sexuality is, after all, just another manifestation of our uniquely individual personalities and in some it will play an important part and in others less so.

Whatever the personality of a child though, as in all other areas of its development, the best we can hope for is that he or she will grow up to have a balanced view of their sexuality that will enable them to relate well with members of both sexes and to be able to create and maintain relationships with members of the opposite sex, eventually in a long-term pair bond of some kind. Whatever the future for sexuality in western culture it looks as though some kind of one-to-one bond will continue to be the basis for child-rearing for the foreseeable future. If this is so it makes sense to bring children up to be as successful at this kind of relationship as possible. Unfortunately, many of us enter adulthood lamentably ill-prepared for this vital part of our lives. Perhaps with more insight and fewer inhibitions we could help our children do better than we as a generation have done.

PART V

SOME EMOTIONAL AND PSYCHOLOGICAL CONDITIONS

There are numerous events and conditions that could affect a baby or young child emotionally or psychologically. In the space available I have concentrated on those that affect the child most deeply and arguably most commonly. I have quite deliberately omitted social conditions such as divorce, separation, poverty, addiction, and so on. Perhaps this will be the subject for another book.

AGGRESSION

Some degree of aggression is perfectly normal as a part of dealing with life's threatening situations. We saw on page 68 how it was that a baby learned to be aggressive towards his mother and it is almost certainly here in the cradle that we all first learn how to be aggressive.

It will be obvious to most mothers just how aggressive babies *can* be, especially when their needs or desires are thwarted. It makes sense to try, in every possible way, to ensure that a baby does not have to become aggressive and angry, if only because such behaviour can become a learned pattern which he or she will resort to later in life and perhaps too readily. Many mothers claim that it will 'do the child good' to be made to wait for things but there is no evidence that this is so. What mothers with lots of experience say is that in reality such behaviour makes for anxious, angry and aggressive babies and, later, similar children.

Perhaps more serious still is the observation that a child whose needs are not met reasonably wholeheartedly and quickly can turn the aggression it feels on to itself and there are many who feel that this sets the scene for later depression. In the short term it can undoubtedly cause a failure to thrive, as well as various emotional difficulties.

As a baby grows into a toddler he or she often becomes aggressive when told not to do something. The secret here is to handle the matter firmly and in a predictable way and never to become aggressive yourself. Young children of two or three often become aggressive towards other children when things don't go their own way. They bite, kick, scratch and so on, much to their mother's horror. This does not mean that you have a delinquent on your hands but that your child has not yet learned that such behaviour is socially unacceptable.

Most children of this age play *alongside* others rather than *with* them. As they mature they come to take the needs of others into account and their naked emotions are modulated by experience of what their parents, and others, think is acceptable. An aggressive child at this age usually needs more love, not more telling off.

An older child who is aggressive might need professional help. Start with your family doctor. Such aggression usually points to a deeply felt emotion as a result of family troubles or problems at school. As children grow, their normal aggression can be channelled into socially acceptable activities like sports or healthy competitive activities with other children. The problem many parents have is how to control their child's aggression so that it is used positively and not negatively. Physical activity is one possible outlet but there are many others including creative pursuits.

Perhaps here it would be helpful to make a distinction between aggressive *feelings* and aggressive *acts*. As I have pointed out, the emotion of anger is normal but it is usually socially unacceptable to translate it into verbal or physical assaults on another person or destructive acts against objects. Clearly we should help children learn to recognize anger for what it is, to acknowledge and own their anger and not to feel anger inappropriately. For example, it is helpful to assist them to see other people's points of view and to recognize that other people's actions which provoke anger need have nothing whatever to do with the child. In short, whilst it is appropriate to feel anger in certain situations it is also undoubtedly true that many people are triggered into anger too frequently. Even when anger *is* justified it has to be dealt with realistically and in a way that is socially acceptable.

Dealing with other people's aggressive children can be difficult when they are playing at your house. It makes sense to tell them that such behaviour is unacceptable to you. This is better than becoming physically involved with the child or even shouting at him. Your own children must learn how to be able to cope with normal aggression and to be sufficiently assertive to get their own views heard and acted upon. However, this should never need to include physical aggression. Perhaps the best principle in this matter is to run one's life along the lines of 'Do as you would be done by'.

Unfortunately, many children are aggressive because they are imitating their aggressive parents. Some adults are amazed and annoyed by their child's aggression yet do not realize that they too are aggressive much of the time. Such a parent might be verbally aggressive, rather than physically, though as yet the child may not have picked this up. All he knows, perhaps quite unconsciously, is that high-key emotional activity is the order of the day in his home and that aggressive tones of voice and actions are the norm. For some children television supplies aggressive inputs that they mimic. Several studies have found that violent programmes can affect children in this way.

ANXIETY

Anxiety is a common experience in everyday life both in adults and in children. It is perfectly natural and understandable to be anxious if a particular situation feels threatening – indeed Nature intended us to be anxious so that we would have sufficient motivation to put an end to the upsetting trigger factor that provoked it. Often such triggers are perceived to be life-threatening in some primitive sort of way even if in the reality of modern life they are not so.

A child who feels anxious has a fast heart rate, sweats a lot, and feels restless, shaky and jumpy. There are also feelings of impending danger, apprehension, worry and fear. If any or all these symptoms are triggered by a reasonable situation then such a child can hardly be said to be unnaturally anxious.

However, some children are like this a lot of the time and in response to all kinds of harmless stimuli that leave other children quite unaffected. Clearly such children have a problem that needs help. Such an anxiety is often accompanied by obsessional (see page 244), phobic (see page 223) or hysterical symptoms.

Such anxiety-prone children are often said by their parents to have been different from their brothers and sisters from the day they were born. Just why this should be is not known but, as I have pointed out earlier, no two children are brought up in the same way, even by the same parents. There can be little doubt that some children are exceptionally sensitive to anxiety right from the cradle. Perhaps they have had intra-uterine experiences that made them so. Only time and a lot more study will throw more light on such complex matters.

Occasionally anxiety states are set off by an obviously frightening experience, such as a death in the family, an operation, or even a terrifying film or book. There is also no doubt that some whole families are 'anxious' and that such parents infect their children with their anxiety right from early on in life. Such parents are often reluctant or inept in their parenting and some realize it. They then act indecisively as parents and their children pick this up. The whole family then spirals downwards in anxious preoccupation with almost everything with which they come into contact.

Even in a normal family with normal children a child can be made to be anxious about almost anything. Such anxieties usually reflect parental attitudes to the subject and as such are to some extent preventable. For example, many parents are anxious about potty training and their anxiety often adversely affects the process. Parental anxiety at mealtimes, especially with toddlers and young children, is often so obvious to an outsider that it is hardly surprising that such moods and feelings affect a child so insidiously. Yet to the family themselves it is often not apparent because it is a part of their everyday lifestyle.

Many toddlers and young children show their anxiety by becoming 'clingy' or shy. The answer here is not to push them away, as many mothers do, with the hope that this will make them more resilient or 'grown up' but to lavish more affection on them and to let them be close if they need to be.

There are two important points worth considering here. First, there is abundant evidence that exposure to feared situations is an essential part of overcoming that fear. Of course, exposure itself is not enough because it is important that it is done in the context of security, confidence and an ability to cope with the situation. The crucial point is that avoiding feared situations perpetuates the fear.

Second, simply being more loving will not necessarily make a child less fearful of a given situation. Certainly it is true that by seeing you, the parent, coping well with the problem the child will learn by 'modelling' but there is no evidence that love alone will deal with the fear.

Most anxieties in children can be defused by the parents, and especially the mother, calming the child and reassuring him or her that all is well. Children have to learn that certain things in the world around them *are* frightening and anxiety-provoking and that when they feel such powerful emotions the threat to their stability of mood isn't so serious that things will never be the same again. As parents we can stabilize our children's emotional state in such situations by being there, by being calm and reassuring and by showing them that, however awful things might seem at the time, life will continue much as before and soon all will be well again.

This means putting anxiety into context and this can be difficult. No child should be ridiculed for becoming anxious when it is sensible to be so, yet we need to help our children cope with anxiety when it seems inappropriate to us as adults. This can often mean looking at life through the eyes of the child and not the way we see it. Anxieties at any age are often totally irrational and can all too easily come about as a result of ignorance or fear. Children are bound to be more affected in this way because they have not yet had sufficient experience of life to be able to have learned what is a realistic cause for anxiety and what is not. Once more, as with so many such areas in life, it helps to enlist the help of your partner. We all have our inbuilt anxieties about certain situations and these problems for us are also bound to infect our children, however unconsciously. Discuss between you the areas that you feel anxious about (for example, going to the dentist) so that the one who doesn't have this problem can deal with the children when it comes to *them* going to the dentist.

Being honest with children can also work wonders. If children know that feeling anxious in certain situations is understandable then they won't feel so panicky about it and will be able to learn from you as their parents that such feelings can be coped with. Those parents who shield their children from feelings they are experiencing do them no favours because then the children believe that in order to be normal, like Mummy and Daddy, you shouldn't have any powerful feelings, and especially not negative ones. Even a reassuring remark such as, 'I used to be anxious about X when I was your age but I soon grew out of it', can be all that is needed to make a child feel that its feelings are valid and that one day he or she will be able to cope with the world in an adult way.

BED-WETTING

Although most children become reliably dry in the first three years some still wet the bed at night for one of many reasons. The most usual cause is that the sensations of a full bladder don't awaken the child. Even if he does wake he may be too tired to call for his parents or he may be unable to get out of bed and find a potty or go to the lavatory.

Because of these very real problems most mothers keep their young children in nappies at night if there is any chance of their wetting the bed. A potty by the bed is only of any value if the child does not have a nappy on.

Most children become dry at night in the second or third year but some take much longer. Half of all two-year-olds are still wet at night and one in ten five-year-olds are unreliable in this respect so don't panic if your child is not dry at night for much longer than you might have thought. All children become dry eventually, so don't worry.

Bed-wetting, although slightly more common in children with lower than average IQ, is no sign of poor intelligence. Although there are many causes of bed-wetting, in a book such as this it makes sense to restrict ourselves to the emotional upsets that can bring it on. Parental rows, a new baby, anxiety over going to playgroup, moving house, fear of the dark or even a fear of wetting the bed can all play their part, even in a child who has previously been dry. Reassurance and physical affection usually help to get most children over such problems. Telling a child off never works. It's much better to praise him when he is dry than to chastise him when he isn't. In the vast majority of children the bed-wetting occurs because their nervous system isn't yet sufficiently mature to signal to them when they are likely to wee in the bed. No amount of parental pressure will make their nerves develop any faster!

If a child isn't dry at night by the age of five it probably makes sense to have him looked at by a doctor to see if there could be some sort of abnormality of the urinary passages but it's vital to play the whole thing down to the child and not to make him feel like a medical 'case'. Other members of the family can be cruel to the bed-wetter so try to keep teasing down to a minimum. Some children, if they are not washed every morning, can come to smell of urine and this can become the source of jibes from friends at playschool or nursery.

Once a child is reliably dry a return to bed-wetting usually means that something is going on in his life that is upsetting him. He is, quite unconsciously, regressing to baby-like behaviour perhaps because he needs baby-like caring from his parents. It always makes sense to look very carefully at what is happening in the family or at school if a child suddenly starts bed-wetting. Usually the answer is obvious but if it isn't it might make sense to talk to your family doctor.

The prevention of bed-wetting is only patchily successful. Some parents find that if they lift their child when they, the parents, go to bed he'll pass water on the lavatory even in a semi-sleepy state. Some children remain apparently asleep throughout this procedure. Others wake up completely and then remain awake which can be a nuisance. You'll have to experiment to see how it works. Restricting the intake of fluids from early evening onwards can also help but certainly isn't a reliable method in all children.

In summary then the best way to handle bed-wetting is to take all reasonable practical precautions (plastic pants over a nappy, a plastic sheet on the bed and so on) so that as a parent the whole thing doesn't annoy you too much. This in turn will take the pressure off the child and he'll stand a better chance of maturing at his own pace without the added anxieties that he picks up from you. If he starts to wet the bed after being dry, don't become alarmed or make too much of an issue of it.

Look for the cause and stay calm and patient. Many's the parent who, by their own alarm and concern, perpetuates the very thing they want to stop.

BEREAVEMENT

Death is an integral part of life and children should learn from an early age that people and pets die. It is our duty as parents to ensure that our children come to see death as something that comes to us all. Having said this, the way a child reacts to bereavement depends greatly on his or her age.

Children under five are mainly self-centred and are usually only affected by bereavement when it directly changes their life in some way. The loss of a parent – especially a mother – if she was the child's main care-giver, is bound to affect a child's life profoundly. A father's death usually has less of an effect if only because in so many families the father is present for less of the time and plays a relatively small part in the child's everyday life even when he is there. However, the effect of a father's death on his wife will usually be profound and this can, of course, subsequently have a negative effect on the child.

A young child may be very accepting of a loss within the family but he may not remember the person for very long unless the individual is kept alive in the child's mind by discussion within the family. This is one reason that it can be so helpful to talk about the person who has died. Many adults find this much more difficult than do their children, especially young ones. Little children have no concept that death is taboo and all too often simply take the whole thing in their stride, rating it as no more important than the washing machine breaking down. This doesn't make them heartless but shows us as adults how we interpret things rather differently from young children. As a child matures he realizes that the death of someone dear to him is indeed an important event in his life and both consciously and unconsciously becomes more aware that he too will die one day. Most *young* children never think about their own dying.

Discussing death with young children is never easy for parents but it can be a lot easier for those who have some kind of spiritual belief or a belief in an afterlife. This can often be the first time that many parents declare their beliefs in such matters to their children and a spiritual dimension certainly seems to help put the inexplicable into perspective for young children.

But it is not just philosophical and metaphysical questions that arise at such times – there are many very practical ones too. 'Why do people have to be burned?' 'Why can't we keep Grandad at home with us?' and so on provide many a parent with trying moments around the time of the bereavement. Odd though it may seem these strange-sounding questions can be far less annoying than they first appear and can, in practice, help to defuse a tense situation. It is often found that children help to take a lot of the pain out of bereavement in the family, partly just by being there and partly because they need looking after and have to be comforted themselves. This all helps take the parents' minds off the situation, at least to some extent, and this can ease the pain, if only a little.

Some young children respond to the death of a loved one with profound feelings of guilt because they feel that somehow they might have caused the death. This may seem preposterous to an adult but a child who has ever wished harm to or even the death of a person who subsequently dies can really believe that he or she actually brought the death about. It is wise to talk this through with the child whose brother or sister dies during pregnancy (the mother has a miscarriage) or at birth (a stillbirth) because the child may believe that all subsequent babies will also die. Simply being aware that this is a potential problem is all that is needed so that you can reassure your child as things progress in a future pregnancy that the chances are that everything will be all right next time.

A young child, and many older ones too, will mourn the death of a pet. This can, with intelligence, be used as a talking point about death generally. Once again, the problems are often more noticeable among parents who become emotional and give out all kinds of unconscious messages about the death when the child him- or herself would not have rated the event that highly. Many children are more balanced about the death of a pet than are their parents or the other adults around them and some, to the consternation of their parents, actually appear to be totally unaffected. Many's the parent who tells of the death of a much-loved pet being shrugged off by their child as if it were something that happened every day of the week. As judged by adult standards this appears uncaring or even callous but from the child's point of view it *is* simply another happening in his or her life and one which has no great significance. As children get older, and certainly in the pre-teens, this changes and they start to adopt more adult views and emotions about the death of pets, and indeed of others around them.

Grieving is a natural human response to the death of a loved one and children of school age onwards are upset about the death of someone they know or love just as are adults. The way they show their grief can be very variable, however. Some children go off their food and become quiet and morose and others will appear almost totally unaffected. As adults we can

212

identify more readily with the former because that is how we perceive that sad people should behave. But as with all such behaviour there is no 'right' or 'wrong' way to react. We are all unique and how any one person reacts will depend very much on how they are feeling at the time of the death; the circumstances of the death; how others around them react; the implications the death has for them and their lives; and of course their intrinsic personality. In certain circumstances a death in the family will have profound implications for the future of the whole family and the way they live. This is especially commonly seen today with the loss of young fathers from heart attacks in the prime of life. Living in a fatherless family becomes a very different way of life, especially if there are young children.

The first reaction that most bereaved people feel is shock and disbelief and children, once of school age, are no exception. Death seems a somewhat remote possibility until it hits us personally when someone we know or love dies. Suddenly it makes one's own mortality only too apparent and children of all ages will one day have to face up to the fact that the only thing we can be sure of in life is that we will all eventually die.

Once the shock and disbelief are over many children start to question their possible part in the death, as we have seen. Many, and not just young children, fear that something they said or did could have accelerated the death and feelings of remorse and guilt are extremely common. 'Should I have been nicer/kinder/visited him or her more often/sent her presents/told him or her I loved them?' and so on are the sorts of things that go round and round in a child's mind. All of this needs talking through because very often the fears and guilts are unfounded. After all, there's little that a twelve-year-old could have done to affect his grandfather's smoking which gave him his lung cancer that killed him and he needs to talk this over with his parents or someone else who really cares for him.

Whenever someone older than ourselves dies (and this is especially true of children if only because almost everyone else *is* older than they are) we realize, however unconsciously, that we are getting nearer the top of the pile. As a result, some children whose parents die when they are quite young feel duty-bound to take on the mantle of the dead parent and to assume responsibility for the remaining parent or even for the whole household. There are many teenagers who have been expected to become little mothers or fathers when a parent has died but this can be hazardous to the child's future, especially if such decisions are taken during the grieving stage which can last for two years or even longer. Many such children, but especially girls, feel they ought to make amends for any past transgressions and evil thoughts about the dead parent by jumping into the empty parental role. The grieving parent who is left may feel that such an offer is too good to turn down but it is important to remember that the child is a *child* and that the death of the parent has done little to advance his or her

213

maturity and may even have halted it temporarily. To treat such a willing child as a surrogate adult is quite wrong because they simply are not ready to cope and can later find it difficult, or even impossible, to behave in an appropriate way with their own family when they have children. Clinical experience shows that some such girls especially are tired of mothering and all its responsibilities long before they have their own children and that, ironically, such a teenage apprenticeship has put them off rather than encouraged them. They have become 'responsible' too young and have short-cut their adolescence to their detriment.

Perhaps the least understood part of bereavement is the time-scale of the whole thing. The stage of initial shock and disbelief can be understood by anyone, even by someone who has never been bereaved themselves. After this things get much more difficult. After a few weeks' practical help, support and sympathy tend to fall off and the bereaved child can be left with the living burden of sadness, guilt, shame and worry which few people recognize as being linked to the death. Many people, both adults and children, produce all kinds of physical symptoms, many, if not most, of which can be explained as a part of the grieving process.

Studies of all kinds of grieving have shown that the average person takes about two years to overcome the effects of the death of a loved one and some people even longer, depending on their relationship with the person who has died. During this time the child will feel all shades of many different negative emotions and it is important for those around him not to tell him to 'snap out of it' if only because such advice is a waste of time and is heartless. Practical and emotional support is what is needed, including an opportunity to be listened to when the child feels like talking. Often such discussions with older children can be a real help to the remaining parent and can help him or her to come to terms with the loss too.

It has been said that there are now only two taboo subjects left in the West. One is incest – and that is fast becoming less of a taboo – and the other is death, which shows no signs of loosening its grip on us. There are few signs that anything will change much in this area because our society is very much a here-and-now one which stresses the importance of materialism (to which death is the absolute end) and puts down spiritual concepts almost entirely. In societies in which spiritual matters are more important in everyday life or that acknowledge the attractions of an afterlife, things are very different. Death to such peoples is not seen as a terrible end-point but rather as a stepping stone to another world. This certainly takes the sting out of death. Indeed, at one extreme are those who welcome death because it brings to an end their stay on this all-too-imperfect planet and marks the start of a new life which they perceive to be preferable.

Whatever your views about death the subject will always have at least some negative overtones to it. Perhaps the best that we can do for our children is to treat death as a fact of life and to help them as best we are able given the nature of the society in which we live. Strangely enough it is often through a death in the family that adults and children alike start to think not only about their own mortality but also about spiritual notions that may have lain dormant for years. In such circumstances then, death can become a point of growth and can lead to conversations with children that enhance their ability to cope with the real world. The sensible parent can use a death in the family to enrich his or her children but all too often, unfortunately, such opportunities are lost, often for ever.

CHRONICALLY ILL CHILDREN

Children who have long-term physical disease such as epilepsy, diabetes, cystic fibrosis, deafness, blindness, or cancer often also experience some degree of psychological and emotional distress either in themselves or in their family.

The links between physical illness and psychological symptoms are difficult to explain. It could be that a particular personality type is more prone to certain physical disease. This is an attractive theory but one which has yet to be proved. It could be that a child with a set of physical handicaps develops abnormally. Here again evidence is lacking. Perhaps chronic illness directly affects brain functioning in some way. This is plausible in some illnesses such as cystic fibrosis and others that affect nutrition, for example. Some children unquestionably become 'institutionalized' by their illness or, more accurately, by the adults around them and their reaction to it. A child who is made to feel 'an epileptic' rather than a child who happens to have epilepsy is a classic example. Any long-term illness affects the whole family, of course, and there can be no doubt that the extra work, worry, expense, anger, grief and so on at work in such families creates a shift in the balance of the family with resulting psychological ailments, perhaps not only in the child but in the parents or other children. It is clear that a 'normal' child with an illness can be made 'ill' psychologically by its parents' reaction to the illness. Lastly, it is possible that the stresses and strains imposed by the burden of the illness on the child himself could result in psychological ailments and disease.

A child who is ill for a long time cannot be looked at in isolation from his family, relatives and friends. The illness shapes that family, perhaps for ever, and it will suit certain family members and not others. We all have very different abilities to cope with disaster and have varying and varied views on ill-health. We thus react rather differently to such a situation and sometimes this will say more about *our* personalities as parents than about that of the ill child. Some parents looking for an ongoing 'rescuer' role will, unconsciously, encourage their child to be ill or remain an 'invalid' so that they, the helper parents, have a role. Some people are near-compulsive helpers, even helping those who do not seek help. A sick child gives them the perfect excuse to continue this pathological behaviour and at the same time look wonderful in the eyes of the world.

That this is indeed pathological should be clear to any reader who has come this far. An ill child still needs to retain his or her own sense of dignity and independence, still needs to learn how to cope. A parent who takes over the child's life and 'controls' it does him or her no favours in the long-term. That child will probably have to go on dealing with the world long after the parents are dead and must have the independence of mind and spirit to be able to do so. Once more this is about allowing our children to grow and mature in their own way, a way that will be relevant to them as unique individuals in the future. The temptation is to try to 'own' a chronically sick child but ironically the inherent dangers are greater even than in the healthy child.

Striking the balance between being there to be supportive to a sick child or taking over his life and making the child's condition answer some need, however unconscious, that we, the parents, have can be very difficult. Many parents cope well but for those that don't professional help is probably sensible.

CRYING

Crying is an expression of fear, loneliness, frustration, anger, boredom, pain, and in a baby, hunger.

A baby has relatively few ways of expressing himself and cries for one of many reasons. At first it might seem strange that such a non-specific type of communication works to the baby's best advantage but it does. Research has shown that mothers can recognize their own baby's cries by the third day after birth, and recent French research has found that there are many different types of cries in any one baby. This fits in with what mothers have been saying for centuries – that they can tell if their baby is crying for a feed, because he is angry, wet, or lonely. The French study found that when cries were analysed acoustically each stimulus (such as hunger) produced a cry with a unique sound signature. These signatures had not only auditory effects on the mothers but also other physiological effects. For example, the mother's pulse, heartbeat, and blood pressure were also altered.

All this proves yet again, in my view, that mothers and their babies communicate with one another in a way that is unique to them and I believe that this communication goes on from the very earliest days in the womb. The outputs of this communication system from her baby mean something to the mother and cannot be ignored. A mother who is tuned in to her baby's communications can no more ignore them than fly to the moon. This puts the lie to the 'letting him cry it out' philosophy that still runs rife in our culture. We don't let others cry themselves to distraction, at least most of us do not, so why do we do it with children and babies in particular? A child who is left to cry soon learns that the world is a pretty unpleasant place to be in and many such babies eventually stop crying only because they know that it produces no result. Some then go on to produce, quite unconsciously, other ways of gaining attention and love. Dis-ease and frank illnesses are just two ways that they can achieve this. The trouble is that babies and young children are so at our mercy as their parents that it is difficult to remember just how helpless they are. Just imagine how you would feel if all the important decisions in your world were taken by others who did not take your feelings and needs into account. Just think how maddening it would be and then add on something for the fact that a baby cannot rationalize as you can and so must be in even more confusion and emotional pain.

Some babies are exceptionally prone to crying and this annoys and frustrates the parents because they cannot see what to do for the best. If in doubt give the child more love and closeness, play with him more and be on the lookout for signs of illness. If this doesn't improve matters seek professional help because there may be something physically wrong with him. Many a first-time parent is so anxious that he or she makes the baby feel anxious and this alone may make him more likely to cry. Many's the parent who says that as they had more children they became more relaxed and as a result so did their babies.

A baby or young child's cries are always a sign that something needs to be done for him – he is expressing a need. The day you can easily hear him cry and not feel compelled to do something to answer those needs it makes sense to look seriously at your relationship with him, and maybe with those around you too. It could be a sign that you are feeling depressed or that parenting is getting on top of you. Talk to your partner about it if you can and then take the trouble to a professional for help if things cannot easily be sorted out. A child's cry is an important signal to its parents and it is one that cannot and should not be ignored.

As a child grows up it will express its needs in ways other than crying. Now crying takes on a different role – that of showing distress of some kind. Just as you would acknowledge the distress of an adult it makes sense to take a crying older child very seriously indeed. If communication has so broken down that crying is the only way a child can tell you that something is wrong, things have usually got fairly serious and the child needs time and love if it is to get the matter off its chest. Sometimes a good cry, especially a real sobbing cry, can in itself be therapeutic. Research in the US has found that the content of tears varies considerably and that those shed in this type of sobbing are different from those shed after cutting an onion, for example. People have known for a long time that a good cry can make them feel better and it is suggested that removal of certain hormones from the body via the tears (as can be proven to occur) might explain why this is.

Having said this, an older child who cries a lot may well be depressed. This needs to be taken seriously. For more about depression see page 219.

DEFIANCE

A defiant child is one who is trying to find out how far he can exert his or her own will over its parents' will. He or she is trying to push you to the limits to see what will happen. Such a child may be copying other children; may be trying you out on a particular matter; may be sickening for something; might be trying to point out an unfairness as he sees it; or may be unhappy about something that has happened to him that day and doesn't know how else to show it.

Children of all ages defy their parents – indeed it is a normal part of testing parental limits. The worst ages are between eighteen months and two and a half years old but many parents find there is another peak at about four. Of course, teenagers can be extremely defiant but this book does not deal with children of that age. Perhaps the best way to deal with defiance is to *tell* the child to do something if it is important rather than ask him to. If you say 'Will you do so and so?' the child thinks it has a choice and, given the choice, might well say 'NO'. If you *can* give him a choice about things then do so because by involving him in the decision-making process you will make defiance less likely to occur at all. This is particularly important in strong-willed children. Try to keep a sense of proportion in deciding what to put your foot down about and *tell* him to do and what you can negotiate over and so allow him to influence the decisions.

A toddler or young child who is defiant and gets his own way all the time will not be well served by such behaviour. He soon becomes concerned because his parents no longer seem to be in control and this worries him. Sticking to your guns does not mean being violent, either physically or verbally, but it does mean being firm and assertive. Most of all it means being consistent so that the child knows where he stands.

Countering defiance with punishment does nothing to make the child any happier. Try to find out why he's behaving like this and then answer his needs. Instead of running down his behaviour praise him when he does things well. The positive reinforcement of 'good' behaviour works wonders in a defiant child. Some children use defiance as a means of seeking attention, perhaps because when they behave well their parents ignore them. Do things with such a child throughout the day so that he does not have to express negative emotions to gain your attention.

DEPRESSION

Many if not most children experience times of sadness and low mood, just as do adults. Most of them regain normal mood quite quickly and feel happy again. Such transitory mood changes are easily understood by parents and as such are not too worrying.

However, some children, and possibly all children at some time in their lives, become truly depressed in response to something in life.

Unfortunately depression in children is something of a minefield amongst the experts. On the one hand there are those who feel that there is no such thing as childhood depression and, on the other, there are those who are convinced that it is common. One of the problems is that children often don't have the same signs and symptoms of depression as do adults. But as the distinguished British paediatrician Dr John Apleyt said, 'childhood can neither be understood nor taught by extrapolating back from adults', and nowhere is this more true than when dealing with depression. The other problem is that, even among children as a group, depression manifests itself differently according to the child's stage of development, age, and degree of attachment to its mother.

In the first few weeks of life a baby's emotions are often expressed in a negative way – it cries when things go wrong. As the months go by the baby still lets its mother (or mother-substitute) know when things are not as it wants, by crying. At some time in the first six months, a baby becomes capable of distinguishing its mother from other people and from this time it becomes anxious if she isn't there. Such anxiety is often accompanied by obvious sadness and misery. As the infant becomes more demanding of its mother's attention it also gets frustrated and angry when she doesn't respond. This anger is often accompanied by sadness and anxiety.

All through their development, children are very greatly influenced by their mother and her moods. A considerable amount of research has shown that young children of depressed mothers are more likely to become depressed as children and that depressed adults, when asked about their early childhood, are more likely than average to report poor parenting because of mental ill health in their parents (usually the mother). It is easy to understand that small children could model themselves on their depressed mother and to see how a slowed-down, apathetic, apparently non-caring mother could deprive a young child of emotional warmth. Some children reared in a normal family, but with a depressed mother, end up behaving just like those reared in an institution. They want a lot of body contact and have difficulty in forming lasting relationships. Studies have shown that depressed mothers have a profound effect on their children, so it is not surprising that such children are more at risk emotionally. One major study, for example, found that depressed women were excessively involved in their children's daily lives, had difficulty in communicating with them and were only too aware that they had stopped being affectionate towards them. Over half of the children of such mothers had social or behaviour problems. Even quite young children become depressed if their mothers are depressed, often because they feel somehow responsible for their mother's low mood and can never please her. The depressed mother is also given to extremes of unpredictable mood-swings which further perplex the child.

A quarter of a century ago Dr John Bowlby's research on children separated from their mothers set the scene for our modern understanding of childhood depression. He found that infants separated from their mothers in institutions became miserable, expressionless and withdrawn, all symptoms close to those of adult depression. But although this has been widely recognized and accepted as a type of depressive reaction, just how depression manifests itself in later childhood cannot be agreed upon. It can be very difficult making a diagnosis of depression in a child and the diagnosis is usually made from the clinical impression the doctor gets when talking to the child and his family.

The whole concept of depression is difficult enough to define even in adults, and in children things are even more confusing. People of any age can feel miserable but depression involves far more than feeling unhappy. In particular it involves feelings of worthlessness, and hopelessness and other negative emotions about life's circumstances. Such depressive feelings seem to be less common in childhood and to take a giant leap forward at around puberty. What we do not know is whether the lower rate in young children is due to their inability to recognize or express such feelings or whether their stage of mental and emotional development renders them incapable of having such feelings.

Later on in childhood, depressive illness may first show itself as a refusal to go to school or in the form of other misbehaviour such as aggressiveness, stealing or truancy. At this age, though, bodily symptoms tend to predominate and poor appetite, headaches, excessive crying, loss of weight, sleep difficulties, and abdominal pains are very common symptoms of depression. Just how important these physical symptoms can be is shown in a pair of research studies, each of 100 children with recurrent abdominal pains. In only 8 per cent and 6 per cent respectively was any physical cause ever found for the pains.

Conduct disorders can be difficult to distinguish from emotional disorders in children, but they do differ in a number of ways. Conduct disorders are very much more common in boys, whereas emotional disorders occur with equal frequency in both sexes. Boys with conduct disorders have a high rate of educational problems; those with emotional problems don't. Children with emotional problems usually become socially well adapted in later life, whereas those with conduct problems don't. Both groups of children are equally miserable and sad.

Sadness in children is a difficult emotion to assess, for both parents and doctors. Several leading researchers in the field see sad children as very different in important ways from normal ones, but whether or not they are depressed is difficult to say. Very tense, miserable children may lash out when provoked and may find themselves in a lot of trouble as their behaviour becomes increasingly antisocial. Such children can end up in custodial care of some kind if their depression is not recognized. Having said this though, it is not unusual to find depressive symptoms and sadness in children with disorders that are not depression. Children with learning difficulties, hyperactivity and even behaviour problems are known to have poor self-esteem and to feel sad a lot of the time.

Quite often, depressed children are 'loners' who cannot enjoy playing and doing things with other children. Sometimes these children are profoundly miserable and at other times they tease and behave sadistically towards their peers. In some children an abrupt shift in behaviour may suggest depression. A previously alert child who suddenly becomes withdrawn, apathetic and unable to study may be becoming depressed. Some depressed children are hyperactive (overactive) but whether this is a parallel to adult mania is not known.

Bereavement, separation from parents, or an illness in a parent can cause depression in children in a parallel way to that experienced by adults. Separation from other members of the family and from their peer group can also adversely affect a child emotionally. Some children are depressed when they move away from a close friend. As we have seen, depression or mental illness in a mother can also separate her from her child. In many cases, there is a long gap between the loss of the key person in the child's life and the onset of depression.

Just how depression in childhood should be treated is not known. Some experts are convinced that anti-depressant drugs are of use and others feel they should be absolutely forbidden.

Family therapy can, on occasions, be useful. Many miserable or depressed children need more love and attention within the family and a general practitioner, child psychiatrist, psychologist or paediatrician can often try to get something moving in this direction. Sometimes the problems lie with parents who are unable to give their children the support and love they need and, as with so many family problems, the child may never really develop to its full potential as long as he or she remains at home. Temperament and personality incompatibilities occur in families just as in other groups and sometimes these are not capable of resolution. It has been shown that excessively strict and uncompromising standards give a child a feeling of hopelessness and helplessness because she or he can never match up to parental standards. Repeated tellings-off reaffirm the child's feeling of being unworthy of parental love and that whatever he or she does will be a disappointment to them. Some children respond to this type of upbringing by becoming excessively industrious 'goody-goodies' but deep down they are often depressed and feel inferior. Others keep their guilt and sense of unworthiness inside them and carry it with them into adult life, when it can be triggered to a full-blown depression.

Even being a favourite child can backfire in emotional terms. Such children are often unconsciously fearful of arousing envy and jealousy in others and some even develop a pattern of behaviour that involves drastically underselling themselves. The conflict between carrying the family banner and having to make everyone like them, at whatever personal cost, plays havoc with the child's emotions and this will often come out as depression eventually, perhaps even as late as middle age.

Of course, children, just like adults, can become depressed because of an underlying physical process. Leukemia, infectious disease (such as the common childhood infections), diabetes, disorders of the pituitary gland, nutritional and vitamin deficiencies, and serious physical disabilities can all produce depression.

FAVOURITES

Whenever I hear someone say that they have no favourites among their children I find myself looking at them somewhat askance because it is almost impossible to like or even love all one's children equally, all the time. It is certainly possible to admire them or even love them for different attributes and to find certain facets of the personality of one annoying and those of another pleasant but it is a rare parent who, in the privacy of the consulting room, does not admit having a current favourite child. I say 'current' favourite because any child's lovability changes as he matures. So today's 'favourite' can be tomorrow's perishing nuisance.

It is inevitable that we should find a particular child more likeable or even more lovable than another. The sex of the child makes a considerable difference, according to some mothers. Many's the mother who is bitterly disappointed when a baby turns out to be of the 'wrong' sex at birth. The love affair she planned throughout pregnancy with her fair-haired, blue-eyed boy has to be quickly re-thought when she gives birth to a dark-haired girl. Features that remind her of other, perhaps unfavoured, family members make the forming of a relationship difficult and can militate against the child's being accepted as he or she might otherwise have been.

Few of us can say that we are delighted by everything about our partner's personality and it is inevitable that some of their unattractive features will come out in our children. This can make the child less attractive to us because although the features are bearable, or even lovable, in our partner because we have a different sort of love for him or her, they are not easy to deal with in a child. Perhaps even worse is seeing our *own* faults in our children. This endears some parents to their child but upsets others, who worry that they have perpetuated the trait in yet another generation.

First-borns by and large tend to be favoured for their efforts and their achievements. They tend, on balance, to achieve more, as judged by worldly success, and are life-long addicts of parental approval. They seek approval in many ways and in doing so perform along lines that please the parents. This makes them likeable, if rather intense. The baby of the family usually gets his or her fair share of favouritism – and often more than a fair share. Women particularly seem to cherish this last product of their womb in an almost symbolic way of which they are usually quite unaware consciously. It is children in between that need extra special loving because it is so easy for them to fall between all the stools and lose out. This is exceptionally sad because middle children are often so 'nice'.

I think parents should be honest with themselves as individuals and as a couple if they feel that they favour one child above another. By acknowledging it they can then make arrangements to ensure that the other children are not disadvantaged by it. Sometimes both parents will favour one particular child but this is not usually so. As I pointed out before, favouritism may well shift with the passing of the years. It is almost impossible to hide one's favouritism for a child. The other children pick up the messages however clever we think we are at concealing them. What we can do though is to lavish more love and attention on the non-favoured child(ren) so that they do not feel left out or unloved.

Life is not fair, to any of us. And it is certainly not fair to our children. Some children, like some adults, are immediately likeable and are favoured by most people they meet whereas others are always somewhat disadvantaged in this respect. Giving a non-favoured child a sense of self-respect and self-esteem is, perhaps, one of the most difficult tasks we are called upon to do as a parent. All the world loves a winner and attractive, bright children are easy to love and favour. Alas, the world is not composed solely of the attractive and bright. The real test comes when we try to love the unlovely or the difficult little monster. Perhaps one of the heartening things that helps redress the balance is that all·too often today's ugly duckling turns out to be tomorrow's swan.

FEARS AND PHOBIAS

We all experience fear at some time or another – indeed it is a normal emotion that helps us become aware of dangers in the environment. In the earliest months of life a baby's fear is related to actual events but as a child grows so too do his or her abilities to fantasize and imagine. Sometimes these fantasies and imaginary images are frightening. With the development of skills the child starts to foresee the implications of things for the future and these too can start to make him or her afraid.

To be afraid, or at least to have the ability to be afraid, is almost certainly natural. Jung, the great Swiss psychologist, thought that we all share what he called the collective unconscious. This is why, he claimed, peoples all over the world tend to be afraid of the same things. For example, a child does not need to be taught to be afraid of the dark or of snakes, he just is. Jung maintained that such fears are primitive and are inherited quite unconsciously as part of our heritage.

Be this as it may there is little doubt that fear is also learned as the result of experience. Children fear all kinds of things, many of which are seemingly quite irrational to adults but which are, nevertheless, very real to the child. An example of this is the fear that he or she might be adopted. Many a child treated badly (or less well than it thinks it should be) wonders how it is that their parents could behave in this way to them. The only answer that seems to fit, according to the child, is that it is actually not the parents' real child. One patient of mine made a scrupulous search of the entire house looking for adoption papers, so convinced was she that she was adopted.

Handling a child's fears is often not easy if only because many of them appear to us as adults to be trivial or even nonsense. However, the emotions are very real to the child and must never be negated or ridiculed. A vital part of learning about the world is to be believed, and especially when feelings run high. Reassurance and love will usually help most children cope but telling them 'not to be silly' is not helpful.

Any adult who has a fear, say of heights, will know how infuriating it is to be told to 'pull themselves together', and how impossible it is to do so and this is set against the background of adult abilities to think and rationalize – abilities a child simply does not possess.

Phobias are emotional disorders in which the individual has a real dread of something, be it an object or a situation. A young child who is terrified of spiders will almost always grow out of it and whilst they might not ever much like spiders they are not subsequently terrified when they see one. The phobic child though does not grow out of the problem and remains in dread of things that other people find acceptable or perhaps only mildly upsetting. There are numerous psychological models that explain phobias, and they all have some value, but the most practical finding from clinical experience is that some children's phobias are maintained by their mother's anxious responses to certain situations. Some researchers have found that treating mothers *with* their children gave the best results.

The commonest phobias in children are of death, animals, insects, noise, the dark and school.

Many different techniques have been used to treat fears and phobias, and most of them work. Usually, the best results are obtained if the family is involved in the treatment so that attitudes held by the parents, and especially by the mother, can be detected and dealt with. Confrontation with the feared object usually forms a part of most types of treatment but this should be done in a clinical setting in which the child can learn to respond to the feared situation in the hands of expert professionals who can then teach him to cope with it.

Parents can, if they are cautious and sensitive about the matter, greatly help their children overcome their phobias. Many a family with a child who fears dogs, has, for example, overcome the problem by having a tiny puppy with which the child can cope. Most fears of water can be successfully overcome by shallow-end games gradually leading to swimming with arm bands and so on. A fear of school at five can usually be overcome by confident, warm insistence that the child will go. If simple do-it-yourself methods such as these do not work it will make sense to seek outside help so that the phobia does not become too deeply ingrained as a part of the child's life.

GOING TO SCHOOL

Going to school is one of the biggest upheavals that any child can experience and in the UK children start school very young. Many, if not most, other western countries start their children at full-time school at the age of six or seven but in the UK it's around the child's fifth birthday. Having said this, in most countries where children start school later, the majority go to nursery school.

Not only is starting school a major event in a child's life, it's a milestone in his or her parents' life too, especially if the child is the first or the last to go to school. From now until the child is about 16 or 18 he will be full-time away from home during term time.

To help surmount the change from being all the time at home with his mother to all day at school many parents choose to send their children to some sort of nursery school, if only for a few half days a week so that he can gently get the feel of being away from home. Having said this, some children are not ready to leave their mothers at all before the age of five and there is a small number that are not ready even then. In any case it is a fallacy to claim that you will avoid school starting problems by getting the child used to being separated from you sooner – what in fact happens is that most of the problems will occur but you get them sooner, when the child is younger and so less able to cope with them. Even starting off at a nursery school is not necessarily the whole answer because there is still a change to be made from the nursery to the real school and this can be just as difficult or even more so than starting at the nursery class. Some schools now allow their youngest children to attend half-time for the first half term and this can work very well if only because a whole day is simply too tiring for many five-year-olds.

Starting school is the end-point of what should be a long preparatory time. Getting a child ready to start school could be said to start in the cradle. By providing a happy and stable home background you will make it more likely that he will be secure enough to be able to leave you to go to school happily. By encouraging an interest in books, reading and writing, you will have at least given him the idea that you think it is important that he learns about such things. To many children whose parents never read to them and never encourage them to learn the whole business of school comes as a stark contrast to home and appears, to the young child, to be somewhat remote from what his parents think is important. By letting him use crayons, teaching him to cut things out and helping him make cards, invitations, notices and so on for the home he will be ready really to enjoy the better equipped and skilled teaching situation that school can supply.

By giving him every opportunity to make friends of his own age before he starts school you will help him develop the social skills which will be so vital when he starts to interact with other children at school.

By teaching him to dress and undress, wipe his nose and manage in the lavatory you will give him confidence that he won't let himself down on these simple things later in front of other children.

By teaching him to behave in a considerate way towards others you will ensure that he stands the best possible chance of being liked by the other children, which in turn will make him happy because he will positively look forward to going to school to see his friends.

Throughout the pre-school years, talk about schools to him as you pass the school he will be going to, or indeed any other. See if you can go into his school at some stage near the time he will be starting and if possible meet the teacher he will have ahead of time so that he can see what she is like. Get to know some of the other children at the school and have them round to tea so that your child can hear what the school is like. Their enthusiasm could be a great help and in some cases makes a child really keen to get started. It is a good idea to find out who else is going to be in his particular class when he starts and to have a little party for a handful of them and their mums a few weeks before the starting date. This is valuable for you as parents too – not just for the child.

Whether or not your child settles down easily and quickly at school depends on many things. However well you have prepared him you will still be almost totally unable to predict how things will go so don't spend too much time worrying in advance. The child's personality is the most vital factor in the whole thing. The naturally outgoing child will cope well, as will the child who has another brother or sister at the school already, but quieter, shy, unhappy, depressed or disadvantaged children (for example if their parents are divorced or separated) may take more time to settle in. Such children will be more cautious of new environments and wary of situations in which they feel threatened or likely to be ridiculed. Children desperately want to be like the others around them and anything (even things that seem quite unimportant to us as adults) can make them feel abnormal and therefore less acceptable in the eyes of their peers. Sometimes the shyest of children surprise everyone and settle in very quickly, blossoming when they go to school. Don't forget that some children are unhappy at home and see school as a welcome escape from domestic pressures and personality battles.

Most children find the first few days quite stressful but if a child still seems unhappy after a week or so ask him why. Is it that he is missing home or his mother? Is it because he doesn't like the teacher? Is it that someone has said something that he perceives to be critical or harsh? Is it that after having a one-to-one relationship with his mother (or nearly so in larger families) that the business of having to compete with others for the attention of the only adult there proves too stressful? Is he actually being shunned by others, for example because he wears glasses or has a birthmark? The causes are many but a sensitive parent should be able to sort out the most obvious ones. Some very articulate children say that they can't bear the thought of being away from home for so much time for so many years to come; others consciously or unconsciously believe that school is some form of punishment that their parents are putting them through for something they have done wrong and that one day in the near future they will be allowed to stay at home again just like old times. If you can't fathom out why the child is not happy have a word with the teacher to see if between you you can sort out what is wrong. Many teachers of children of this age are exceptionally sensitive to the problems of starting school and some will suggest that the child go home early on some days in the first term. In a few schools parents are encouraged to go in to help with practical classes such as art and handiwork if their child is having difficulties and this can work wonders in a very short time.

Almost all children settle down eventually at some time during the first year. The main thing is not to make too much of anything in your child's behaviour. It is amazing how many parents start to make all kinds of generalizations about their child from the way he or she behaves in the first few weeks at school. This is almost always nonsense and can be dangerous for the child because some at least of these erroneous notions will get through and stick to the child. Many's the quiet or even school-phobic

227

child who turns out to be a bundle of extrovert fun within no time at all. It is, as is so often the case in such matters, our reactions as parents that are more important than the child's. We have all kinds of conscious and unconscious aspirations for our children and if they settle into school quickly and well we feel we can at least take some of the credit. Yet this is probably not so and it can be one of the earliest and hardest knocks for any parent to come to terms with. Some, mothers especially, find it hard to believe that their darling little child who was so dependent on them until a few weeks ago can seem now to need them so little. This causes such mothers a lot of heartache, especially if the child is the last to leave the nest. Many a mother sits down and howls her eyes out on her last child's first day at school but the tears are for herself and for the passing of an era, not for the child. The day your last child starts school is a major landmark that ranks almost as high in the family stress stakes as the day the last child leaves home – and the two have many similarities. It is not too fanciful to suggest that at least a few mothers will try, however unconsciously, to keep their child at home if they, the mothers, are looking to the child to answer needs in their lives. Some such mothers produce children who are school refusers (see page 249).

GUILT

Guilt is a normal human emotion that arises when we think we have done something wrong. Some children are brought up to believe that almost anything they do can or might be disapproved of. This is especially seen in girls and in those families which make great demands on their children to be 'perfect'. Such children are so prone to failure that they can be made to feel guilty about almost anything. Some are so sensitized to feeling guilty that they do so even when they are not, actually, at fault. It doesn't take much imagination to see how badly such children fare as adults.

Of course, some children who have been brought up normally can also feel that they are to blame for something that is not their fault. For example, some children believe that they have caused the death of a baby or grandparent by something they have said or done to them. A child who believes this can be profoundly unhappy because of the guilt he or she feels, yet no one latches on to the reality of the situation and the child goes on suffering, even perhaps becoming truly depressed.

Sometimes a child will be off colour emotionally for no apparent reason and it can take persistent but gentle probing to find out what it is all about. Don't bully, nag or threaten him but gently give him the opportunity to talk over what is worrying him. This often happens best on neutral ground rather than at home. The object of the exercise is to enable the child to feel free to spill the beans without any concern for your reaction. The way you handle this sort of situation early on in life will greatly colour how the child opens up to you in the future, so go gently and sensitively. Under safe and loving conditions a child will often declare that he is feeling guilty about something he has done wrong. Sometimes the wrongdoing will be over-estimated and so seems all the worse to the child, but even if it is something you are cross about be sure to praise him for telling you. The relief at such a response together with his delight at having got the matter off his chest will usually make him a lot happier very quickly. Once he feels more stable emotionally discuss why you think what he did was wrong and why he should not do it again. This will do far more good than a harsh telling off and will make him more likely not to do it again. Loving guidance such as this does more good than physical or verbal violence.

The children I'm far more worried about are those who have little or no sense of guilt and who do not care about the effects of their actions on others. Often such behaviour is the result of harsh, overbearing parenting – the child dare not admit such negative emotions, even to him or herself, for fear of ending up believing that what their parents say about them might be true. Such a child then denies his or her feelings of guilt and may behave badly in other ways as a means of venting the pent-up emotions.

Some children feel angry with their parents or other authority figures and then end up guilty about doing so. Many children wish their parents dead at some time or another and some feel very bad about it on reflection. In the event that something untoward happens to the parent the child believes that, in some magical way, he or she has brought it about. Such a child may then become a goody-goody to make amends. What we as parents can best do is to let our children know that negative emotions are quite acceptable, but that one has to be careful how one expresses them.

Any child who is constantly criticized in a negative way will grow up with poor self-esteem and will almost constantly feel guilty at not having lived up to his parents' expectations. Nine times out of ten children like this are not wicked or failures in any way, it is their parents' expectations that are at fault. What such children need most is praise when they do things right and the minimum of comment when they don't.

Of all the subjects about which children are made to feel guilty perhaps one of the greatest is sex. Although it isn't always easy to feel at ease when your child masturbates it makes sense to ignore it (unless it is in public, which is unacceptable in our culture) rather than making him think he is dirty, naughty, or sinful. It is in the very first few years of life that many children are brought up to be guilty about their bodies and their sexuality and this can leave a legacy that dogs them throughout the rest of their lives. Be as open and relaxed as you possibly can on such matters and you will end up with a child that has no real guilt about sex.

But children don't just experience guilt directly: they also pick up their parents' guilt. Many's the parent who feels guilty about things they have or haven't done with or for their children. Working mothers can easily feel terribly guilty; those who send their children off to playschool very young can do so too; some parents feel guilty about having been too strict, and others about having been too lenient; some mothers are riddled with guilt after a miscarriage or a stillbirth; and yet others feel guilty because they don't fall in love with their baby the minute it's born. The list is endless. This comes about partly because of the way we rear girls in our culture to have such a poor image of themselves that they feel they are in the wrong even when they are in the right. Such feelings are the very stuff of much marital and sexual therapy. Most women can be made to feel guilty about almost anything and this is a terrible indictment of our culture's views of women. As a result of all of this the guilt of a mother can infect her child partly because it hampers her ability to mother effectively and openly and partly because the child knows instinctively that something is wrong. If the child fears, as is often the case, that its mother's moods and dis-ease are caused by him or her it doesn't take much imagination to see how it is that he or she then feels guilty about having made the mother so unhappy. So it is that young girls, especially, can grow up to feel motherly towards their own mother. They start to shoulder the burden of the mother's guilts. This can often be the start of a lifetime's feeling that they have to bear the burden of others, often in preference to even recognizing their own needs, let alone dealing with them. So it is that in our culture we perpetuate guilt from generation to generation, and especially among females.

Any mother who feels guilty easily should try to get to the heart of what is going on, perhaps with the help of a professional. Only by doing so will she be able to deal with the unconscious matters that could so easily infect her child, and especially her daughters, who so strongly identify with her. Only in this way will we be able to break the destructive circuit of guilt, especially in women.

THE HIGHLY-STRUNG CHILD

This is a non-medical term for those children who are almost always edgy, nervous, cry easily, and who are more anxious and moody than are other children. They seem to be 'too highly tuned' and to react to things in the environment in a way which makes them anxious and at a disadvantage. Quite clearly much of this has to do with inherited temperament but there is also a learned component to such behaviour, as can be seen from children who adopt the highly-strung behaviour patterns of the adults around them.

The problem with a highly-strung child is that he or she is such hard work both for themselves and for their parents. So many situations make them anxious or unhappy that they need almost constant reassurance that all will be well. With lots of love and attention most such children grow up to be perfectly normal, albeit still somewhat over-sensitive to the big wide world – but having said this it takes all types to make the world go round and at the other end of the scale are those who are introverted, quiet, and seemingly unaffected by anything much.

So long as such a child isn't so nervous that he or she cannot cope with life all that is needed is for the parents to spend more time loving and caring for him or her so that their underlying fears, whatever they might be (and they are usually quite unconscious) can be dealt with and even defused entirely. If a child like this becomes so highly-strung that he or she can no longer function well it probably makes sense to seek professional help. It is also sensible to get help if a previously easy-going child starts to become highly-strung. There is almost always a reason, if only we are clever enough to find it.

Just why some children are highly-strung is anyone's guess. Certainly genes play a part but this is not the whole story, in my opinion. It's easy to see that a child who has highly-strung parents, and especially such a mother, is likely to have experienced all kinds of influences antenatally, however unconsciously. A mother like this is bound to have been more anxious than normal during pregnancy and may well have fussed or panicked about her health and the baby from very early on. It is not yet scientifically provable but it is my belief that this type of mother pre-sensitizes her child to being anxious and edgy even while he or she is in the womb. Prevention, if I am right, lies in helping the mother, which brings me back to my plea earlier in this book for much more psychological and emotional work to be done with women during and even before pregnancy. In this way a lot of potentially highly-strung and anxious children and their families could be saved a great deal of unnecessary stress.

HYPERACTIVITY

The subject of hyperactivity is a very controversial one if only because the term cannot be easily defined. In order to be able to say what hyperactivity means one has to be sure that one knows what is normal, a difficult enough task at any time, especially with children. All young children are hyper-active compared with the middle-aged and elderly and all vary a great deal in their level of activity according to their state of health, their mood, their personality, things that are exciting them in their environment, how much sleep they have had, the time of day, and many other things. Hyperactivity is really only a relative judgement of how a particular child is when compared with himself. Many such children are not only very active but also find it difficult or impossible to focus their attention on anything for long. Their brains are as overactive as their bodies.

As with so many behaviour problems in children definitions are confused. What one can probably say with some certainty is that there are two conditions to be discussed here. The first is overactive *behaviour* and the second, the hyperactivity *syndrome*. The latter is probably somewhat over-diagnosed in the United States and under-diagnosed in Europe. Nevertheless there is good research on both sides of the Atlantic to show that there is a very real syndrome involving overactivity and serious difficulties with concentration, both of which have been present from the pre-school years and which are often associated with mild delays in development. Children with this syndrome are provably helped by stimulant drugs in the short term. However, just how good they are in the long term is in doubt – and this is important because the hyperactivity *syndrome* is a long-term condition.

What is also important is that it seems highly likely that there are many secondary problems associated with hyperactivity and attention difficulties. One of the important findings with the use of stimulant drugs is that they tend not only to improve the child's behaviour, but to lead in the short term to improved patterns of family interaction. I emphasize the short term because the implication is that long-term benefits may well depend on using this opportunity to enhance and maintain improved family functioning by methods other than drug treatment.

In many ways, the most controversial areas concern the role of food allergies. A trial at the Hospital for Sick Children, Great Ormond Street, showed that a diet that was rigorously constructed to avoid the specific allergens that are relevant to each individual child was surprisingly effective in a carefully controlled double-blind study. However, the children were attending a paediatric hospital and many of the hyperactive children had a variety of bodily complaints as well. The main doubt, therefore, lies in how far the findings can be generalized to apply to other groups. There is no question but that the claims on the value of the Feingold diet, a hypo-allergenic diet which has been used widely, are unwarranted but it does now seem that the extreme scepticism of some doctors is also unjustified.

I would draw four lessons from this. First, that most hyperactive children do not have an allergy problem but a few have and it remains uncertain how big this minority is. Second, that the Feingold diet as such is not the most satisfactory form of treatment, in that it is necessary to tailor the specific diet to the needs of the individual child. Third, that dietary treatment is both difficult and demanding on the child and family, as well as potentially dangerous in unskilled hands. And fourth, that the much advertised tests to identify allergies by examination of children's hair and the like are highly dubious procedures. It makes sense to be very cautious about claims being made in this area, especially if you are feeling desperate. High hopes dashed could add further to your desperation.

Being overactive is not a disease in itself but can be a sign that something is wrong. Most normal children under five become overactive and over-excited at times and older children who are emotionally or intellectually active become over-excited on occasions. There are a few medical conditions that cause a child to become overactive much of the time and more recently much research and effort has been spent looking at food allergies as a cause. Often no cause is found.

Several forms of behaviour therapy have been tried, with varying degrees of success and they are less successful when tested in trials than are drugs. Self-control training produces mixed results; counselling can be useful in some instances; family therapy has its followers; and some experts try to combine several of these methods with drugs.

Most hyperactive children whose condition is not caused by a food allergy need careful management to bring out the underlying personality and family problems that might be producing it. Follow-up studies show that hyperactivity can influence personality development and even predispose to certain types of personality disorders, so clearly anything that can be done to treat the condition is well worthwhile.

JEALOUSY

Jealousy is one of the most powerful of emotions. In adults it can be actually dangerous and some people are killed every year because of it. In children it is an overwhelming emotion too, bringing, as it does, its fair share of aggression and destructiveness. Children can be jealous of other children, their parents, other adults, material objects, and situations that keep their parents away from them, to mention but a few.

Jealousy of a new baby is so widespread that it could be considered normal. It is easy to see why this should be so. The newcomer takes over its mother's time, emotions and much else for what, to the child, feels like a very long time. Almost all young children are egocentric and very much want to be the focus of attention. Anything that deflects attention from them they find hard to take and understandably they fight to retain their position. It will have been explained to most young children that a new baby is on the way and at first they will feel able to be generous to the little interloper. This honeymoon period is usually short-lived, however, as realization dawns that he or she will not go away.

Although the matter is very complex there are several points worth bearing in mind when thinking about such jealousy.

First, it is usual for there to be a change in the pattern of parental

233

interaction with the first child when the second child is born. This particularly takes the form of a reduced amount of positive interaction, and an increase in prohibitions and confrontations. It is, of course, an understandable pattern in terms of the parent's involvement with the new baby and concern that the older child be sufficiently responsible to behave 'well' and respect the baby. When this pattern is marked it does tend to increase the likelihood that the older child will respond negatively to the new baby. Second, jealousy and negative behaviour towards the new baby tend to be most marked when the older child has had a good relationship with the mother. It is easy to see why this should be but many parents are especially upset that their loving and much loved child should behave in such a horrible way to the new baby. Third, it seems that the jealous behaviour of the first-born has a tendency to increase the very pattern of parental behaviour that predisposes to jealousy. In this way a vicious circle builds up. Last, it is important to remember that a child's temperamental qualities also influence the likelihood of his or her jealous reactions towards a newcomer.

Jealousy towards a new baby can show up in many ways. The most common is attention-seeking. The older child seems to make endless demands, day and night. He or she might go back to infantile behaviour (such as bed-wetting) in an unconscious bid to get the attention focused back on them again. Some older children are actually aggressive towards the new baby and even the most 'loving' of young children in this situation can give the new baby's hand a hard squeeze 'accidentally' while playing with it. Some children are open about their hostility whilst others hurt the baby when no one is around.

Older children keep their jealousy to themselves but feel it none the less. Children of any age can react by becoming sad, moody, tearful, rude, or by going off school. Of course some children have no open hostility at all and cope with a new baby perfectly well.

But jealousy is part of the ambivalence that we all experience when we try to keep negative and positive emotions about those we love in balance. 'I hate him but I still love him' is what we feel. And, just as in adulthood, a child's feelings of jealousy are to some extent self-centred rather than other-centred. Along with jealousy at almost any age goes quite a lot of self-pity. We feel sorry for ourselves at the unfairness of it all. 'Why should this be happening to me?' is what we ask. And coping with these feelings of unfairness can be a real handful for a child. It is difficult enough for an adult who can rationalize about the world and its twists and turns but for a child the whole thing can seem unbearably desperate.

The aware parent can do quite a lot to reduce feelings of jealousy in older children about to go through the experience of a new baby in the family. Loving preparation helps a great deal and a little present 'from the baby' when you take the older children to the hospital to see the baby for the first time works well. Encouraging an older child to take an active part in doing things with the newcomer usually involves making that extra special effort to tell them and show them that you love them. Try, when the baby is asleep, to make time to do things with the older children. This is probably far more important than doing the housework. Let that go undone for a few weeks, or at least do only the basic minimum.

As children grow up they can also feel jealous about some of the things we adults do. The answer here is to let your children know that you are at ease with their negative and painful emotions just as you are with their positive ones. Many children think that they are naughty if they have such feelings and they need reassurance that we all have negative thoughts about people and that they have to be dealt with.

But not all jealousy is justified and it is our job as parents to help our children recognize the difference between jealousy and envy. Many's the child who says that they are jealous of a friend's house, car, toys, father or whatever. They really mean that they envy them these things and that they wish they could have them. As parents we can help our children look at the world more realistically and should point out the fact that we are all different in our likes and dislikes and in what we choose to do with our lives. Just because a friend of theirs has a better car, or whatever, does not mean that they are necessarily a better person, and so on. Children are, understandably, suggestible to such pressures and some even say that they would rather be a child in another family because life seems better there. This is a time to explain the value of material things and the value of personal relationships and to relate them to one another. Material objects often seem very important to a child, especially as he or she approaches the teens, but given that we, as human beings, seem to have an almost inexhaustible ability to be dissatisfied it behoves us as parents to try to put all this in perspective for our young children. This can be an uphill job in a materialistic culture but we do our children no service if we leave it undone. It is a nettle that has to be grasped and I think the earlier it is done the better.

Many children are jealous of the time their parents, and especially their mother, spend with other people, her job, her hobbies and even her husband. At around the age of three to five most children go through a phase of feeling close to their opposite-sex parent and this can go hand-in-hand with powerful feelings of jealousy. Many such children wish the same-sex parent dead, or at the very least that they would go away and let them alone with their 'loved one'. It is vital for the normal, healthy growth of a child's personality that they don't achieve this ambition. They have to learn that however they feel about the parents' relationship it is an enduring thing that they cannot destroy.

As long as human beings form close emotional bonds with others, jealousy, the fear that they might be broken or lost, will always be with us. The individual child or adult's reaction to the threat of loss will vary greatly according to his underlying personality and temperament but there will almost always be some sort of reaction, even if it is masked and pushed into the unconscious. I feel that jealousy is better out than in, better expressed than suppressed, and to this end I think that we should encourage our children to express such emotions in a way that makes them feel safe and totally loved. A child who can recognize jealousy, talk about it and come to terms with it, will be well equipped for adult life with its far greater potential for jealousy. When he or she then meets it, rather than crack up or become irrationally destructive they will have learned how to deal with it and will accept it as just another of life's inevitable hurdles to be jumped.

LONELINESS

Human beings are social creatures who crave the company of others. Babies want to be with their mothers and in many parts of the world they are alongside their mothers both day and night for the first few years of life. In our culture however, we try our best to separate ourselves from our babies and young children whether by sleeping in another room or putting them in a different room from the family when they sleep during the day.

It is a criminal matter in my view that so many children, and babies in particular, feel lonely so much of the time. There is no reason, for example, why a baby cannot be with its mother all the time wherever she is. He can be in the kitchen alongside her while she cooks; can be taken around in a baby carrier much of the time; and can even sleep alongside the family where the action is. Such a child is never lonely and will, as a result, tend to have a more positive view of the world.

I believe that it is best to get babies off to sleep in the company of a parent or older child rather than to leave them on their own awake for a long time. Many's the baby or young child that is put to bed only to lie awake, perhaps afraid of the dark or the loneliness. Almost all children prefer to go to sleep in the company of others so try putting a baby or young child in with other children, either actually in their beds or in a cot in the same room.

Loneliness in babies and young children should and could be a thing of the past. Older children, however, can become lonely as their brothers and sisters go off to do things. This is a problem especially for the youngest child who has come to rely on the older ones for company. When they start to get out and about in the world the youngest can become very lonely. We, as parents, can give more time and attention to them to make up for this and can encourage them, perhaps earlier than the others, to have their own friends.

Loneliness can often be linked to boredom. It is very much easier to become bored if one is on one's own. First-borns are better at amusing themselves and dealing with loneliness and boredom than are later-borns. It is useful for any child to know how to amuse itself on some occasions but the time to teach this lesson is not in babyhood, as many parents fool themselves. I say 'fool themselves' because many's the parent who has told me that they think it good training for the future to leave their baby alone to deal with his or her loneliness. There is no evidence that this is, in fact, helpful. On the contrary, such arguments are parent-centred much of the time. It is the parent who wants to be alone so he or she projects this wish on to the child. Children learn about independence by being loved securely, *not* by being left alone in the early years. Of course, parents have needs too and there will be times, hopefully rarely, when a baby or very young child will have to be left alone.

As a child grows up, and certainly by the age of three or four, he or she will be able increasingly to amuse themselves. This they start to do by seeing that we as parents do things alone some of the time. This is the time to start to get across the message that being alone doesn't mean being lonely. Many of us enjoy being alone, in the bath, in the greenhouse, or just driving in the car and these are times of value to seek respite from the world and to recharge our emotional and psychic batteries. Children too, once of about school age, start to enjoy being alone for much the same reasons. However, an older child who seems to want to be alone a lot of the time needs careful watching in case the desire to be alone is the sign that something more serious is wrong. If you have any such doubts, seek professional help.

LYING

To tell a lie means to speak untruthfully with the intent to mislead or deceive someone. Very young children (of one and two years old) couldn't lie if they wanted to – they don't have the verbal ability. Some bright two- and three-year-olds though may well be able to mislead when asked a direct question about something they know they shouldn't have done but few people are truly deceived by a child of this age because they are so obviously guilty about it. This is the age to start to tell a child that it is wrong to lie and that it is best if he tells the truth.

If you insist that your children tell you the truth it's vital not to get cross if you promise that you won't. Whatever the 'crime' is that a child is lying about he must be made to feel that his parent's response won't be so severe that it is better to lie than to face it. If a child is afraid to own up or tell the truth it makes sense to look at whether your system of punishment is too fierce. (See more on discipline on page 135.)

Children are easily confused by little white lies that their parents tell. Sometimes these are told to make life go more smoothly, or to prevent someone's feelings being hurt, and this seems quite justifiable to the adult. To a child, however, they seem wrong in the context of his being taught not to lie. Explain as clearly as you can why you sometimes have to lie so as not to hurt others.

Older, school-age children often find themselves telling lies to keep up with their peers. The 'my Daddy has a speedboat' (or whatever) lie is commonplace, especially among little boys who are already beginning to explore the competitiveness of life. Such lying is really a form of boasting and often forms a part of the child's fantasy world. Don't forget that young children live in a fantasy world a lot of the time and on occasions they get carried away and cannot see reality for what it is. This is perfectly normal within reason but if a child persistently lives in a fantasy world then it makes sense to talk it through with him quietly and lovingly. It could be that he feels disadvantaged compared with his friends or unloved by his family. The trouble is that we give our children such confusing messages. On the one hand we tell them off for lying, or exaggerating (especially material possessions or personal achievement) – 'My Dad's a pop star and drives a Porsche' – and on the other hand we strive for such things ourselves and, however unconsciously, make it clear that such things matter to parents. We tell our children that material possessions are not really that important and that happiness is what matters, then work twelve-hour days to provide them with possessions. Perhaps a lying child should make us as parents look at what we say, how much *we* lie and what our standards really are.

MOTHER-SUBSTITUTES

This is a thorny subject that raises many hackles so I shall try to be as unemotional as possible on the subject.

Whilst it was, until recently, a fact that most children in western cultures were looked after mainly by their mothers there have always been those children whose mothers died, were in hospital for long periods, or who had to be away from them for one of many reasons. In almost every family a child is looked after, at least for some of the time, by someone other than the mother.

Of course this alternative care-giver does not have to be the child's father. In societies throughout the world close female relatives and friends have always looked after one another's children and indeed mothering is a shared role in many such societies. But having said this, although a baby or young child can form attachments to many people experience shows that he or she usually has, and wants to have, one particular person who is special. So although there is often a hierarchy of loved ones *an* individual is always more important than the others. This is usually the baby or child's mother.

Whoever the mother figure is, and it can be a man, the baby or young child seeks to form a close, loving bond that ensures that he or she will be cared for, fed, loved and protected. Quite clearly these functions can be performed by almost anyone who has the skills. But whoever performs them the main thing is to ensure that there is consistency and continuity for the child. Babies and young children seem to crave reliability and appear, from clinical experience and also from studies, to do less well if there are many, shifting mother-type relationships.

In our culture there are many possible mother-substitutes. A father may do the job, as may an older child, a close relative, a granny or even a close friend. Even a baby-sitter is a form of mother-substitute, if only for a few hours a week. Paid substitutes include nannies, mother's helps and au pairs. When choosing such a person it is vital to ensure that they are warm, loving and truly caring. No matter what their head knowledge from courses and training it is their heart that needs to be in the job if they are to be successful for your child.

Whoever is the mother-substitute she is likely to form a good bond with the child if she is with him or her a lot and gives loving attention readily. This, needless to say, means that the mother-substitute could well end up having a closer bond with the child than does its own mother and this can be a bitter pill for the mother to swallow. When a young child falls over and runs to its mother-substitute rather than to its mother it takes a tough woman to remain emotionally unaffected.

Clearly, mother-substitutes are valuable, necessary and welcome if a woman cannot, for whatever reason, mother her own child. However, today the matter has attained massive importance as a result of so many women going out to work very soon after the birth of a child. This has thrown some new stresses on to family life and on to at least some of the children who are left with substitutes.

While it is almost impossible to be sure about anything in this area I have been able to come to a reasoned position over many years of working with young families and with adults who are affected, however unconsciously, by their upbringing. The way I see this subject now is as follows:

A baby during its life in the womb is entirely dependent on its mother for all its needs, be they nutritional, emotional, or whatever. They form a dyad that is inseparable. This nine-month period comes to an end at a fairly arbitrary time, in my view, when the baby is ready to start to breathe air rather than remain in the watery environment of the womb. From this time on the second part of the pregnancy begins – that time when the baby is still totally dependent on its mother but is now outside the womb. This period lasts for at least another three months but some say *should* last for another nine months. I agree with the longer time. During this period mother and baby should not, in my view, be parted for any length of time; the baby should ideally be breast-fed; and all its main needs should be answered by its mother. The love affair that started in the womb should be allowed to continue.

According to mothers who have brought up different babies in different ways, babies nurtured like this are perceptibly calmer, happier, sleep better, are more smiley, and are a joy to be with. Of course there are exceptions, but as a generality this seems to be true.

Just as it is difficult for anyone else to mother a child when it is in the womb I contend that during these first few months of life outside the womb the baby's mother is still the most vital person. Just why this should be is difficult to say and it is also not what most young women want to hear but I believe that it has to do with the bonds that are formed at a higher level – spiritual and other bonds at the highest levels of consciousness and indeed unconsciousness. There is a great deal of unspoken communication going on between a mother and her baby, both inside and outside the womb and in time we shall be able to 'prove' this. Many psychically aware women know this to be true and some have, on occasions, told me so.

As the months pass a baby becomes ready to allow new people into the relationship with his or her mother and of course the father and other significant people will have started to have a relationship with the baby that is important to *them*. And so it should be. Having said this though I think the main relationship of importance is that between the mother and the child and so I cannot recommend the use of mother-substitutes for really young babies for more than the shortest of times except in dire circumstances of ill health, or similar times.

Many of my strongly held beliefs in this area come from working with adults. One of the most powerful emotions that most of us are aware of, whether consciously or unconsciously, is that associated with separation from the one we love. There are few emotions that rate as highly in the production of depression and even suicide than the loss, or even the threatened loss, of someone we love. The emotions, sometimes murderous, associated with sexual jealousy also arise out of fears of the loss of someone we love and need.

Clearly the loss, real or imagined, of those close to us plays a vital part in the sum total of all human unhappiness.

It is my belief that we are, quite unnecessarily, sensitized to this loss early in life when, in our culture, many of us experience the loss of our mothers far too early. This is a wound from which many never recover. This might seem a crazy assertion but it is all the more easily seen, strange to tell, when the mother is physically present but emotionally absent from her child or baby. Such a mother may feel unloved herself (perhaps because her man–woman relationship is bad); she may have post-natal depression; she may feel completely at a loss as a mother and so 'retire' from the field of battle, wounded and unable to continue; she may be physically ill; or one of many other things. Any or all of these can come between her and her baby so as to make her unable, often for quite unconscious reasons, to mother her baby effectively. Such children, when adult, often show signs of anxious attachment, never really believing that anyone will be able to care for them, or deal with them as they really are. For all of these reasons I think it is vital to offer all the help possible to women with babies and very young children because the best thing must be to rehabilitate the mother rather than to take the child away and promote a mother-substitute in her place.

This has a far greater application than might at first appear to be the case. Today's mother often says that she will 'go mad' or words to that effect if she stays at home with her baby. As a result many go out to work and leave their young children with a mother-substitute. The problem, though, has been settled in a way that suits the mother but which might well not suit the baby. Almost all young children, when asked, say that they would rather be with their mother than with a substitute, especially in the first two or three years. Some are not happy to leave her until they go to school.

A book such as this is no place to go into the contentious matter of working mothers but there can be little doubt that many mothers go back to work because they feel bored, socially isolated and to seek the company of both men and women. If women were able to make a social life other than in the workplace, as they have always done for centuries, then children would be better served, especially in the first few vital years. I suggest that we look, as a culture, at the needs of women and try to answer them so that they, in turn, can be better mothers.

As with so many other things in the emotional and psychological life, and one particularly sees this in the sexual lives of many couples, people try to do the absolute minimum with which they can get away. So it is that in this context a woman 'plans' her baby, rather like buying a washing machine, and then proceeds to plan her life so that the baby intrudes as little as possible into it. This often means rejecting the child early in life in favour of a return to work. Such a pattern is common in the United Kingdom but is even more widespread on the continent of Europe. Few women now think of full-time motherhood as a career – it is a temporary nuisance that has to be tolerated.

It is hardly surprising, then, given the prevalence of this view, that mothers tend to feel that the sooner a substitute can be found to take over the task of mothering the better it will be for them. And this is what is happening all over the world – including the Third World.

Just what the long-term effects of all this will be I cannot say but I feel that they are likely to be negative as more and more of us suffer the ill effects of being rejected by the one we most want to love and as we learn that love bonds are easily shattered and are of little value. No one who works in the marital field can but be impressed at the link between all this and the increasing breaking of love bonds in adult life. Divorce rates are soaring everywhere and soon one in two western marriages will be affected. This is hardly surprising to me because most of us have been divorced before – from our mothers.

It is hardly fanciful to suggest that we learn to make a meaningful, loving, trusting, one-to-one bond in the earliest years of life and that we first learn this with our mother. Certainly, other people are important but in the scheme of things a child's mother is central to his early years. Because of this I feel that, unless there are extreme circumstances that make it impossible, all children should be looked after almost entirely by their mothers for at least the first year of life and preferably for longer. If we have to change certain facets of society to achieve this, then so be it. I think it would be a change worth making.

Perhaps it would be salutary, if a little below the belt, to say that I have discussed all this with many a former mother-substitute over the years and the most heart-rending memories that I have are of those who have told me that it is obvious to them that they never treated their charges as they subsequently treated their own children. I think this says it all.

I started off by pointing out that this is a complex matter which raises many hackles. Perhaps in conclusion it would be sensible to balance the views expressed here with some further thoughts that undoubtedly have equal validity.

First, it can reasonably be claimed that the quality of interaction between the care-giver and a child is more important than who the care-giver is. However, a crucial component of that quality is continuity. Multiple changes of care-givers are not a good thing.

Second, the wellbeing of babies and children will be influenced by the wellbeing of those who look after them. For this reason alone one cannot ignore the effects of arrangements for child care on the parents. Women vary enormously in how they want to arrange their lives and it is clear that the satisfaction of a mother has an important effect on the wellbeing of her child. This is so whether one is dealing with mothers remaining at home with their baby or with mothers who have gone out to work.

Third, and as an extension of this point, it is usually desirable to have a degree of shared care. This is where fathers and other family members have a crucial role to play. There is no evidence at all that sharing in this way is anything other than beneficial for the child.

Fourth, children benefit from the ideas and interests that their parents provide for them. This is especially so with older children and it is important that mothers, as well as fathers, have sufficient interests and experiences outside the home so as to be able to give what is necessary to the children. For most women this means having some kind of absorbing interest outside the home, although this need not necessarily be a paid job. This need is in no way incompatible with mothers giving up such interests for periods of time to look after young babies but it is a consideration in terms of planning the pattern as a whole and in terms of the length of time over which mothers do this. Because of individual needs, it is unwise to recommend too fixed a pattern.

Last, there is an important difference between what is needed in terms of care for children over the age of two or three and the situation with babies and young children. The evidence on substitute care for the older pre-school group is pretty reassuring provided that the quality of care is good. This last caveat serves as a reminder, however, that a lot of group care falls short of these standards. The evidence is much more contradictory with the younger age group. It would not be right to say that it has been shown that substitute care is damaging but recent evidence has raised queries about the possible dangers for some children of full-time group care outside the home. It is clear, even at that age, that the quality of the care is the most important factor but it does seem possible that, at least for some children, the usual patterns of group day care may be less than optimal if this occupies the whole of the child's day.

NIGHTMARES AND TERRORS

Unpleasant and frightening dreams which may wake a child up are not at all uncommon after the age of about four. Before then, it seems, the child's imagination is not powerful enough to create such problems. A child may have dreamed about something he or she saw on television, in a film, in a book or one of many other places. It is interesting that one of the most popular types of book with six- and seven-year-olds is the horror story. They love to be frightened, perhaps to learn to come to terms with fear in a controlled and 'safe' environment. Sometimes a physical sensation such as a cold in the nose can trigger off nightmares as the child fights for breath in his sleep. There is little doubt in my mind that many foods cause nightmares in both adults and children.

The cure, or rather preventive, for these causes is usually all too obvious once you are aware of them. Much more difficult though is the child who wakes terrified at night for no apparent reason. Such a child clings to his parents and will not be left, so real are the dreams.

This is not the place to explore their significance, but there is no doubt that people of all ages have horrifying dreams, if only from time to time. As adults we can usually deal with the powerful emotions that they create and we don't wake up crying for our parents. Having said this, some people do just this, if only symbolically, and some wake up their partner for reassurance and comfort as if they were indeed a parent.

Children are highly perceptive about what is going on around them at home. They are, in my view, also every bit as intuitive as are adults, and many are more so. All of this makes them susceptible to working out their responses to such moods, and as we adults do, they deal with them in their dreaming sleep. Children are also much closer to fairy tales, fantasy and the other ancient symbolism of nursery rhymes than are their parents so it is hardly surprising that many of them have much more vivid dreams than we do. It can be argued that children are closer to the collective unconscious than are adults and that, as a result, their unconscious does not filter out the primitive demons, ghouls and other beasties that ours does.

Any child who persistently has bad dreams or nightmares or wakes terrified at night, should be considered very carefully. It could be something fairly obvious that is at fault such as frightening tales at bedtime. A secure bedtime routine helps and an opportunity to talk things through just before going to sleep can be of great value.

If, after all these simple, first-aid measures have been tried things still don't improve, seek professional advice just in case there is something much more troublesome at the heart of the matter. Those of us who work with adult dreams find that powerful, dangerous, worrying, or disturbing dreams almost always take place against a background of considerable unconscious activity. Often the nightmares or terrors are the only signposts to an otherwise well-hidden problem.

OBSESSIONS

Obsessions are persistent, repetitive thoughts or actions that a person seems to have to carry out if he is not to become unacceptably anxious. They may involve touching specific things, smelling, feeling the texture of objects, handwashing, complex rituals, and so on.

Almost all children have at least some rituals especially at bedtime or when dressing and these are generally thought to be helpful, if only in practical terms. Many children feel compelled to touch certain things or to walk only on the cracks in the pavement, and so on.

All of this is fine when it is controlled and does not alter the child's life unduly. Sometimes, though, a child will become ruled by his or her obsessions and help is needed. One problem with obsessions at any age is that they are so consuming of time and energy. The time spent in endless handwashing, for example, not to mention the chapping of hands, can make life a misery for both parent and child. Normal compulsive behaviour can be fairly easily given up but true obsessive behaviour cannot.

Most adults, realizing that their obsessions are socially disruptive, try to keep them to themselves, but this is more difficult for children. Many of them involve their parents in the obsession, sometimes in a somewhat aggressive way. Indeed, many adult obsessions are characterized by a lot of aggression. Such children discover that their compulsive behaviour can be used to control their parents and soon they find that this manipulation gives them a sense of power. A parent who is also compulsive may well go along with the child for some time before realizing that they have been led into a trap. Once having realized this they often become hostile themselves. It has been suggested that of all the neurotic tendencies in childhood, obsessions are the most closely linked to parental behaviour. In one study such behaviour was present in three-quarters of all the family histories of obsessive children.

It appears that ritualistic and obsessional behaviour is learned from the cradle onwards. Such families also tend to place high importance on morality, etiquette and personal cleanliness and one study found that potty training was rigid, prolonged and punitive in those children who were obsessional.

Obsessional symptoms usually begin at about the age of six but most parents take no action for another four years or so. In nearly half of all cases there is some sort of precipitating factor and about half the children also have phobias. Affected children appear to be of above average intelligence.

The prevention of obsessions starts with the parents becoming less rigid, more tolerant generally, less strict about potty training, more flexible about the 'shoulds' and 'oughts' in life and more forgiving when their children behave like children rather than robots. Given that about 70 per cent of all children with obsessions go on to have them in adult life it makes a lot of sense to do all that we can as parents to ensure that we control our own obsessive and compulsive behaviour and, if necessary, to seek professional help to combat it.

PSYCHOSOMATIC DISEASES

In recent years in the West there has been an increasing acceptance of the fact that diseases occur as a result of many factors, some of which are physical and others psychological or spiritual. Some conditions appear to have a more physical cause and others a more psychological one but it has long been the contention of the most ancient systems of medicine in the world that both play a part in almost every type of ailment that human beings are heir to.

Just as such principles apply to adults so too do children have the same forces at play in their lives, their ailments and their illnesses.

To say that the mind can influence the body so as to produce disease or dis-ease seems too trite on the one hand but remains profoundly true on the other. There are few illnesses that are not influenced, at least to some degree, by the way the child reacts to them; the progress of a particular illness is also affected by the family's behaviour and beliefs; and there is undoubtedly at least some psychological predisposition in families to certain ailments. So it is that a seemingly purely 'physical' disease can have psychological or emotional roots, and that once a particular condition takes a hold in a child the child himself, or the family in which he lives, can either enhance or reduce the effects of the disease.

There are numerous examples that could be chosen to illustrate these points but here are just a few.

It is often said, rather glibly, that children need love if they are to survive and thrive. However, what most people do not know is that this is literally true. Some babies and young children fail to thrive and are taken to their doctors with feeding problems, poor growth, vomiting or inexplicable diarrhoea. Some such children also show a slowed mental and intellectual growth. Sometimes there is a physical cause for such a story but there often is not. In many children in the latter group there is often a story of social disorganization and family deprivation. Frequently the relationships within the family are disturbed and marital problems between the parents abound. The child may be under-loved or even frankly rejected by one or both parents and this rejection may well date back to birth or even before. Research suggests that tender loving care is vital for the *physical* wellbeing of a child, as well as for his psychological and emotional health.

All this evidence means that any child who is not thriving as he or she should deserves to be looked at in a much wider context than simply dealing with the diet. Quite often a psychiatric assessment of the family discovers undetected problems which, when resolved, enable the child to thrive, perhaps for the first time ever.

Obesity is a common problem in our culture, affecting perhaps one in ten children. Just why it is so common is not known, but the contribution of eating habits and styles within families and inherited predispositions to fatness cannot be ruled out. Just how psychological factors might influence the story is not clear but several researchers and many individual practitioners have the impression that mothers of obese children feel guilty with regard to their children and express this as a need to keep them physically close. Such parents then encourage overeating, quite uncon-sciously of course. Such children soon come to realize that to please their mothers they must eat and so the scene is set for life. These children often resort to eating when the going gets tough in later life, partly because of other long-term effects of their mother's guilt. It is not unusual for children from such families to have had longstanding battles over food in various guises. This kind of battle is the norm with many toddlers but does not usually persist into older childhood. It appears that many such children know, however unconsciously, that they have been programmed in this way, and try to rebel against it. The mother often feels rejected and hurt if they do and so has a lot of emotional investment tied up in promoting the eating. We look at this in more depth on page 147.

Obese children do not have an especially high level of neurotic or psychiatric problems. On the contrary, they may even have fewer than normal. This has led at least some experts to suggest that obesity might be a very successful coping mechanism which, if not present, might have meant that the child would have succumbed to other psychological or emotional disorders. Obese children, like obese adults, are not well thought of by their peers. They are less likely to be wanted as friends; are rated as less worthy of being friends than are children with other physical handicaps and as a result come to have a rather poor self-image over the years. So it is that many obese children become teenagers who have a somewhat distorted body image including an overestimation of their size.

Obviously the treatment of obesity in childhood, as at any other time of life, involves the careful control of food intake but in those children who do not respond well to this simple approach other more family-based and psychological approaches deserve attention.

Asthma is a common childhood condition, arguably one of the most common 'diseases' that afflict children. Whilst there is no doubt that many factors, most of them physical, play a role in triggering an attack there can also be no doubt that psychological factors have an effect too. It used to be said that there was a specific relationship between the personality of the parents of asthmatic children and the children themselves but this has not been definitely proven. What can be said though is that the emotional state of the parents can greatly influence the outcome of an attack once it has started. One research team found that leaving asthmatic children in their homes (exposed to all the same environmental factors) but removing the parents resulted in a dramatic improvement in at least some of the children. It could be said that these children were allergic to their parents! In many asthmatic children any form of excitement or emotional trauma induces an attack, though, to be fair, it is not only the child's parents who are responsible for these conditions.

Treating an asthmatic child then may involve more than simply giving the appropriate medicines and avoiding triggers in the environment.

Epilepsy occurs in about eight children per 1000 and can be very distressing for all concerned. Psychological factors alone are not thought to cause the condition but it is thought that emotional and psychological triggers can spark off a fit in at least some children. Such a link has indeed been substantiated by research using electroencephalographs.

247

Children with epilepsy have several times as much psychiatric disturbance as do children in the rest of the population and substantially more than those suffering from other longstanding disorders that do not affect the brain. This suggests that it is the effect of the condition on the brain itself that causes the problems. However, even children with newly diagnosed epilepsy have a higher-than-expected rate of psychological abnormality.

Abdominal pain without any evidence of a physical cause is not at all uncommon in children. This is especially true of those children who refuse to go to school. There are those who claim that much, if not most, such pain is caused by psychological and emotional stresses but perhaps this is too harsh a judgement. Certainly with increasing knowledge of lactose and other food intolerances and allergies such strange and previously inexplicable tummy aches can be understood in other ways. Migrainous and non-migrainous headaches are often linked to tummy aches and emotional disturbances and some paediatricians assert that there is a sort of abdominal migraine in children whose family has a history of ordinary migraine.

Of all children who have longstanding tummy aches about a half continue to have them in adulthood. The children of such parents (with recent tummy aches) seem only to suffer their tummy aches when the *parents* have symptoms. Just why this should be is not known but there could be an inherited underlying condition or it could be that the parents' emotional reactions, mainly anxiety, infect their children.

Obviously, a child's reaction to chronic illness or disability, his ability to deal with cancer, and a host of other examples will be greatly influenced by his family's response to the condition. Even something as apparently 'organic' as a cancer might be influenced by psychological and emotional factors. It was known by the Ancients that breast cancer was more common in 'melancholy' women and increasing knowledge of the influence of the mind over the immune system must make this an exciting area for future research.

Without a doubt many children suffer from what appear to be purely 'physical' diseases as a result of emotional and psychological influences in their families. Even the accident-prone child could be said to fall into this category, as we saw on page 108.

Many readers will no doubt raise their hands in horror and think they might be to 'blame' in some way for their child's apparent physical illness. Whilst in no way wishing to be alarmist I firmly believe this is a possibility that as parents we cannot afford to ignore. If only by our example, and the way we handle or do not handle stress, we could be predisposing our children to smoking, overeating or other self-destructive behaviour. Without being too dramatic I feel that it makes sense to bear all this in mind if we are to hope to rear balanced, healthy children for the future.

SCHOOL REFUSAL

It has been calculated that about one in ten of all schoolchildren in Britain are absent from school at any one time, with about four out of five of these being kept away because of illness. Just how real much of this 'illness' really is is open to debate because there is a group of children who do not want to go to school and will no doubt create symptoms or at least make the most of existing ones so that they are not made to go to school.

Over the years truants have been recognized by school authorities and parents alike. Such children either run away from school or absent themselves on a fairly regular basis. But school refusers are really school phobics – they are terrified of school just as some people are frightened of spiders or heights.

One study compared truants with school phobics and found some very convincing differences. School refusers came from families with many neurotic problems, had less experience of maternal absence in babyhood and childhood, were more often passive, dependent and overprotected but usually showed a higher standard of work and behaviour at school. Their refusal to go to school was usually a symptom of anxiety or depression.

The truants, on the other hand, were from larger families, where home discipline was inconsistent. They had changed school frequently and their standard of work was poor. Their general behaviour was bad and some were even delinquent.

The problem of school refusal is a complex one. It starts with general complaints about school with perhaps a reluctance to go at all and ends with a total refusal to attend. Most such children show signs of anxiety even at the mention of school and many of them cannot even make the journey all the way there – they turn around and come back home. The condition affects boys and girls equally.

Just how much of all of this reflects the emotional and psychological condition of the parents of such children is not known but it has been found that one-fifth of the mothers of school refusers are suffering from some kind of psychiatric disorder, often depression.

Young children usually become affected slowly but older children and adolescents can have a more dramatic onset. At any age triggers such as illness, a stay in hospital, an accident, a school holiday, a new house, the loss of a schoolfriend or marital or other family disharmony can precipitate school refusal.

Once the child becomes phobic of attending school he or she clings to the mother and can become stubborn and argumentative, perhaps for the first time ever. Such children often have a history of finding change difficult. They also sometimes have recurrent physical problems, such as headaches, vomiting, fainting, tummy aches, limb pains, or a fast heartbeat. Such complaints, when present on school days, should always make a parent think of school refusal under another guise.

Clearly, starting school is a major upheaval in a child's life. Until this time he or she is safe in the domestic environment that is largely controlled by known factors. At school the rules are new and different, the child has almost no control over what happens, his parents cannot do much to alter the way things are run there, new skills have to be learned, new friends to be made, and there is, perhaps for the first time, a sense of competition in his life. Because of all of this most children have at least some difficulty adjusting to primary school. One study found that about 80 per cent of children experienced difficulties in junior school, of which half were moderate to severe. From the age of six to eight the problems were worse in only children and those who were middle-class. Such children usually had problems of being over-dependent on their parents. Having said this we do tend to send children to school rather young in the United Kingdom and it could be that many are simply not yet sufficiently secure to make the transition without protest or pain. School refusal is commonest at three ages. When first starting school (between the ages of five and seven); at around the age of eleven as children change school and sometimes have a variety of neurotic disorders; and again at fourteen or older.

No one knows why it is that some children are particularly prone to school refusal but it makes sense to me that they have suffered in some way that makes them exceptionally dependent on their homes generally and are anxious rather like a juvenile type of agoraphobia. But it is not just the children who have problems. As we have seen, they often have mothers who are neurotic and there is little doubt in my mind that at least some such children are being unconsciously used by their mothers to fulfil their, the mothers', needs rather than those of the children. It is quite possible for such a woman, quite unconsciously, to so over-value herself to her child that he or she sees the mother as indispensable. Clearly such behaviour, however unconscious, is harmful to a growing child who needs to learn about independence if it is to function at all normally in the real world outside the home.

Dealing with school refusers takes time and patience because, as we have seen, it often involves not only the child but other members of the family too. Various kinds of therapy have been tried from anti-depressant drugs to family therapy and many things seem to work in certain families and to some degree. Young children fare better with treatment than do the over-elevens.

Treating such a child can be difficult because there are often many pulls that make a single-minded approach difficult or even impossible to implement. The best method is to be firm and to seek out the help of someone the child likes and respects, perhaps a particularly kind teacher, to encourage him to return. It is vital not to become sidetracked on issues such as whether the child should change school (unless, of course, there is a very obvious reason why the school is wrong for him) or the knotty matter of home tuition. Some parents will, unfortunately, become embroiled in all this, and more, in an unconscious effort to control the child and keep him at home.

When a group of female school refusers were followed up for 14 years in the United States it was found that most were able to make an independent life away from their parents but that their social contacts were limited. Those that were married were very dependent on their husbands. Most of them had done well for themselves in the world in spite of their absence from school.

Most school refusers go on to become normal adults but some are at particular risk of suffering from psychiatric illness in adult life.

SEXUAL ABUSE

Almost everyone in our culture agrees that the sexual abuse of children is unacceptable and because of this it is also illegal. Having said this, however, it is nevertheless very commonplace with about one in five women having been abused (though not necessarily physically) in one way or another by the age of eighteen.

Sexual abuse of children raises very strong feelings, and rightly so, but there are no simple answers to its prevention and the key almost certainly lies with children themselves, as we shall see.

Most people, when thinking about the sexual abuse of children imagine that intercourse is the main activity that they have to be protected from. This is not so. Certainly some child abusers do have intercourse with their victims but much more commonly the contact is less overt and many more children are subjected to unwelcome fondling, petting, genital manipulation, exhibitionism, or even obscene phone calls. Even a parent who forces a child to be close or overly intimate with another adult with whom the child feels ill at ease could be said to be abusing him or her.

Child sexual abuse is very common indeed and the majority of abusers are men and the abused, girls. The crime usually starts when the child is around the age of ten but some girls are abused from their pre-school days. In the vast majority of cases the man is known to the child – indeed it is often a man that the girl thinks she can trust. Fathers, father-substitutes, step-fathers, uncles, grandfathers and professionals such as teachers, are the commonest groups involved.

A book such as this is no place to go into why men sexually abuse children but put at its simplest it appears that some men are 'into children' and will try to find emotional and sexual satisfaction with them whether they are related to them or not. These are dangerous men who might put any child at risk. The second, and far more common group, are those who are insecure, immature characters, often with a religious background who abuse their children in many ways, one of which is sexual. Such men also sometimes abuse their wives and it is this that makes the crime so difficult to detect. Many of the wives of such men are fearful of reporting the wrongdoings and, as a result, things go on for years. It has been found in one study that the average duration of child abuse within a family is seven years.

Whatever the nature of the sexual abuse most children who are involved feel guilty because they imagine that they must have brought it on themselves. Many girls carry this guilt with them throughout their lives and some are unable to make good man–woman relationships. It is hardly surprising that many such abused girls have difficulty being well-balanced parents themselves – they are exceptionally ill at ease with the emerging sexuality of their daughters as it re-kindles old memories. Such a woman is very likely to be prudish towards the sexuality of her own daughter; may quite unconsciously retard her progress with boys; and will, in short, do anything to ensure that she doesn't attract the sexual attentions of her husband, or other men in her life.

It is an extraordinary fact that women who were themselves abused as children are more likely to marry men who will abuse their own children. Other women are so tyrannized by their husbands that they can do little even when they are sure something is going on.

For the child who is being abused there is a terrible dilemma. To tell or not to tell? If clinical evidence is anything to go by the majority say nothing and carry the burden for ever. But many do want to tell yet can't find a way or the opportunity to do so. This makes it important for parents to be alert to the fact that a child could be being abused even for quite some time yet be unable to draw attention to the fact and have it stopped.

The following list gives just some of the tell-tale signs that a child might be being sexually abused. Of course, such signs do not definitely point to such abuse but they certainly mean that something is seriously wrong which needs sorting out. Such a child needs listening to.

- The child may seem depressed and low in spirits.
- There may be a fear of a particular individual, perhaps manifesting itself as an unwillingness to be in his or her company alone.
- Withdrawal and inward-looking behaviour. The child may want to spend long periods alone.
- Running away from home, or the threat of it.
- Bed-wetting in younger children.
- An inability to concentrate.
- Nightmares and sleeping difficulties.

- Sudden school problems, including truancy.
- Making allegations that are obviously false as an indirect way of drawing attention to the problem.
- A general lack of trust in adults.
- A lack of trust in an adult the child knows well.
- An aversion to sex or any mention of it.
- Displays of knowledge on sexual matters that are ahead of the child's years.
- Unexplained bruises, scratches or bite marks.
- Eating disorders – but mainly a poor appetite or compulsive eating.
- Pain in the genitals, itching, VD, or genital damage.
- Suicide attempts.
- Prostitution.
- Unwanted pregnancy.

  Make time for your child so that there is an opportunity for him or her to tell you. Some children find that their parents are too busy or preoccupied with their own lives to make time to discuss anything much, let alone something as difficult as this.

  But supposing the child does confide in you, how should you handle it?

- Perhaps the first rule is to be very open and understanding and to stay calm. Children will often have put off saying anything for years for fear of the effect that the revelation might have on their parents, their family and themselves. It can take real bravery to declare what has happened. If Mum then throws a fit or has a breakdown, the child could wish she had kept quiet.
- Find a place where you can talk privately – perhaps outside the house – on neutral ground. This will make disclosures a lot easier.
- Ensure that the child knows that you are pleased that she has told you. Make it clear that she will not be punished for telling.
- Until proven otherwise, believe what the child tells you.
- Even if you think the child is to blame, don't say so.
- Reassure the child that now that you know you will do something about it. Be sure to live up to your promise.
- Don't be over-intrusive about the detailed goings-on. It will be too painful for the child and she might wish she'd kept quiet.
- Get some help for yourself. Start by talking it over with your general practitioner or even a close friend. Or go straight to the police, the National Society for the Prevention of Cruelty to Children (NSPCC) or your local Social Services Department, because you will be unable to stop the abuse on your own. You can't be with your child twenty-four hours a day. You haven't, for whatever reason, been aware of what has been going on so far and the chances are that whatever the abuser says, it will all happen again sooner or later. If you decide to keep things to

yourself, then you must accept the risk that the abuse will continue.

- Even though you may feel very incensed and indeed highly emotional about the revelations, don't keep bringing the subject up at home and don't make the child relive the experience by telling you about it again and again.
- Try to avoid attacks on the offender in front of the child.
- Contact a specific sex abuse organization.

  Child sexual abuse is a very common crime and one that is almost impossible to prevent by tackling the adult end of the problem. The only answer is to bring children up to be aware of the dangers and to tell someone they trust as soon as anything happens that makes them feel uneasy.

  There are three basic rules that every modern child should be made aware of from the earliest age at which they can understand:

- Your body belongs to you. If ever anyone tries to touch you in a way that makes you worried or scared, tell them to stop and make sure you tell an adult you can trust.
- If any adult tells you to keep a secret of something they do to your body, tell at once.
- If the first adult you tell doesn't believe you, tell another one until someone does.

These simple guidelines, if applied universally, would defuse many a potentially dangerous situation early on before it took a hold of either child or adult. We cannot rid the world of men who are liable to perpetrate this crime but we can teach our children to see the dangers early and avoid them.

SIBLING RIVALRY

This is a normal state of affairs in which children within a family compare themselves with one another and often actually compete. This behaviour starts when they are young but can go on for a lifetime.

Competition between brothers and sisters in a family can be present from a very early stage and can even start before a baby is born. The actual amount of rivalry that goes on depends on the child's personality and how we as parents handle the situation. At the heart of sibling rivalry is the fact that children in a family have to share not only their parents' time and material resources but also their emotions. Each time another child is born the size of the piece of emotional cake that any one child can have is reduced and the first-born becomes further removed from the centre of the stage. But however well organized and aware parents are, new babies always take more than their fair share of their parents' time and emotions because they are so demanding compared with an older, more independent child. This will always seem tough to the older children. A way around this is to try to give that much more attention to the older children than you otherwise might have done. This will, to some extent at least, redress the balance.

A child who has always been sat upon or beaten in competitive situations at home may grow up with an unconscious desire to do better than his siblings. What's more, he may succeed if his determination is strong enough. The quiet one who always came second may be the one who grits his teeth and works hard so that he passes exams, gets into all the teams and so on. Sibling rivalry can go on for a lifetime. It is not by any means always obvious but is always there to some degree, mingled with all the other perfectly normal feelings towards one's brothers and sisters such as love, protectiveness, pride, a desire to see them do well, and jealousy.

Danger can creep in if a child believes that because he is stronger than his brother, for example, he's intrinsically a better person and loved more by his parents as a result. It is important to teach your children that you love them for what they are, warts and all, and always will do. *Never* imply or tell one child that you love him more than another (even if you do). This could stick in his mind for ever and do him a lot of harm. It's a question you will be asked because each child wants to know how much you love him and comparison is a good way of estimating his worth. Tell him that you love each child the same.

Sibling rivalry can make one child feel a failure and another a bully. It's up to you to smooth things over, to help each child accept himself and to show that you love everyone.

Clinical experience with this phenomenon suggests that for the older child, siblings who are one or two years younger are not a serious problem but siblings who are say three to six years younger can produce real difficulties. Unfortunately, research does not bear this out and the matter will remain subject to debate for some time. Being a younger child can also cause problems because of the jealous hostility of an older one. To a small boy, a girl who is four or five years older is partly a mother and to some extent shares the image he has of his mother. In practice this can be a reality because older girls are often turned into deputy mothers by their mothers. The girl may be nervous in this role, or be overburdened and blamed if anything goes wrong during her period of custodianship. She may well feel jealous too, although it is usually mixed with loving feelings. The element of her which is hostile may later affect the boy's attitude towards women and make him somewhat fearful of them. Similarly, a girl may be tested, rejected and bullied by an older brother which, in turn, may tend to make her fearful of men later. Even if a brother and sister love each other a lot it can still give rise to problems later because the attachment they feel towards each other may interfere with their subsequent relations with the opposite sex. Some seek a replacement brother or sister in the shape of a wife or husband but often only with difficulty because they want the old relationship (the real brother–sister one) to spring back into life as it once was.

The sex of siblings can affect the issue in another way. If a younger sibling of the opposite sex is seen as being especially favoured by one or both parents, but especially by the opposite-sex parent, an older child can begin to imitate the younger one so as to compete and may even begin to feel that one needs to be of the opposite sex to be really loved. Parents, too, may have their preferences for the sex of a child and this can, in some cases, profoundly affect children of the 'wrong' sex.

Regardless of 'right' or 'wrong' sex, the middle child of three is often in an especially difficult situation. The eldest has all the privileges and the youngest the emotional love, often leaving the middle child in a vacuum all round. Unfortunately, this can't necessarily be overcome by treating all the children the same because their needs for love, affection, attention and so on will vary enormously.

Apart from which sex the child is, the general reactions to a younger sibling are to resent the mother for producing him or her; to resent the older child; and to try to punish him. Unfortunately, signs of hostility towards the younger child usually bring a sharp rebuke which is why so many adults repress the memories of their childhood jealousies and see them as something of which they are ashamed. However, all this is well understood and perfectly normal. The *third* thing that happens in such situations is to come to see oneself as being inadequate. This is understandable. Young children cannot reason, they can only feel. Mothers often say there is no reason for their older child to have felt jealous because she divided her attention equally between them and did her best for both. The reality is different though because new-born and very young babies are slave-drivers towards their mothers, especially in the first few months after birth. This almost always means that a baby *is* given priority over older children however hard the mother tries. Even if what mothers claim were true, the older child has still lost half of the love and attention he or she was getting, as we saw above. Out of a fear of further loss of love such an older child can become over-sensitive to parental instructions and emotions. When it comes to sexual matters this can lead to the suppression of sexual interests and can even have a psychosexually castrating effect, especially on girls who are desperately keen not to further lose their parents' love and affection.

In an effort to retain a bigger share of love, the older child usually makes strenuous attempts to gain parental approval and if the family is one in which achievement, academic or otherwise, matters, the child can easily become a compulsive over-achiever. First-born children form a larger proportion of the 'successful' in any career one looks at – possibly because they were 'only children' for at least some of the time and had more attention lavished on them as a result. Less happily, some become so anxious, as a result of the emotional implications of testing situations (such as school exams) that their performance deteriorates and they become under-achievers. The damaging effect this then has on their emotions and self-esteem can weaken them to a point where they become under-achievers in all areas of life, including their dealings with the opposite sex.

SLEEP PROBLEMS

Of all the letters that arrive at mother and baby magazines those on sleep problems rank as the most numerous, along with questions on feeding. It certainly seems that sleep problems worry many parents – often for years on end.

Unfortunately, we bring many of the problems upon ourselves as a result of the way we treat children in our culture. Young babies are taught from very early on to expect to sleep on their own, apart from the rest of the family, often in their own room. They are expected to go off to sleep at a predetermined time whether they are tired or not and are then expected to sleep throughout the night. The fact that babies quite normally wake during the night is either not known or is ignored in favour of a desire on the parents' part for an undisturbed night.

One in five one-year-olds is still waking at night and the proportion at two is about the same. Some children go through the night from babyhood only to start waking during their third year, for example.

It seems from experience that babies sleep best in the company of others, be it their brothers and sisters or their parents. Many's the waker who, when put into a bed with another child, sleeps the night through. This is hardly surprising when one looks at other less industrialized cultures in which children, and often parents too, all sleep together for comfort, warmth, safety and reassurance.

Once a child is out of the parental bed and sleeping alone in a bed, albeit still in a room with brothers and sisters, problems can occur if he wakes at night and wants to play or be active. Most parents find that the answer is to be firm and to make it plain that night-time is not for playing but sleeping. Perhaps, lie down with the child and pretend to go to sleep or alternatively, if it suits you better, take him into your bed. Either of these strategies can, however, lead the child to expect that you will always lie down with him to get him off to sleep. If this suits you, fine, but it could become a burden. The main problem under such circumstances is to get enough sleep as a parent – few toddlers and young children go so short of sleep that it harms them. The child who wakes very early can be shown how to play until getting-up time. This is much more easily achieved if there are other children for him to play with.

There is little doubt in my mind that more babies would like to sleep in their parents' bed, or perhaps in the same room in a cot near their bed than ever have the opportunity to do so. This makes breast-feeding easier and even an older child can be the more easily cared for if he or she is close at hand. There is no evidence of which I am aware that shows that it is better to let a child 'cry it out'. On the contrary, a child who wakes at night needs *more* love and attention, not less. It is, of course, possible to condition a child to cry less or even not at all at night and some 'experts' think this advisable. I see it as a form of mental cruelty that is totally unnecessary.

Dealing with night-time crying will be dictated to some extent by the age of the child and when the crying occurs. Babies crying in the night are one thing and school-age children crying to get parental attention are quite another. Moreover, a crucial distinction needs to be made between the difficulties (including crying) in getting children to settle down to sleep and the problems associated with a child waking distressed during the night. So far as the latter is concerned, it is always wise to go to the child to see what is the matter and to help him or her settle down again. It would be unusual for this to be an attention-seeking manoeuvre.

The situation with respect to children settling down at night is quite different and there are plenty of circumstances in which it is wise, having assured oneself that the child is all right, to insist that he or she remains in their room and to ignore crying. This should not be done as a first resort and even when it is an established problem it is sensible for parents to go the first time if only to check that the situation is not a different one because of some new factor – emotional or physical. However, it is not mental cruelty to ignore attention-seeking behaviour in this fashion. Moreover, there is evidence that this works better than other ways of handling the problem.

Having said this, any particular parent's abilities to deal with crying babies or children will be coloured by their own upbringing and personality type. It is quite impossible for some parents to leave their baby or young child crying for any length of time yet others can do so with apparent callousness.

Certainly there are problems with parental sex with a baby in the bed or the room, if this is the way that you choose to get around the problem. Beds are not large enough in many households for a baby as well as the parents; some parents are concerned about smothering their baby or young child in their bed even though there is no evidence that this is a danger unless one or the other is drunk, heavily drugged or extremely obese; and so it goes on. But for many parents a lack of sleep becomes a real drain on their own lives and indeed on their relationship and desperation can overcome them. It is often better to find ways around such problems and to keep the baby or young child with you.

I think the way out of this is to look at how the child could be given more time and love and how night-times could be made more child-centred. It always appears to me that parents who try to make their children sleep for twelve hours pay for it somehow or other, unless they are lucky. There are, of course, some children who will sleep this long but they are the exception rather than the rule. There are vast individual variations as to how much sleep children need. On balance, they need much less than their parents think. The truth, as I see it, is that in many if not most families the subject of children and sleep is a vexed one. It makes sense to me to seek the easiest way out that is compatible with doing no harm to the child. This will usually involve being closer to the child in the day; allowing him or her to remain with you longer in the evenings; encouraging sleeping together, if not in the same bed then in the same room; using bedtime rituals to get children off to sleep calmly; and accepting the fact that few young children will sleep for a solid twelve-hour stretch.

A child of any age who sleeps badly needs to be looked at by the parents to see what could be causing the problem. Could it be that he or she is so stimulated before going to bed that they get off to a bad start? Could he or she be allergic to a food which makes him or her hyperactive in the night, as in the day? Could there be environmental factors such as draughts, excessive heat, insufficient covers, or other children disturbing them? Could it be they are drinking something too soon before going to sleep so that they always need to get up to go to the lavatory? The possibilities are many and common sense will usually sort them out.

More difficult though are the relationship problems within a family, the marital discord, the family with high levels of tension, and so on. Many children lie awake listening to their parents rowing, or worry about their parents' relationship. All of these concerns are real and help needs to be sought so that they can be dealt with, perhaps with the assistance of a professional.

SOILING

This uncontrollable passage of bowel motions can be very slight, resulting in only a minimal staining of a child's underpants or can be true defecation with all the mess and embarrassment that this entails.

Some parents are so keen to have their child out of nappies that they try too early and then find that he cannot cope. Even a child who has been carefully potty trained in a relaxed way can still have the occasional accident, especially if there is something stressful or emotional going on in his or her life. The safest thing is to put such a child back into nappies and to have another go at potty training once the stressful situation is over. Although most such children soil themselves quite unknowingly there are a few who have the awareness that doing so brings them the kind of attention they seek in a stressful situation, such as when a new baby arrives.

Older children who soil present more of a problem but the most common cause is constipation, which is treatable. This might at first seem strange but what happens is that hard, bulky masses of stool block the lower bowel and liquid stools flow around them and leak to the outside. The cure here is to deal with the constipation.

The psychological background to soiling is not clear-cut but there are some interesting findings from research studies. One such found that nearly all the children who soiled showed signs of emotional disorders and that many came from 'unsatisfactory' homes. In another study well over half of those children who soiled themselves had been harshly potty trained with many of them having experienced what the researchers called 'the battle of the bowel'. Such potty training is probably only one factor in soiling though. Another study found that the mothers of soiling children were anxious, unreliable, emotional, overprotective, and indulgent and that they reacted to soiling in boys by punishing them angrily. A 1974 study found that there were high levels of family disharmony and marital problems in the families of children who soil.

Obviously a child who soils because he is constipated must have his constipation treated but if this is not the cause several other treatments can be tried. Individual and family psychotherapy both produce promising results.

The main problem with soiling, and especially in the older child, is the awful embarrassment of it all to the child. To him or her it is just like being a baby again. A soiling child needs treating with care, love and tact. Never let him or her wear smelly clothes longer than you have to and be sure to go around prepared for the worst. Always have tissues, wipes and a spare pair of pants with you so that any mishap can be cleared up quickly. A polythene bag to put the dirty pants in is also a must.

Such a child is all too aware that this behaviour is socially unacceptable so there is no need to punish him in any way. The majority do not soil themselves deliberately and so can do nothing to prevent it. Whilst it can be a real nuisance for the parents it is usually short-lived if handled sensitively.

As with so many things at this stage of life it is important to have insights into your own behaviour so that your unconscious does not harm the child or punish him in any way. Most of us are only too glad to get our children out of nappies as soon as possible and any regression to babyhood is greeted with at least an inward groan. As long as we can be aware of our negative feelings we have a better chance of keeping them to ourselves and allowing the child to progress at his own pace to becoming clean again.

STEALING

Children under school age often take things that don't belong to them but this can hardly be called stealing because often they have no real understanding of what is theirs and what isn't. This is particularly true up to the age of about four. Often the idea of ownership is hard to grasp and in many cases a child doesn't think of something as 'owned' at all. Sensible, gentle handling of the situation is all that is usually required. Never scold a child of this age or accuse him of stealing in the adult sense of the word. Many young children borrow things intending to return them but never get around to it because their memory is not up to it or because they don't realize that it matters to do so.

Once over the age of four or so a child does begin to understand possessions and whom they belong to. He now realizes that certain things are of value to him and that others have similar views about their things. After this age, then, real stealing can occur but I feel it is unwise to call a child a 'thief' except under the very greatest provocation. This sort of label has a nasty habit of sticking and a child branded like this might just oblige you by acting up to his reputation.

Much more important is to find out why he or she stole in the first place. One major study found that boys who stole were much more likely to have been separated from their mothers early in life than non-stealing boys. Some children indulge in 'comfort stealing' – taking things from home (money from the mother's purse is common) as a way of making life more acceptable. This is somewhat akin to the woman who, although fat, keeps on eating whenever the going gets tough emotionally for her. Older children who steal (above primary school age) usually have other signs of delinquency.

Comfort stealing is almost always a sign of feeling unloved by the parents. It can occur in all types of family, even the well-heeled. Such children are usually over-controlled, fear the expression of anger or indeed of any negative emotions, and often express such feelings as physical symptoms. They also often lie and both behaviours make the parents cross – the very response the child seeks to avoid. The child now craves affection even more and his anger at not receiving it comes out at school and at home.

A few parents get second-hand, if unconscious, kicks out of their children's stealing and then come down on them very hard as a projection (see page 110) of their anger at their own unconscious desires. They punish their child for their own (uncommitted) offences.

I believe that stealing deserves carefully looking into by the parents. No happy, loved child will steal, or at least not persistently so. Stealing should always be treated as a cry for help until proven otherwise.

APPENDIX

WHAT IS 'THERAPY'?

Throughout the book I have often referred to 'therapy' so I thought it would make sense to say a few words about what it actually is, in the context of this book.

The sort of therapy to which I am referring is psychotherapy – the use of the mind, instead of physical or drug treatments, to help cure people.

There are many different types of therapy including classical 'talk' therapies, which are usually one-to-one; body–mind therapies involving the use of physical bodywork; group therapy in which many people take part and act as 'therapists' to one another; and so on. There are probably well over 140 different therapeutic disciplines widely practised in the western world.

What they all share is a trusting relationship with another human being in which the person seeking help examines his or her values, ideas, needs, aspirations, fears, behaviour and so on in a way that alleviates their current life predicament. How long all this takes depends upon what is to be achieved and the method used to achieve it.

People often get confused between counselling and therapy and this is understandable because the two are closely related. Counselling usually involves more superficial dealings with the person's unconscious whereas true psychotherapy involves tackling defence mechanisms (see page 109), personality structure, dream interpretation, encouraging the person to get back to the feelings of childhood, and much more. The simplest of counselling can produce results in a few short sessions; intensive psychotherapy can last for years. The sort of therapy I have mainly referred to in the book is one-to-one psychotherapy lasting some time, perhaps weeks or a few months.

Counselling and psychotherapy services are increasingly available throughout the UK. The best place to start to find a counsellor or therapist is with your general practitioner. He will probably know a good local person or will tell you of someone who does. The Citizen's Advice Bureau locally is also a good source of such information. Personal recommendation from friends can work well but just because someone has suited a friend does not mean that he or she will suit you. Try and see how you get on over the first interview or two.

Other sources of counselling or therapy help include:
The British Association of Counselling, 37a Sheep Street, Rugby, Warwickshire CV21 3BX.
National Council for Civil Liberties, 21 Tabard Street, London SE1 4LA.

Parents Anonymous for Distressed Parents, 6–9 Manor Gardens, off Holloway Road, London N7 6LA, tel. 01–263 8918. This organization helps parents who have battered or fear they might batter their children.

In extreme desperation or if you become suicidal *The Samaritans* can be a real help. Their number is in the local directory. They are increasingly involved in non-crisis help too. *Brook Advisory Centres* are to be found in most major cities. They offer counselling about sex and birth control problems to young people. Phone them or just walk in.

The National Marriage Guidance Council, Herbert Gray College, Little Church Street, Rugby, Warwickshire CV21 3AP, runs clinics for couples over sixteen (whether they are married or not) all over the country. They deal with many forms of personal problems, not just those to do with marriage. Look up the nearest branch in your local directory. As this book went to press this organization was changing its name to *Relate*.

British Agencies for Adopting and Fostering, 11 Southwark Street, London SE1 1RQ, gives advice on adoption and fostering nationwide. *Gingerbread* is a self-help organization that specializes in single-parents and their problems. They are at 35, Wellington Street, London WC2 E7BN.

Another useful address for single parents is the *National Council for One-Parent Families* at 255 Kentish Town Road, London NW5 2LX.

USEFUL ADDRESSES

Although this book is not about abnormal children there are some addresses that might be of help to parents who find that they need more help or advice with a child who has special problems of various kinds.

Advisory Centre for Education (ACE), 18 Victoria Park Square, Bethnal Green, London E2 9PB. 01–980 4596

Association for All Speech Impaired Children, 347 Central Markets, Smithfield, London EC1A 9NH. 01–236 3632/6487

Association for Improvements in the Maternity Services, Hon. Sec. Elizabeth Cockerell, 21 Franklin Gardens, Hitchin, Hertfordshire SG4 0NE.

Association for Post-Natal Illness, 7 Gowan Avenue, Fulham, London, SW6 6RH. 01–731 4867

Association for Spina Bifida and Hydrocephalus (ASBAH), 22 Upper Woburn Place, London WC2H 0EP. 01–388 1382

Asthma Society and Friends of the Asthma Research Council, 300 Upper Street, London N1 2XX. 01–226 2260

British Diabetic Association, 10 Queen Anne Street, London W1M 0BD. 01–323 1531

British Epilepsy Association, Anstey House, 40 Hanover Square, Leeds LS3 1BE. 0532 439393

British Institute of Mental Handicap, Wolverhampton Road, Kidderminster, Worcestershire DY10 3PP. 0562 850251

British Migraine Association, 178A High Road, Byfleet, Weybridge, Surrey KT14 7ED. 093 23 52468

British Polio Fellowship, Bell Close, West End Road, Ruislip, Middlesex HA4 6LP. 089 56 75515

British Pregnancy Advisory Service, Austy Manor, Wootton Wawen, Solihull, West Midlands B95 6DA. 021-643 1461

The British Red Cross Society, 9 Grosvenor Crescent, London SW1X 7EJ. 01–235 5454

Brittle Bone Society, Unit 4, Block 20, Carlunie Road, Dunsinane Industrial Estate, Dundee DD2 3QT. 0382 817771

Centre on Environment for the Handicapped, 35 Great Smith Street, London SW1P 3BJ. 01–222 7980

Down's Syndrome Association, 12–13 Clapham Common Southside, London SW4 7AA. 01–720 0008

Fair Play for Children Safety Committee, 248 Kentish Town Road, London NW5

Family Planning Information Service, 27–35 Mortimer Street, London W1N 7RJ. 01–636 7866

Foresight – The Association for the Promotion of Pre-conceptual Care, The Old Vicarage, Church Lane, Witley, Surrey GU8 5PN. 0428 794500

The Foundation for the Study of Infant Deaths, 15 Belgrave Square, London SW1X 8PS. 01–235 0965

The Haemophilia Society, 123 Westminster Bridge Road, London SE1 7HR. 01–928 2020

Hyperactive Children's Support Group, Sally Bundy, 71 Whyke Lane, Chichester, West Sussex PO19 2LD. 0903 725182

Invalid Children's Aid Nationwide, Allan Graham House, 198 City Road, London EC1V 2PH.

La Leche League of Great Britain, BM Box 3424, 27 Old Gloucester Street, London WC1N 3XX. 01–404 5011

The Leukaemia Care Society, PO Box 82, Exeter, Devon EX2 5DP. 0392 218514 (secretary)

Meet-a-Mum Association (MAMA), Kate Goodyer, 3 Woodside Avenue, South Norwood, London SE25 5DW.

The Migraine Trust, 45 Great Ormond Street, London WC1N 3HD. 01–278 2676

Muscular Dystrophy Group of Great Britain and Northern Ireland, Nattrass House, 35 Macaulay Road, London SW4 0QP. 01–720 8055

The National Association for Gifted Children, 1 South Audley Street, London W1Y 5DQ. 01–499 1188

National Association for Mental Health (MIND), 22 Harley Street, London W1N 2ED. 01–637 0741

The National Association for the Welfare of Children in Hospital, Argyle House, 29–31 Euston Road, London NW1 2FD. 01–833 2041

The National Autistic Society, 276 Willesden Lane, London NW2 5RB. 01–451 3844

National Children's Bureau, 8 Wakley Street, London EC1V 7QE. 01–278 9441

The National Childbirth Trust, 9 Queensborough Terrace, Bayswater, London W2 3TB. 01–221 3833

National Children's Homes, 85 Highbury Park, London N5 1UD. 01–226 2033

The National Child-Minding Association, 8 Mason's Hill, Bromley, Kent BR2 9EY. 01–464 6164

National Council for the Divorced and Separated, 41 Summit Avenue, Kingsbury, London NW9 0TH. 01–205 8316

National Council for Voluntary Organizations, The Information Department, NCVO, 26 Bedford Square, London WC1B 3HU. 01–636 4066

National Deaf/Blind and Rubella Association (SENSE), 311 Gray's Inn Road, London WC1X 8PT. 01–278 1005

The National Deaf Children's Society, 45 Hereford Road, London W2 5AH. 01–229 9272

National Eczema Society, Tavistock House North, Tavistock Square, London WC1H 9SR. 01–388 4097

National Society for the Prevention of Cruelty to Children, 67 Saffron Hill, London EC1N 8RS and local addresses. 01–242 1626

Parents Anonymous, 6–9 Manor Gardens, off Holloway Road, Islington, London N7 6LA. 01–263 8918

The Patients' Association, Room 33, 18 Charing Cross Road, London WC2H 0HR. 01–240 0671

Pregnancy Advisory Service, 11–13 Charlotte Street, London W1P 1HD. 01–637 8962

Pre-School Playgroups Association, 61–63 King's Cross Road, London WC1X 9LL. 01–833 0991

The Psoriasis Association, 7 Milton Street, Northampton NN2 7JG. 0604 711129

Royal National Institute for the Blind, 224 Great Portland Street, London W1N 6AA. 01–388 1266

The Royal National Institute for the Deaf, 105 Gower Street, London WC1E 6AH. 01–387 8033

Royal Society for Mentally Handicapped Children and Adults (MENCAP), Mencap National Centre, 123 Golden Lane, London EC1Y 0RT. 01–253 9433

The Royal Society for the Prevention of Accidents, Cannon House, The Priory, Queensway, Birmingham B4 6BS. 021–200 2461

The Samaritans, 17 Uxbridge Road, Slough SL1 1SN. 0753 31011 and in local telephone directories

The Spastics Society, 12 Park Crescent, London W1N 4EQ. 01–636 5020

Spinal Injuries Association, 76 St. James' Lane, Muswell Hill, London N10 3DF. 01–444 2121

Toy Libraries Association, Seabrook House, Wyllyotts Manor, Darkes Lane, Potters Bar, Hertfordshire EN6 2HL.

Twins Clubs Association, Judi Linney, 198 Woodham Lane, New Haw, Weybridge, Surrey.

Voluntary Council for Handicapped Children, National Children's Bureau, 8 Wakley Street, London EC1V 7QE. 01–278 9441

FURTHER READING

The literature that I have drawn upon when writing this book is large and consists of books (both professional and 'lay') and learned papers in medical and psychological journals. This list is a short one consisting of some of the more readily available books that the reader will enjoy.

Barnes, B. and Colquhoun, I., *The Hyperactive Child, What the Family Can Do*, Thorsons, Wellingborough, Northants., 1984

Bartz, W. and Rasor, R., *Surviving with Kids*, Ballantine, New York, 1980

Berne, E., *Games People Play – The Psychology of Human Relationships*, Penguin, Harmondsworth, 1968

Campbell, Dr R., *How to Really Love Your Child*, Victor Books, Wheaton, Ill., 1977

Collange, C., *I'm Your Mother*, Arrow Books, London, 1987

Dally, A., *Inventing Motherhood – the consequences of an ideal*, Burnett Books Ltd., London, 1982

Davenport, D., *One Parent Families – A practical guide to coping*, Sheldon Press, London, 1979

Dobson, J., *Dare to Discipline*, Kingsway Publications, Eastbourne, 1982

Dobson, J., *Preparing for Adolescence*, Kingsway Publications, Eastbourne, 1983

Dodson, Dr F., *How to Discipline with Love (from crib to college)*, The New American Library Inc., New York, 1978

Donaldson, M., *Children's Minds*, Fontana, London, 1984

Erikson, E., *Childhood and Society*, Hogarth Press, London, 1965

Faber, A. and Mazlish, E., *How to talk so kids will listen and listen so kids will talk*, Rawson, Wade, New York, 1982

Freud, S., *On Sexuality*, Penguin, Harmondsworth, 1984

Genevie, L. and Margolies, E., *The Motherhood Report – How women feel about being mothers*, Macmillan, New York, 1987

Gibran, K., *The Prophet*, Heinemann, London, 1986

Goldman, R. and J., *Children's Sexual Thinking*, Routledge & Kegan Paul, London, 1982

Gots, R. and Gots, B., *Caring for your Unborn Child*, Bantam, New York, 1979

Green, Dr C., *Toddler Taming*, Doubleday, New South Wales, 1984

Greenleaf, B., *Children through the Ages, A history of childhood*, Barnes and Noble, New York, 1978

Harris, T., *I'm OK – You're OK*, Pan, London, 1970

Hauck, P., *How to bring up Your Child Successfully*, Sheldon Press, London, 1982

Hodder, E., *The Step-Parents' Handbook*, Sphere Books, London, 1985

Holt, J., *How Children Fail*, Penguin, Harmondsworth, 1984

Holt, J., *How Children Learn*, Penguin, Harmondsworth, 1985

Inglis, R., *The Good Step-Parents' Guide*, Grafton Books, London, 1986

Kaplan, L., *Oneness and Separateness: from infant to individual*, Simon and Schuster, New York, 1978

Leman, Dr K., *The Birth Order Book*, Dell Publishing, New York, 1984

Lewis, D., *The Secret Language of Your Child*, Pan Books, London, 1978

Liedloff, J., *The Continuum Concept*, Futura Publications, London, 1976

McConville, B., *Mad to be a Mother*, Century Hutchinson Ltd., London, 1987

McKee, L. and O'Brien, M., *The Father Figure*, Tavistock, London and New York, 1982

Odent, M., *Birth Reborn*, Souvenir Press, London, 1984

Pogrebin, L., *Family Politics*, McGraw-Hill, New York, 1984

Price, A. and Parry, J., *How to boost Your Child's Self-Esteem*, Golden Press, New York, 1982

Ridgway, R., *The Unborn Child – How to recognise and overcome pre-natal trauma*, Wildwood House, 1987.

Roeber, J., *Shared Parenthood*, Century Hutchinson, London 1987

Rosenberg, E., *Getting Closer*, Berkley Publishing, New York, 1985

Sarnoff, S. and Sarnoff, I., *Masturbation and Adult Sexuality*, Evans and Co., New York, 1979

Segal, L., *What is to be done about The Family?*, Penguin, Harmondsworth, 1983

Skynner, R. and Cleese, J., *Families and how to survive them*, Methuen, London, 1985

Spock, Dr B., *Raising Children in a difficult time*, Simon and Schuster (Pocket Books), New York, 1985

Stanway, Drs A. and P., *The Baby and Child Book*, Pan, London, 1983

Stanway, Drs A. and P., *Choices in Childbirth*, Pan, London, 1984

Stanway, Drs A. and P., *Pears Encyclopaedia of Child Health*, Pelham, London, 1977

Teyber, E., *Helping your Children with Divorce*, Simon and Schuster (Pocket Books), New York, 1985

Verny, T. and Kelly, J., *The Secret Life of the Unborn Child*, Sphere Books, London, 1982

Whelan, Dr E., *A Baby? . . . Maybe*, Bobbs-Merrill Co., New York, 1980

Williams, P., *Nourishing your Unborn Child*, Nash Publishing, New York, 1974

Winnicott, D., *Home is Where We Start From*, Penguin, Harmondsworth, 1986

Wolff, S., *Children under Stress*, Penguin, Harmondsworth, 1983

York, P., York, D. and Wachtel, T., *Tough Love Solutions*, Bantam Books Inc., New York, 1985

INDEX